Methodist Preachers

in

Georgia

1783–1900

A Supplement

HERITAGE BOOKS
2024

HERITAGE BOOKS

AN IMPRINT OF HERITAGE BOOKS, INC.

Books, CDs, and more—Worldwide

For our listing of thousands of titles see our website at
www.HeritageBooks.com

A Facsimile Reprint
Published 2024 by
HERITAGE BOOKS, INC.
Publishing Division
5810 Ruatan Street
Berwyn Heights, MD 20740

International Standard Book Number
Paperbound: 978-0-7884-2966-8

Publication of this book was made possible by a grant from the
R.J. Taylor, Jr., Foundation
which is gratefully acknowledged

INTRODUCTION

W hile this volume serves as a supplement to *Methodist Preachers In Georgia, 1783-1900,* and gives additional information on preachers already listed in that work, it offers fresh compilations in the following areas: 1) birth, marriage & death dates on many local preachers in Georgia abstracted from the *Southern Christian Advocate* newspapers from 1862-1878; 2) citations of letters and articles on churches, circuits and districts as they were reported in the *Southern Christian Advocate* for this same period; 3) additional personal data on preachers, itinerant and local, furnished by family members collected since 1984. In considering these three features, the value of this supplement becomes obvious. Since there is little to nothing in print in the conference journals or in the handwritten minutes of the conferences regarding local preachers prior to the 1850's, their data will be given here for the first time. Because the conference journals never listed the churches on circuits prior to the turn of the 20th Century, many can be found in the writings on revivals and meetings and other subjects authored by the preachers and given under their listings. A convenient place index at the end of this book is a quick cross reference of this data.

Inasmuch as possible, the scholarship of these preachers is cited under their listings, though many wrote under pen names and are unidentified in the newspaper articles they authored. The majority of these writings, however, are cited, and their titles give evidence to the influence wielded by the preachers through literary expression. These articles, like the ones on church events, range from columns of data to small paragraphs, depending upon the editorial limitations in each issue. They point toward an informed and involved clergy who wrote exhaustively for other transient publications as well. Sadly, there is no way to document the full extent of such writing, though the references here offer a sample of it.

Access to the film of the *Southern Christian Advocate* for the purpose of gaining the full materials which are referenced in this work is not a simple matter. While some university libraries may have the film, there is a problem with acquiring the film. Masters of the film have been misplaced at the South Carolina Library in Columbia, SC. In my own copy of the film (purchased many years ago), years 1860-62 are missing. There are four abstracted volumes of marriage and death notices from the paper which have been done by Brent Holcomb of Columbia, SC. Two of these are currently out-of-print from Southern Historical Press. Two are recent publications, one of marriages and the other on deaths for the years

1867-1878. The cut-off year of 1878 is the year that the *Wesleyan Christian Advocate* became the instrument of the Georgia conferences. While these four publications abstract data on marriages and deaths, they do not reference the articles which were generated by preachers about their churches or circuits.

As in the former volume, this one deals with many abbreviations which require the reader to refer to the abbreviation page. Unless one does so, he or she may confuse abbreviated listings. For instance, the designation lp or LP means licensed to preach, not local preacher. The designation for a local preacher is (L). Unfortunately, the utilization of complete words or designations would make the volume unwieldy and littered with senseless repetitions.

In the preface to the original volume, there are guidance pages at the beginning which deal with the interpretation of the entries. While they are not repeated here, the reader is encouraged to check them there before attempting to utilize this resource. The organization of the listing is the same as in the first volume; only in rare instances is there any repeated data; and, in some instances, there is correctional material on entries or variations given for birth or death or marriage dates. As with the last volume, this one goes no further than the lives of those persons admitted on trial in 1900. Those coming in in 1901 and later will not be found in these pages.

Information from books and articles not abstracted for the first volume will be found in this supplement. There are also references to the materials from the archival depository of the parent conference of South Carolina located at Wofford College, Spartanburg, SC, which give added information on early Georgia preachers operating under the auspices of that conference.

Using this supplement as a companion volume to the larger work, these two should give the fullest listings possible on Georgia preachers for the period covered. While genealogical data will continue to be forthcoming from those who have access to private papers and non-published materials, these compilations represent the bulk of what can be found in printed sources as well as what has been offered for inclusion from private records and files.

Harold Lawrence 1994

FOREWORD

The Reverend Dr. Harold A. Lawrence, Jr. is an avid historian. He loves Georgia and the Southland, and has written books and poems about both. More than that he loves The United Methodist Church and all of its predecessor organizations. He has already blessed us with his book, *METHODIST PREACHERS IN GEORGIA 1783-1900*, which was published in 1984. That book gave us many important details of the lives of ministers who served in Georgia for more than a century.

Now Dr. Lawrence has blessed us with a new volume entitled *METHODIST PREACHERS IN GEORGIA 1783-1900: A SUPPLEMENT*. The Supplement is an amplified version of his first volume which gives us greater detail about ordained and lay pastors in Georgia Methodism. This has been a very exacting and difficult work. Only one who has self-discipline and the love of the Church would be able to do the detailed work of tracing through conference newspapers, film in state libraries, and other documents which have rendered sometimes small but vital information about our forebears.

This volume is a very high tribute to those who went before us in preaching the Gospel and sharing the faith during the tumultuous nineteenth century. We should never forget their sacrifices and the excellent work they did with very little resources.

In some cases Dr. Lawrence was not able to glean much additional information. But there are wonderful vignettes of the lives of some of these Gospel heroes. For example, Young J. Allen, who was converted at age 17 at the Salem Campmeeting in Newton County, Georgia, later became one of the first missionaries to China. According to Dr. Lawrence's account, the Reverend Mr. Allen has literary works that would comprise 250 volumes. This book contains a listing of the articles written about work in China by Young J. Allen.

Georgia Methodism is indeed indebted to the Reverend Lawrence for his careful, painstaking work in helping us understand more of our past. I commend this splendid book to libraries of our colleges, universities, churches, and individuals.

James Lloyd Knox, Resident Bishop
The Atlanta Area
The United Methodist Church

12 October 1994

Abbreviations

A.B.	Batchelor of Arts
ABS	American Bible Society
AME	African Methodist Episcopal
AMEZ	African Methodist Episcopal Zion
Assoc.	Associate
Asst.	Assistant
b.	born
B.A.	Batchelor of Arts
B.S.	Batchelor of Science
Bapt.	Baptist
bp	back page
bur.	buried
bv.	birth date variable
CA	Christian Advocate
C.H.	Court House
cem.	cemetery
cert.	certificate
CG	Campground
ch.	church
Chap.	Chaplain
chrn.	children
cir.	circuit
CL	Class Leader
CMC	Congregational Methodist Church
CME	Colored Methodist Episcopal
Col.	Colonel
Conf.	Conference
CSA	Confederate States of America
cvt.	converted
d.	died
dau.	daughter
D.D.	Doctor of Divinity
dist.	district
D.S.	District Superintendent
dv.	death date variable
(E)	Elected
ed.	educated
ed.	editor
EUQ	Emory University Quaterly
EUQR	Emory University Quarterly Review

EWO	Encyclopedia of World Methodism
FC	full connection
FC	Female College (with institution)
fp	front page
FP	Family Puzzlers
Gen.	General
Gen. Conf.	General Conference
GHQ	Georgia Historical Quarterly
GR	Georgia Review
grad.	graduated
HH	Historical Highlights
H.S.	High School
inf.	infant
(L)	Local Preacher
le	licensed to exhort
lp	licensed to preach
m/	married
m.	mile(s)
M.A.	Masters of Arts
MBC	Methodist Bishops Collection
MC	The Methodist Church
M.D.	Medical Doctor
MEC	Methodist Episcipal Church
MEC(N)	Northern MEC
MECS	Methodist Episcopal Church, South
MH	Methodist History
Mis.	Mission
MM	Methodist Magazine (The)
MM&QR	Methodist Magazine & Quarterly Review
MPC	Methodist Protestant Church
MR	Methodist Review (The)
MQR	Methodist Quarterly Review (The)
MRQ	Methodist Review Quarterly (The)
mv	marriage date variable
n.	north
nd	no date
np	not published
nv	name variation or variable
nv	not verifiable
obit.	obituary
ord.	ordination
OT	Admitted on Trial

PC	Preacher in Charge
PE	Presiding Elder
PF	Profession of Faith
pp	private printing
pp.	page no.
QC	Quarterly Conference
QR	Quarterly Review
ref.	referenced
reg.	regiment/ regional
ret.	retired
rpt.	reprint
RS	Revolutionary Soldier
(S)	Supply, supplied
SCA	Southern Christian Advocate
SMR	Southern Methodist Review
SpCl	Special Collections
SS	Sunday School
sta.	station
Sup.	Superannuated
Supy.	Supernumerary
Supt.	Superintendent
surv.	surviving
tf	transferred
t/f	transferred from
t/t	transferred to
tw.	twin
UGA	University of GA
UMC	United Methodist Church
up.	unpublished
uv.	unverified
v	variation
vet.	veteran
WCA	Wesleyan Christian Advocate
WFMS	Woman's Foreign Missionary Society
w/o	without
Wof.	Wofford College

Adams, Habersham J.

"The Revival In Covington." *SCA*, 6-24-1858, p. 15.
"Savannah, GA Conf." *SCA*, 6-23-1859, p. 223.
"Lexington Cir., GA Conf." *SCA*, 10-16-1856, p. 79; 6-19-1856, p.11.
"Bethel, GA Conf." (near Milledgeville). *SCA*, 10-30-1862, p. 166.
"Covington, GA." *SCA*, 5-13-1858, p. 199.
"Griffin FC." *SCA*, 7-16-1863, fp.
"Athens Dist., GA Conf." *SCA*, 10-26-1865, np.
"Atlanta Dist., N. GA Conf." *SCA*, 8-16-1867, p. 130; 8-30-1867, p. 138;
    9-20-1867, p. 150; 11-8-1867, p. 178.
"A Sunday In Oxford." *SCA*, 9-20-1867, p. 150.
"Griffin, GA." *SCA*, 6-12-1868, fp; 11-6-1868, p. 178; 12-10-1869, p. 198.
"Letter from Griffin." *SCA*, 4-16-1869, p. 62.
"LaGrange District Conf." *SCA*, 8-9-1871, p. 126.
"To the Official Members of the Church in the Rome Dist." *SCA*,
    4-8-1870, p. 54.
"Episcopal Districts, i.e. Diocesan Episcopacy." *SCA*, 5-13-1870, p. 74.
"The Rome Dist. Conf." *SCA*, 7-15-1870, p. 110; 7-22-1870, p. 114;
    9-30-1870, p. 154.
"Grove Level, Dalton Cir." *SCA*, 9-23-1870, p. 150.
"LaGrange Dist., N. GA Conf." *SCA*, 3-15-1871, p. 92; 6-14-1871, p. 94.
"LaGrange Dist." (series). *SCA*, 1-10-1872, p. 2.
"Dalton Dist." *SCA*, 11-22-1871, p. 186.
"LaGrange Dist. SS Celebration." *SCA*, 4-2-1873, p. 50.
"St. James, Augusta." *SCA*, 8-25-1875, p. 134; 10-13-1875, p. 162.
"Milledgeville," *SCA*, 3-29-1876, p. 50; 5-16-1876, p. 78; 7-11-1876,
    p. 110; 9-12-1876, p. 146.
"Growth of Methodists at Milledgeville." *SCA*, 10-24-1876, p. 170;
    10-31-1876, p. 174.
"Sparta & Milledgeville." *SCA*, 1-2-1877, p. 2.
"Sparta, GA." *SCA*, 6-5-1877, p. 90; 8-21-1877, p. 134.
"The Revival at Sparta." *SCA*, 8-28-1877, p. 138.
"The Church in Marietta, GA." *SCA*, 1-29-1878, p. 14; 4-16-1878,
    p.58; 4-23-1878, p. 62.

Adams, John M.

wife Agnes Melita Hulme (2-24-1814 - 7-5-1875); b. Elbert Co., GA;
d. Madison Co., GA. Parents of Rev. Thomas J. Adams.

Adams, Thomas J.

m/ 6-24-1873, Eliza C. Tucker of Elbert Co., GA.

"Crawfordville Cir., N. GA Conf." *SCA,* 3-4-1874, p. 34; 11-4-1874, p. 174.

Adams, W. H. (d. 1874)

b. Elbert Co., GA; cvt. Oct. 1839; Tribute Elbert Cir.

(L) N. GA CONF. 6-11-1870, Deacon

Ahern, John George

See: *WCA,* 4-25-1888.

Akin, Eldridge K.

"Dallas Cir., N. GA Conf." *SCA,* 10-18-1871, p. 166.
"Powder Springs Cir., N. GA Conf." *SCA,* 8-21-1872, p. 130.

Ainsworth, James T.

"Carrollton Cir., GA Conf." *SCA,* 9-23-1858, p. 67.
"Roswell Cir., GA Conf." *SCA,* 10-13-1859, p. 286; 11-10-1859, p. 303.
"The New MC in Roswell." *SCA,* 12-1-1859, p. 315.
"Columbus, GA." *SCA,* 5-26-1864, np.
"Buena Vista Cir., GA Conf." *SCA,* 3-30-1866, fp; 9-21-1866, fp; 9-27-1867,
   p. 154.
"Camilla Cir., S. GA Conf." *SCA,* 10-8-1869, p. 163; 9-23-1870, p. 150;
   10-7-1870, p. 153; 9-20-1871, p. 151; 10-4-1871, p. 159; 12-6-1871,
   p. 195.
"Cairo Cir., S. GA Conf." *SCA,* 8-22-1876. p. 134.

Ainsworth, William N.

Grad. A.B. 1891 Emory; D.D. 1905.

"Our Essential Unity," *WCA,* v99, n42, 10-2-1935, p. 12.
"Summary of Keynote Address" (Anti-Saloon League of America, St. Louis,
   12-1-1935) *WCA,* v100, n5, 1-31-1936, p. 12.
"Where To Begin," *WCA,* v100, n1, 1935, p. 8.
"Who That Fears God Will Stand For Repeal In GA," *WCA,* v100, n46,
   5-21-1937, pp. 4-5.

Akin, Warren

1878 - Tribute by Cassville Church.

Alexander, W. J.
m/ 1-14-1872, Celestra J. Sadler

Alexander, William
Cert. for elders orders, 12-27-1829; Recom. to SC Conf. as traveling preacher, 8-8-1829. (Wof.).

Allen, Beverly
"Methodism in Charleston." *SCA*, 11-1-1855, p. 85.
Creitzberg, A.M., "Beverly Allen: The First Apostate Presbyter of American Methodism," *MR*, v19, n3, Jan-Feb. 1896, pp. 368-375.
ref. in Jenkins, James. *Experiences, Labors & Sufferings of*...pp. 35, 50-52.

Allen, George   (1818 - 6-28-1873)
d. Savannah, GA; (L) elder, Trinity & Wesley churchs, Savannah, GA.

Allen, Lemuel Q.
cvt. 10-13-1849; m/1858, Margaret M. Mills, of Jackson Co., AL. 4 chrn. Joshua Soule, Luella, Julian, Clarence. bur. near Lumpkin CG.

"Reidsville Cir., GA Conf." *SCA*, 9-15-1859, p. 271.
"Dade Mis., GA Conf." *SCA*, 7-3-1856, p. 19.
"Lafayette Cir., GA Conf." *SCA*, 9-10-1863, bp.
"Dahlonega Cir., GA Conf." *SCA*, 11-26-1866, fp.

Allen, Richard (d.1830).
"Allen lived in Hepzibah, GA, and invented the Allen plow; m/1796, Elizabeth Anderson in Richmond Co., GA, dau. of Elisha Anderson & Elvina Brack."
(Source says he d. in Columbia Co., GA, and was named Robert, not Richard).
FP, n876, 8-2-1984.

Allen, William G.
cvt. Holbrook CG, Forsyth Co., GA; le, lp, Harmony Grove, Hall Co., GA.

"The Revival on Canton Cir., GA Conf." *SCA*, 10-14-1858, p. 78; 11-25-1858, p.102.
"Blairsville Mis., GA Conf." *SCA*, 10-9-1856, p. 75.
"Ft. Valley Cir., GA Conf." *SCA*, 10-30-1862, p. 165.
"Army Mission." *SCA*, 7-30-1863, bp.
"A Further Appeal to Methodist Preachers." *SCA*, 8-6-1863, bp.

Allen, Young J.

cvt. age 17, Salem CG, Newton Co., GA; attended Emory & Henry College, VA; his literary work would comprise 250 vols; Chinese name: Lin Lo Chih.

"From the China Mission." (series). *SCA*, 11-2-1865, fp.
"The China Mission." *SCA*, 9-21-1866, fp.
"Emory College." (poem). *SCA*, 11-2-1866, fp.
"Letter From China." (series). *SCA*, 11-2-1866, p. 4.
"The Resuscitation of Idolatry in Shanghai." (poem). *SCA*, 11-9-1866, fp.
"The Wreck." *SCA*, 11-23-1866. p. 6.
"Chinese Products." *SCA*, 5-14-1869, fp.
"Letters to the Shining Stars." (series). *SCA*, 9-24-1869, p. 156.

Candler, W.A. *Young J. Allen, The Man Who Seeded China*, Cokesbury, Nashville, 1931.

Allgood, William   (1817 - 1872)

b. Elbert Co., GA; d. Spalding Co., GA.

(L) N. GA CONF.   Villa Rica Cir.

Amos, Asponsal G.

bur. Brunswick, GA.

Anderson, David L.

b. Summerhill, SC; attended Washington College; worked for *Atlanta Constitution*; established Souchow Univ.; Gen. Conf. delegate.
m/12-31-1879, Mary Garland Thomas, Huntsville, AL.

Anderson, Isaac H.

"To the Colored MECS." *SCA*, 3-5-1869, p. 38.

Anderson, John R.

served Union MPC & CG.

Anderson, Josephus

"Methodist Church Government." Serial. *SCA*, 8-16-1855, p. 41;
        8-23-1855, p. 44; 8-9-1855, p. 37; 8-2-1855, p. 33; 7-27-1855,
        p. 29; 8-30-1855, p. 49.
"Bereavement." *SCA*, 10-11-1855, p. 73.
"Quincy, FL Conf." *SCA*, 7-30-1857, p. 37; 7-21-1864, np.
"A Biblical Institute for the Colored People." *SCA*, 3-23-1866, fp.

"Changes In Methodism." *SCA,* 3-23-1866, bp.
"The Baptism of Fire." *SCA,* 6-21-1867, fp.
"The Angels of Heaven & of Earth." (poem). *SCA,* 11-29-1867, fp.
"FL Correspondence." *SCA,* 1-10-1868, p. 6.
"Praise of God - A Hymn." (poem). *SCA,* 3-6-1868, fp.
"The Orphan's View of Life." (poem). *SCA,* 8-28-1868, fp.
"Methodist Unification." *SCA,* 7-1-1870, p. 102.
"Close to Thy Cross, O Christ." (poem). *SCA,* 5-29-1872, fp.
"Soliloquy of the Bereaved." *SCA,* 11-13-1872, fp.
"Christmas Day." (poem). *SCA,* 12-25-1872, fp.
"To A Bereaved Mother." (poem). *SCA,* 9-24-1873, fp.
"Pastoral Visiting." *SCA,* 10-1-1873, fp.
"Tallahassee, FL." *SCA,* 11-12-1873, p. 175; 6-2-1875, p. 86.
"Christian Trust." (poem). *SCA,* 12-10-1873, fp.
"Lines." *SCA,* 2-25-1874, fp.
"Lines on the Death of Mrs. F.E. Choice." (poem). *SCA,* 9-2-1874, fp.
"The Bible & Temperance." *SCA,* 11-4-1874, fp.
"The Offense of our Cross." *SCA,* 4-3-1878, fp.
"Christian Confidence & Hope." (poem). *SCA,* 10-18-1871, fp.

Anderson, William D.
m/ 1-30-1877, Lula Latimer.

Andrew, James O.
d. New Orleans, LA; 1820, Gen. Conf. delegate; 1838, trustee, Covington
Manual Labor School. m/ 1816, Ann Amelia McFarlane; m/3 1854,
Mrs. Emily Simms Childres (1798 - Jan. 1872).

1824, letter to Duke Goodman for books, drayage; 1-12-1825, voucher for
freight & drayage; 12-24-1836, letter to Conf. stating inability to be present re
illness; 1844, report of Com. of Nine & resolution adopted by QC. (Wof.).

"A Call For Preachers," *SCA,* 7-8-1853, p. 21.
"Memoir of the Rev. Hardy H. Andrew," *SCA,* 10-27-1854, p. 81.
"Sketches of Itinerant Ministers," *SCA,* 7-22-1858, p. 29; 7-29-1858, p.33.
"Funeral Discourse before the Louisville Conference at Greensburg, KY."
    9-21-1850 in Bascom, H.B. *The Cross of Christ.* South. Meth.
    Bk. Concern, Louisville, 1851.
"Pastoral Address to the GA Annual Conference." *SCA,* 1-21-1848, p. 130.
"Pastoral Address to the FL Conference." *SCA,* 2-25-1848, p. 150.
"Instruction and Management of Servants." *SCA,* 4-6-1849, p. 173; 4-13-1849,
    p. 177.

Address to Sons of Temperance, *SCA*, 5-25-1849, p. 201.

"A Trip To Caliafornia. *SCA* serial: 2-21-1856, p. 149; 2-28-1856, p. 153;
 3-20-1856, p. 165; 3-27-1856, p. 169; 4-3-1856, p. 173; 4-10-1856,
 p. 177; 4-17-1856, p. 181; 6-12-1856, fp., etc.

"Letter." *SCA*, 9-6-1839, p. 46.

"An Address Delivered at Mississippi & SC Conferences." *SCA*, 9-22-1842,
 p.1.

"Address to Candidates for Deacon's Orders, SC." *SCA*, 2-17-1859, fp.

"Remarks at the Reading of Appointments, SC." *SCA*, 2-24-1859, fp.

"East Florida." *SCA*, 4-21-1859, p. 187.

"A Plea For Sunday Schools." *SCA*, 8-18-1859, fp.

"Letter - Last Days of Mrs. E.M. Lovett." *SCA*, 8-14-1856, p. 43.

"Pastoral Duty." (series) see: *SCA*, 10-9-1856, fp.

"The Christ of History." *SCA*, 2-19-1857, fp.

"Religious Instruction of Negroes." *SCA*, 7-17-1856, fp.

"The General Conference - Duty of the Church." *SCA*, 3-19-1863, p. 44.

"Thoughts For the Fast Day." *SCA*, 3-26-1863, fp.

"Thoughts For the Times." *SCA*, 12-4-1862, p. 185.

"Army Chaplain." *SCA*, 10-23-1862, p. 162

"Support of the Bishops; Publishing House." *SCA*, 12-17-1857, fp.

"Non-Secterian Methodist Schools." "*SCA*, 2-4-1858, fp.

"A Christian Man's Politics." *SCA*, 2-11-1858, fp.

"Immoral Politicians and Unscrupulous Editors." *SCA*, 2-18-1858, fp.

"A Fortnight Among the Missions to the Blacks." (series). *SCA*, 5-14-1857,
 p. 199.

"Are We Sufficiently Sectarian?" (series). see: *SCA*, 12-3-1857, fp.

"Meeting of the Bishop's Missionary Board." *SCA*, 2-11-1864, np.

"The Methodist Church, North & the War." *SCA*, 3-3-1864, np.

"To the Preachers & Members of the MECS." *SCA*, 4-21-1864, np.

"The Times." *SCA*, 10-22-1863, bp.

"Letter." *SCA*, 10-1-1863, bp.

"The Conferences." *SCA*, 10-1-1863, bp.

"Random Thoughts on Pastoral Visiting." (series). *SCA*, 6-23-1864, np.

"A Trip To The Atlanta Salt Works." *SCA*, 8-18-1864, np.

"Extracts of a Letter from ..." *SCA*, 9-29-1864, np.

"Bishop Andrew's Charge & Appeal." *SCA*, 9-7-1865, np.

"The Augusta Meetings." *SCA*, 8-2-1867, fp.

"Our Work on the Pacific Coast." *SCA*, 3-13-1868, p. 42.

"Ministerial Consecration to Christ." (sermon). *SCA*, 5-31-1871, fp.

"Funeral Sermon of Mrs. Andrew" (Wm. Capers). *SCA*, 10-21-1842,
    f. & p. 75.
"Reminiscences of Bishop Andrew." (A.H. Mitchell). (series). *SCA*,
    6-21-1871, fp.

Andrew, John (9-14-1758 - 1830)
son of James (d. 12-5-1770) and (nv) Esther (d. 7-6-1773), members of Midway
Church, Liberty Co., GA. Baptz. 10-14-1758, Midway; RS; bur. 1 m. n.
Farmington, Oconee Co., GA.

"Extracts from Journal, 1789-91" *CA*, 12-1-1841, p. 64.
"Extracts from his Journal." *SCA*, 10-22-1841, p. 74.
"Correspondence w/ Hull, Crutchfield, Ivey." *SCA*, 10-29-1841, p. 78.

Andrews, Christopher C. (6-21-1829 - 7-26-1876)
b. Liberty Co., GA; d. Belton, Hall Co., GA; grad. Trinity College, NC 1858;
m/7-11-1859, Mary S. Robstean of Fayetteville, NC. (L). School teacher,
Belton, GA; past Pres. of Louisburg FC, NC; Thomasville FC, NC; Andrew
FC, GA. bur. Belton.

"Altamaha Dist. Conf." *SCA*, 8-20-1873, p. 130.

Andrews, Gibson C.
dv. 5-27-1907; started Hiwassee Mis. in 1877; m2v/ 1-31-1895,
Georgia Wilhoit. By 1869, he was a preacher in the Free Will
Baptist Church.

"Isabella Mis., GA Conf." *SCA*, 11-17-1864, np.

Andrews, Hansford (d. 5-6-1893)

Andrews, Robert N.
25th GA Reg., CSA.

Ansley, Asa
wife Rebecca Wade (1805 - 7-19-1872), d. Sumter Co., GA., dau. of Moses
& Mary Wade.

Anthony, Bascom
Numerous weekly editorial articles. *WCA*. 1934-1943.

Anthony, George Lucius W. (d. 2-21-1886).
son of Rev. Whitfield Anthony, brother to Rev. J.D. Anthony; died of suicide
at his home in Jefferson Co., GA, the same day his father died.

"Alpharetta Circuit, GA Conf." *SCA*, 10-30-1862, p. 166.

Anthony, James D.
"Sandersville Cir., GA Conf." *SCA*, 7-7-1864, np; 11-17-1864, np.
"Taylor's Creek Campmeeting." *SCA*, 11-16-1866, fp.
"My Sainted Wife." *SCA*, 7-19-1867, fp.
"Dahlonega Dist. Meeting, Cumming Cir., N. GA Conf." *SCA*, 9-18-1868,
    p. 151.

MacAfee, Mildred. "James Danelly Anthony 1825-1899." *HH*, v14, n2. Dec.
    1984, pp. 4-5.

Anthony, Samuel
Colored Mis. in Macon Dist. *SCA*, 10-2-1853, p. 82.
"Forsyth Cir., GA." *SCA*, 11-10-1837, p.82.
"Letter from Covington, GA." *SCA*, 10-19-1838, p. 70.
"Villa Rica Mis. & LaGrange Dist., GA Conf." *SCA*, 11-6-1856, p. 91.
"Americus, GA." *SCA*, 6-9-1864, np.

Anthony, Whitfield
9-26-1831, recommended to conf. at Darlington for Deacon's Orders by
Asbury CG, QC. (Wof.).

Anthony, William W.   (MECS)
FLORIDA CONF. 1861 OT; 1862-63 Colquitt (Tallahassee). Record
incomplete.

Arbogast, Benjamin
"A Home For the Exiles." *SCA*, 11-20-1862, p. 179.
"Rome, GA." *SCA*, 6-1-1866, fp.
"To the Preachers of the Rome Dist., GA Conf." *SCA*, 11-2-1866, p. 4.
"Church Property." *SCA*, 5-17-1871, p. 78.

Ardis, John (d. 1878)
death notice 8-8-1878 from Greenville, AL. Bur. Pioneer Cem., Greenville, AL.

Armistead, Thomas S.
"Camden Cir., S. GA Conf." *SCA*, 7-29-1874, p. 118.
"Leesburg & Smithville, S. GA Conf." *SCA*, 10-27-1875, p. 170.

Armstrong, John M.
"Richmond Cir., N. GA Conf." *SCA*, 10-21-1870, p. 166.

Arnold, Miles W.
m/9-19-1854, Martha J. Baskin (1-22-1835 - 2-16-1870), d. Oxford, GA, dau.
of Rev. Jas. & Henrietta Baskin. m2/2-6-1875, Elizabeth S. Nowell

"Villa Rica Cir., GA Conf." *SCA*, 10-14-1858, p. 78.
"Lawrenceville Cir., GA Conf." *SCA*, 10-27-1859, p. 295.
"Greensboro Cir., GA Conf." *SCA*, 9-22-1864, np; 11-17-1864, np.
"The Bible." (poem). *SCA*, 2-22-1867, fp.
"A Visit To Augusta." *SCA*, 9-6-1867, p. 142.
"Lines." (poem). *SCA*, 2-19-1869, fp.
"Thy Will Be Done." (poem). *SCA*, 2-18-1870, fp.
"The Dying Day of Winter." (poem). *SCA*, 6-10-1870, fp.
"Elegiac Lines on the Death of Rev. Wm. H. Evans." (poem). *SCA*,
    11-25-1870, fp.
"Acworth Cir., N. GA Conf." *SCA*, 11-20-1877, p. 186.

Arnold, Thomas T.
Calhoun Cir., N. GA Conf." *SCA*, 10-4-1867, p. 158.

Arnold, William
"Macon District, GA Conf." *SCA*, 9-13-1839, p. 50.
"The Way-Worn Pilgrim." (poem). *SCA*, 2-15-1871, fp. (rpt.).
"In Memory of Wm. A." (poem). *SCA*, 3-15-1871, fp.
"The Pulpit." (poem). *SCA*, 10-7-1874, fp.

Asbury, Daniel
Letter, 1802, Yadkin Cir. *SCA*, 8-21-1846, p. 41.

Ashmore, Joseph S.
3rd GA Reg., Chap. 25th GA Reg., CSA.

Askew, Josiah (1764 - 5-30-1845)
g.father of Atticus G. Haygood.
11-9-1821, letter to or from Jas. Patterson expressing his belief. (Wof.).
Travis, Joseph. *Autobiography*. pp. 194-196.

Austin, James M.
7th child of John Austin and Elizabeth Copeland; moved to GA in 1826.
wife, Orille Quarterman (10-13-1838 - 9-8-1915), b. Liberty Co., GA, New
Midway Ch. d. Athens, GA. Chrn. Manning (1881 - 1935); Addie, b. 9-3-1859.

"Methodism in Darien, GA." *SCA,* 5-15-1856, p. 199.
"State Line Mis., GA." *SCA,* 7-19-1850, p. 26.
"Prospects in Darien, GA." *SCA,* 2-12-1857, p. 147; 2-19-1857, p. 151.
"Columbia Cir., GA Conf." *SCA,* 10-16-1862, p. 159.
"Revival In Lumpkin." *SCA,* 8-14-1872, p. 126.
"Thomasville Dist." *SCA,* 9-16-1874, p. 147.

Avant, Isaiah L. (6-27-1840 - 9-30-1874)
b. Bibb Co., GA; d. Houston Co., GA; joined church 1849; lp 1863.
Tribute by Crawford Cir., S. GA Conf.

"Revival Meeting in Fort Valley Cir., S. GA Conf." *SCA,* 11-8-1867, p. 178.
"Revival Meeting, Knoxville Mis., S. GA Conf." *SCA,* 9-3-1869, p. 142.
"Knoxville Mis., S. GA Conf." *SCA,* 10-14-1870, p. 162.

Averitt, William N. (1801 - 7-7-1871)   MECS
b. NC; settled in Twiggs Co., GA; moved to FL; then to Early Co.,
GA; then to Decatur Co., GA, where he died. Served in SW GA & FL. 9 chrn.

(L) S. GA CONF.

Avrett, Alexander
bur. Avrett Cem., Ft. Gordon, GA. Chrn. Mary, Sarah, John, Alexander Jr.,
Joseph, Columbus.

"Jefferson Mis., GA." *SCA,* 7-14-1848, p. 22.

Aycock, Emory B. (3-5-1873 - 3-10-1942)
m/ Tommie L. (3-5-1873 - 4-28-1961). Both bur. Nazereth UMC, Barrow
Co., GA.

Bailey, John Palmer
b. Dalton, GA. 9 chrn. Emma Tallulah (3-7-1860 - 5-29-1955); Frances
Elizabeth (10-23-1869 - 3-10-1947); Martha Caroline (d. inf.); Laura Leanora;
Albert Weems; Mary Augusta; Rosa Eugenia (9-27-1880 - 4-30-1973); Annie
Lee; Elizabeth Eloise (d. inf.).

Baker, John   (11-28-1796 - 5-1-1870)

b. Abbeville Dist., SC; d. Polk Co., GA, Bethany Community; bur. Bethany CG; see: 1860 Census, Heard Co., GA.

joined church 1820; le 1829; lp 1835; served New Hope, Henry Co., GA.

Baker, John W.

"Hartwell Cir., N. GA Conf." *SCA*, 8-16-1871, p. 130; 9-20-1871, p. 150; 9-4-1872, p. 138.
"Gwinnett Cir., N. GA Conf." *SCA*, 9-2-1870, p. 138.
"Morganton Mis., N. GA Conf." *SCA*, 9-17-1873, p. 146.
"Atlanta Cir., N. GA Conf." *SCA*, 9-9-1874, p. 139.
"Alpharetta Cir., N. GA Conf." *SCA*, 10-14-1874, p. 162.

Baker, Lawrence   (4-6-1848 - 7-19-1876)

b. Covington, GA; d. Atlanta, GA; cvt. age 10, Salem CG, Newton Co., GA; Class Leader. m/2-24-1870, M.W.J. Smith.

Baker, Thomas

from Mt. Zion, Carroll Co., GA.

Baker, Thomas Richard (7-30-1866 - 3-8-1926)

father of Rev. Rudolph R. Baker, Sr.; g.father of Rev. R.R. Baker, Jr.

Baker, William S.

Chap. 27th GA Reg. CSA, appointed but declined.
wid. Mara A. Beall d. 5-13-1887, Irwinton, GA.

"Wilkinson, GA." *SCA*, 9-18-1872, p. 146.

Baldwin, Benjamin J.

Chap. 31st GA Reg., CSA.

"Trinity Conf., TX." *SCA*, 11-19-1873, p. 179.

Ball, James G. M.   (7-31-1809 - 7-5-1868)

joined church, 2-22-1825; lp 9-27-1837; tribute of respect Weston Lodge # 80. m/ 12-28-1838, Eliza A. ? (12-7-1815 - 12-7-1869), b. Green Co., NC; d. Weston, GA.

Ballew, David L.
"Dahlonega Mis., GA." *SCA*, 4-26-1839, p. 178.

Bankston, Erasmus I. or J.
"Carrollton Mis., GA." *SCA*, 7-9-1841, p. 14; 9-17-1841, p. 54;
    12-31-1841, p. 114.

Barnett, Thomas R.   (MECS)
FLORIDA CONFERENCE: 1859 Holmesville (St. Mary's); 1860 Satilla
Col. Mis.; 1861-62 Holmesville; 1863-64 Black Ck. Cir. (Jacksonville);
1865 Middlebury Cir. & Col. Charge. Record incomplete.

Barnett, William B.
12-12-1820, letter to SC Conf. resigning due to ill health. (Wof.).

Barr, John Wesley (9-3-1827 - 4-17-1893)
b. Lexington, SC; d. nar Marcus, Jackson Co., GA. m1/ Catharine M. Eidson;
m2/ Sarah M. Quattlebaum. 10 chrn.
(L)

Barrett, George W.
"Clothed With Life." (poem). *WCA*, 299A, n28, 7-19-1935, p. 12.

Barry, George L. (2-20-1804 - 12-21-1868)
b. Baltimore, MD; d. Cuthbert, GA; lp 1838, Eufaula, AL; Grand Lecturer
of State of GA in Masonry.

Barton, John B.
"Farewell." (by L.H.S.). *SCA*, 10-25-1839, p. 72.
(a poem about Mrs. Barton at the grave of her missionary husband).

Baskin, James
nv. b. Gwinnett Co., GA; m/1822 Henrietta Harrison. Charter member
Concord Ch., Carroll Co., GA. Chrn. James Lawrence, Rev. C.M., Mary.
m2/ 11-4-1872, Rhoda Bledsoe of Carroll Co., GA.

Bass, Henry Alexander
m/ 1821Amelia Love (1-18-1794 - 10-21-1865), bur. Tabernacle Cem.,
Greenwood Co., SC. Daniel S. bur. nearby.

1822-46, bills and receipts Book Concern; 1865 cert. of standing as an elder;

1813-43, notebook of sermons; 1816, Bible & signature; 1-13-1843, recommendation to itineracy; 1844-46, 5 letters from A.H. Mitchell; 7-10-1844, letter from nephew; 12-10-1850, letter to Conf. (Wof.).
"Cokesbury Dist., SC." *SCA*, 8-19-1837, p. 34; 8-17-1838, p. 34.
"Visit to N. & S. Santee Mission, SC." *SCA*, 12-25-1840, p. 110.
"Providence Campmeeting, Charleston Dist." *SCA*, 8-12-1842, p. 35.
"Charleston Dist., SC." *SCA*, 9-23-1842, p. 59.

Bass, Larkin
(L) M.D. m/ Mary Rabun (1805 - 8-31-1871), bur. Sparta, Hancock Co., GA. dau. of Wm. Rabun. 2 chrn.

Bass, William C.
son of Henry & Amelia Love Bass; m/ nv Octavia Nickelson of Greensboro, GA.

"The Columbus Dist. Meeting." *SCA*, 6-28-1867, p. 102.

Battin, D.
served Mt. Zion, Carroll Co., GA.

Baxter, James H.
"A Vindication of Young Preachers." *SCA*, 7-19-1871, fp.
"Little River Cir., N. GA Conf." *SCA*, 8-30-1871, p. 138; 10-28-1870, p. 170.
"Gainesville Station, N. GA Conf." *SCA*, 7-17-1872, p. 110; 10-16-1872, p. 162.
"Hall Cir., N. GA Conf." *SCA*, 8-21-1872, p. 130.
"Constant Happiness - How Secured." *SCA*, 3-19-1873, fp.
"Dahlonega Dist. Conf." *SCA*, 9-3-1873, p. 138.
"Gainesville, N. GA Conf." *SCA*, 11-12-1873, p. 175.
"The Witness of the Spirit." (series). *SCA*, 4-15-1874, fp.
"Atlanta Dist. Conf." *SCA*, 7-8-1874, p. 106.
"Covington & Mt. Pleasant." *SCA*, 9-30-1874, p. 154.
"Covington, GA." *SCA*, 10-14-1874, p. 162.
"Newnan Sta." *SCA*, 5-23-1876, p. 82.
"Newnan Cir., N. GA Conf." *SCA*, 10-23-1877, p. 170.

Bazemore, Thomas (d. 9-12-1884)
d. Sylvania, GA.

Bearden, Wilbur F.
Revival on Moultrie Mis." *SCA,* 9-10-1873, p. 142.

Bedell, Mahlon Lucius
b. Burke Co., NC; bv 10-8-1806; bur. Kettle Creek Cem., Waycross, GA; son of David Bedell, RS, (4-17-1764 - 3-24-1840) b. Morris Co., NJ, and Ruth Fairchild (9-3-1765 - 2-19-1833). chrn. by m1/ Benjamin Mitchell; Richard; Georgia Ann (1841 tw.); Florida Jane (1841 tw.); chrn. by m2/ Lucius Mahlon (1851-1932); James King (1849-1923). m3/ 6-1-1856, ElizaHammock Moncrief, b. 3-29-1811, Wilkes Co., GA. 1 dau.

cvt. 10-9-1824; le July 1826; lp 8-7-1826.

1-28-1830, Account to Wm. Capers, Book Concern. (Wof.).
"Little River Mis., FL Conf." *SCA,* 8-30-1850, p. 50.

Belin, James L.
"Waccamaw Neck Mis., SC." *SCA,* 9-18-1840, p. 54.

Bell, James M.
m/ 11-4-1873, Amie C. Champion of Greene Co., GA.

Bell, Thomas A.
"Clayton Mis., GA Conf." *SCA,* 6-13-1851, p. 6.

Bell, William B. (10-30-1826 - 7-3-1876)
bur. Old Smyrna Cem., Cobb Co., GA.

Bell, William R. (10-30-1826 - 7-3-1876)
M.D. b. Chester Dist., SC; d. Cobb Co., GA; m/ 11-3-1846, Margaret Ryles; 1865-6 33rd Dist. GA Legislature; built Bell's Chapel in Hall Co., GA. Mason.

Bellah, James (d. 1833)
dau. Margaret A. (d. 1-6-1838), age 16; dau. Rachael A. (d. 1-20-1838), age 13; both of fever.

Bellah, Morgan
"Cuthbert, Ft. Gaines, GA." *SCA,* 10-23-1846, p. 79.
"Forsyth Cir., GA." *SCA,* 9-23-1837, p. 54.
"Kingston Mis., GA." *SCA,* 9-4-1840, p. 46.

"Decatur Cir., GA." *SCA*, 7-7-1843, p. 15.
"From Thomaston, GA." *SCA*, 4-27-1866, bp.

Bellinger, Lucius
"Letter." *SCA*, 9-17-1869, p. 151.
"Bamberg Dist. & Blackville Campmeeting." *SCA*, 11-5-1869, p. 178.

Bennett, Eli
43rd GA Reg., CSA.

"Monticello Cir., GA." *SCA*, 9-2-1837, p. 42; 10-7-1837, p. 62.
"Oglethorpe Cir., GA." *SCA*, 8-28-1840, p. 42.

Benning, Thomas C.
"Report of the Missions in the bounds of the Newnansville Dist., GA Conf."
    SCA, 10-4-1844, p. 68.
"The GA Conference, 1837." *SCA*, 12-29-1837, p. 110; 1-5-1838, p. 114.
"Washington & Mt. Zion, GA." *SCA*, 6-11-1841, p. 206.
"Mt. Zion, Oglethorpe Co., GA." *SCA*, 10-15-1841, p. 70.
"Florida District." *SCA*, 6-17-1842, p. 2; 9-23-1842, p. 59.

Benson, Blackwood K.
m/ 9-5-1869, Mary A. Basford of Columbia Co., GA.

Bentley, Joseph H.
"Loganville Cir., N. GA Conf." *SCA*, 9-19-1876, p. 150.

Berry, John F.
1853 joined church; le 11-10-1857; lp 6-12-1858.

"Butler Circuit, GA Conf." *SCA*, 10-16-1862, fp.
"Ellaville Cir., GA Conf." *SCA*, 10-12-1866, p. 5.

Best, Hezekiah   (4-15-1801 - 1-12-1878)
b. Hagerstown, MD; d. Bartow Co., GA; parents died when he was inf.;
m/1-29-1833, Adaline Ball. Came to GA Nov. 1857; settled in Kingston.

le 8-22-1825; lp 1825; Deacon 1830;
BALTIMORE CONF: (appts). Rockingham Cir., VA; Greenbrier Cir.;
Fredericksburg, VA; Cumberland, MD; Bladenburg; Westminster; Great
Falls Cir.; Lancaster; West River; Severn; 1842 - Seaman's Union Bd.,
Baltimore. 1878 - Tribute by Cassville Cir. (GA).

Betts, Charles   (1-1-1800 - 4-16-1872)
m2/ Anna Godfrey Green

"Santee Circuit, SC." *SCA*, 9-13-1844, p. 53.
"Columbia Circuit, SC Conf." *SCA*, 10-1-1844, p. 65.

Betts, Jonathan
m/ Elizabeth Fondren

Bigby, Thomas
bur. Mt. Gilead, Coweta Co., GA.

9-26-1831, rec. for deacon's orders from Asbury Camp Ground; 9-17-1832, same from Smyrna QC, SC. (Wof.).

Biggers, Thomas Jefferson (5-23-1831 - 6-25-1941)
formed first MPC in Haralson Co., GA. bro. to John M. Biggers.

Biggs, Joseph E.   (Apr. 1792 - 1-5-1874)
b. VA; d. Talbot Co., GA; reared in Clarke Co., GA;
lp 1824; (ord. v) Deacon 1829; Elder 1834.

Bigham, Robert W.
wife Charlotte Elizabeth Davies, d. 6-22-1872; b. Savannah, GA; reared in Milledgeville, GA; d. Newnan, GA.

"The Death Cottage of Rev. L.J. Davies." *WCA*, v50, n39, 9-29-1886, p. 5.
"Lexington Mission, GA Conf." *SCA*, 6-30-1848, p. 14.
"Athens Dist., GA Conf." *SCA*, 10-16-1862, fp.
"Eatonton Cir., GA Conf." *SCA*, 9-7-1866, fp.
"Griffin, N. GA Conf." *SCA*, 11-22-1867, p. 186.
"LaGrange, N. GA Conf." *SCA*, 9-24-1869, p. 154.
"Pew Rent Experience." *SCA*, 10-15-1869, p. 166.
"Christian Liberality - The Pastor's Duty." *SCA*, 11-5-1869, p. 178.
"Dalton & the Dalton Dist." *SCA*, 1-29-1873, p. 14; 9-10-1873, p. 142;
        10-29-1873, p. 167; 11-11-1874, p. 178.
"Letter From Dalton Dist." *SCA*, 9-17-1873, p. 146.
"Itinerancy Being Corroded - Bishops Blamable." *SCA*, 2-18-1874, fp.
"Trip to the Burnt Church, McLemore Cir., Dalton Dist." *SCA*,
        4-1-1874, p. 50.
"Trion - The Judge & the Hazel Thicket." *SCA*, 10-7-1874, fp.

"Augusta & the Revival." *SCA*, 4-14-1875, p. 58.
"Oxford - The Richmond Campmeeting." *SCA*, 9-1-1875, p. 138.
"Augusta Dist. Campmeeting." *SCA*, 9-22-1875, p. 152.
"Augusta Dist., N. GA Conf." *SCA*, 10-6-1875, p. 158; 4-19-1876, p. 62;
    9-19-1876, p. 150.
"Eatonton, N. GA Conf." *SCA*, 9-5-1876, p. 142.

Birch, Edmund P.
"Is It Wrong To Dance?" *SCA*, 8-13-1857, fp.
"Portrait of a Sectarian." *SCA*, 9-3-1857, fp.
"A Sabbath In The Country or A Visit to Old Mt. Zion Church." *SCA*,
    10-1-1857, fp.
"The Successful Appeal." *SCA*, 10-8-1857, fp.
"Hope & Memory." *SCA*, 10-15-1857, fp.
"The Soul's Capacity For Happiness, et al. (poem). *SCA*, 12-1-1864, np.
"Religion The Light Of Life." (poem). *SCA*, 1-17-1864, fp.
"Hope & Memory." *SCA*, 4-23-1878, fp.

Bird, Daniel
"Lincolnton Cir., GA." *SCA*, 8-19-1837, p. 34.
"Black River Mis., GA." *SCA*, 7-10-1840, p. 14; 5-14-1841, p. 190; 7-2-1841,
    p. 2; 11-19-1841, p. 90; 5-27-1842, p. 198; 9-9-1842, p. 50.

Bird, Elijah   (9-10-1786 - 10-21-1869)
b. Edgefield Dist., SC; settled in DeKalb Co., GA, then moved to Polk Co.,
1853.

Bird, Francis
"Dade Mis., GA Conf." *SCA*, 10-29-1847, p. 82.
"Jenkin's School House, GA Conf." *SCA*, 10-21-1858, p. 82.

Bivens, Thomas H.
M.D. m/ 9-2-1873, Eliza Parks of Columbia Co., GA.

Blake, Edwin L.T.
m/Mary A. Myers (1830 - 2-9-1897). Chrn. Edwin, 1851; Jessica, 1856;
Mary P., 1849; Robert Gorman, 1859; Mary, 1865.

"Leon Cir., FL Conf." *SCA*, 8-18-1875, p. 130.
"Election & the Perseverance of the Elect." *SCA*, 2-23-1876, fp.
"Financial Methods." *SCA*, 7-17-1877, fp.

Blalock, David

"Burke Mis., GA Conf." *SCA*, 8-21-1846, p. 42; 4-30-1847, p. 186;
    8-27-1847, p.46.
"Watkinsville Cir., GA." *SCA*, 8-30-1855, p. 51.
"Ft. Valley Cir., GA Conf." *SCA*, 9-10-1857, p. 59; 10-8-1857, p. 75.
"Morven Cir., S. GA Conf." *SCA*, 4-24-1877, p. 66.

Blalock, James M. (3-30-1825 - 6-18-1872)

joined church 1852; lp 1866; d. Carrollton, GA.

Blanton, Benjamin (12-6-1765 - 9-5-1845)

b. NC; bur. in cemetery of old Pope's Chapel Church (Oglethorpe Co., GA),
near Hutchins, GA, on Barrow Mill Rd.; a son, Benjamin Blanton (7-3-1815
- 4-24-1851) and wife Susannah Davis are in the same cem. Blanton's will is
in Oglethorpe Co., rec. Nov. term,1845; another marriage of Blanton's is
m/12-12-1801, Sally Freeman; Miss Huett was probably his first wife. See:
Hill, Lodowick. *The Hills of Wilkes Co., GA, and Allied Families*, pp. 96-97.

Travis, Joseph. *Autobiography*, pp. 196-197.

Blythe, William H.

m/ Bethena Ward (1817 - 7-25-1867), d. Greene Co., GA, dau. of Jonathan &
Bethena Ward.

Boland, Elijah N.

dv Sept. 1862.

Boland, John M.

"The Problem of Methodism," Southern Meth. Pub. House, 1888.
    (*WCA*, 4-4-1888).
"Gaston Cir., AL Conf." *SCA*, 10-16-1862, p. 159.
"Winning Souls To Christ." (series). *SCA*, 1-28-1864, fp.
"Science And Religion." *SCA*. 1-21-1864, fp.
"The Philosophy of Temptation." *SCA*, 8-4-1864, fp.
"Keep Yourself In The Love of God." *SCA*, 8-11-1864, fp.
"Rembert Hills Cir., Mobile Conf." *SCA*, 11-17-1864, np.
"The New York World Vs. Methodism." *SCA*, 7-15-1874, fp.

Bond, J.B.

"Decatur Cir., GA Conf." *SCA*, 8-28-1846, p. 42.

Bond, William M. D.
m/9-12-1843, Margaret Norris (1826 - 9-28-1909), b. Hall Co., GA.

"Wesley Chapel, Columbus, GA." *SCA*, 6-5-1872, p. 86.
"Hayneville Cir., S. GA Conf." *SCA*, 8-26-1874, p. 130.
"Hawkinsville Cir., S. GA Conf." *SCA*, 10-28-1874, p. 170.

Bonnell, John M. (4-16-1820 - 9-30-1871)
"Athens Mis., GA Conf." *SCA*, 6-25-1847, p. 10; 10-15-1847, p. 70.
"Thoughts For Christian Parents." *SCA*, 7-17-1856, fp.
"Popular Education." *SCA*, 7-24-1856, fp.
"Good Education." *SCA*, 7-31-1856, fp.
"Education By The Church." *SCA*, 8-14-1856, fp.
"Graduation Address at Wesleyan FC." *SCA*, 7-16-1863, fp.
"A Bird's Eye View." *SCA*, 10-6-1864, fp.
"Another Shot." *SCA*, 10-13-1864, fp.
"Dr. Whedon on the Two Methodisms." *SCA*, 4-13-1866, bp.
"One of the Days of the Son of Man." *SCA*, 6-8-1866, fp.
"The Young Reapers of 1867." (poem). *SCA*, 7-19-1867, p. 114.
"The Columbus Dist. Meeting." *SCA*, 8-28-1868, p. 138.

Bonnell, William B.
m/3-30-1875, Alice J. Wright.

Bonner, Eaton P.
wife Martha M. (1817 - 3-3-1864), d. Columbus Co., GA.

Bonner, George E.
"Three Years in Clayton." *SCA*, 5-9-1876, p. 74.
"Clayton Cir. & Mis., N. GA Conf." *SCA*, 10-3-1876, p. 158
          11-21-1876, p. 186.
"Homer Cir., N. GA Conf." *SCA*, 10-30-1877, p. 174.

Bonner, John
A charter member of Old Camp, Carroll Co., GA.

Booth, Robert M.
"Worth Mis., S. GA Conf." *SCA*, 11-3-1875, p. 175.
"Calhoun Cir., S. GA Conf." *SCA*, 11-28-1876, p. 190.
"Quitman Cir., S. GA Conf." *SCA*, 11-6-1877, p. 178.

Booth, William G.
Hinesville Cir., S. GA Conf." *SCA,* 10-4-1871, p. 159.

Boring, Isaac
wife Eliza Dean Jarratt (6-24-1814 - 10-27-1872); b. Morgan Co., GA; d. near Americus, GA, having m3/ J.M. Broadfield.

Boring, Jesse
Served Gwinnett Mis., age 15; erected Wesley Chapel, San Francisco, CA; edited *The Christian Observer;* organized the Pacific Conference on 4-15-1852; CSA McCullough's Div., chief surgeon, CSA, AR, and medical purveyor; head of Medical Dept., Soule Univ., Galveston, TX; co-ed. of *Galveston Medical Journal;* founded San Antonio FC; bur. Orphan's Home, Decatur, GA. See: Simmons, J.C. *Pacific Coast,* 1886.

He preached a sermon in Columbus, GA, called "The Judgement Day." It was so powerful the crowd broke out of the church, running up the streets of the city shouting to everyone,"The judgement has come." He wrote 3 letters in the *WCA* which bitterly attacked Paine College, Augusta, GA, and Pres. Callaway. Issues were: 9-5-1883, p. 2; 9-12-1883, p. 4; 9-26-1883, p. 5.

"The California Mission." *SCA,* 2-14-1851, p. 146.
"Prayer For Peace." (series) see: *SCA,* 12-25-1862, fp.
"Support of Missions." (series) see: *SCA,* 3-18-1858, fp.
"Moving To The West." *SCA,* 8-9-1871, p. 126.
"Church Orphans' Home." *SCA,* 11-5-1869, p. 178.
"Fairs, Horse Racing, Tournaments, etc." *SCA,* 10-11-1871, fp.
"Orphan's Home." (series). *SCA,* 10-1-1873, fp.

"Dr. Jesse Boring." (by William Martin). *SCA,* 8-7-1868, p. 126.

Bouchelle, Lewis B.
"A Plea for the Methodists of the S. GA Conf." *SCA,* 10-30-1868, fp.
"Honor To Whom Honor." *SCA,* 12-4-1868, fp.
"Swainsboro Cir., S. GA Conf." *SCA,* 10-24-1876, p. 170.

Bowden, John M.
"Campbellton Cir., N. GA Conf." *SCA,* 10-1-1869, p. 158.
"Franklin Cir., N. GA Conf." *SCA,* 10-7-1870, p. 153.
"Palmetto Cir., N. GA Conf." *SCA,* 10-16-1872, p. 162.

"Hogansville Cir., N. GA Conf." *SCA*, 11-11-1874, p. 178.
"Fairburn Cir., N. GA Conf." *SCA*, 11-17-1875, p. 182.

Boyd, Hugh
m/9-5-1878, Mary Emma Thurman (8-5-1860 - Feb. 1928), d. NY; chrn.
Florence, Clark, Anna, Hugh.

Boykin, John T.
"Meeting at Rehoboth, Troup Co., GA." *SCA*, 8-8-1844, p. 33.

Bradford, Joseph J.
founded & bur. at Bradford MH, Mitchell Co., GA.

Bradford, Joshua
7-21-1848, LP; m/1820, Mary Kirkland (d. 1874). Chrn. Jefferson, David,
Ambrose, Sarah, Lucy, Sytha. m2/ 6-3-1875, Martha Badenbaugh (Mrs.),
2 chrn. d. inf. He was assigned work in 1857 in Lumpkin Co., GA, but
failed to be effective due to ill health. He was employed by the American
Tract Society for 2 yrs. as a Colporteur, distributing Bibles & religious
literature. He pastored the following churches in Gwinnett Co., GA,
Pleasant Hill (now Dacula), Mt. Carmel, Prospect, preached at Flint Hill
CG, Lawrenceville CG, Harmony Grove, organized the Buford church in 1871.
He organized New Hope Methodist Church in Gwinnett Co., GA.
In 1866 at New Hope, he preached a revival in which over 60 were converted
and joined the church. In Aug. 1846, while pastor of the church, his wife,
Mary Kirkland, preached 2 wks. with over 100 converted. 77 joined the church.
His wife was thoroughly consecrated and rendered much assistance to him.
It was unusual for a woman to preach in those days. He was afflicted with
cancer of the face. He prayed that he might be spared a lingering death. His
prayer was answered. He died in his 78th year.

Bradley, Jackey M.
d. 1865, not 1845.

"Charlotte Cir., NC." *SCA*, 10-25-1839, p. 75.
"Deep River Cir., SC." *SCA*, 9-18-1840, p. 54.
"Chesterfield Cir., SC." *SCA*, 10-21-1842, p. 75.
"Montgomery Cir., SC." *SCA*, 9-1-1843, p. 47.

Brady, John Wesley
cvt. 1849; m/1845, Susan Simmons (1830-1876).

"Dade Mis., GA Conf." *SCA*, 11-11-1853, p. 94; 6-23-1854, p. 10.
"Carnesville Cir., GA." *SCA*, 6-21-1855, p. 11.

Bramlette, Nathan (5-29-1789 - 2-20-1876)
an exhorter on the Hall Cir.

Branch, Franklin
12-10-1842, Recommendation to office of deacon by Cokesbury Cir., SC. (Wof.).

Branch, Franklin A.
m3/ 1-9-1860, Martha Turnbull of Monticello, FL.

"Bainbridge Female College." *SCA*, 2-25-1864, np.
"New Bethel Camp Meeting." *SCA*, 11-8-1871, p. 178.
"Fort Valley & Marshallville Cirs." *SCA*, 9-25-1872, p. 150.
"Fort Valley, S. GA Conf." *SCA*, 9-30-1874, p. 154.

Branch, James O.
"Warm Weather Work." *SCA*, 7-17-1872, p. 110; 7-3-1872, fp.
"Letter from CA." (series). *SCA*, 5-30-1876, p. 86.

Brand, Jesse O.
"The Gospel of Appreciation," *WCA*, v99, n41, Oct. 1935, p. 13.

Branham, Walter R.Sr.
"Lack or Decline in Pulpit Power, How It May Come About." *WCA*, v50, n6, 2-10-1886, p.2.
"A Plea For The Aged." *WCA*, v50, n35, 9-1-1886, p. 5.
"Clinton, GA." *SCA*, 8-2-1839, p. 26.
"Watkinsville Circuit, GA." *SCA*, 10-14-1837, p. 66.
"Atlanta Dist., GA Conf." *SCA*, 9-23-1858, p. 67.
"Griffin Dist., GA Conf." *SCA*, 10-20-1862, p. 166.
"Athens Dist., GA Conf." *SCA*, 9-28-1866, fp.
"Oxford & Social Circle," N. GA Conf." *SCA*, 11-5-1873, p. 171.

Branham, Walter R. Jr.
"Subligna Cir., N. GA Conf." *SCA*, 9-18-1872, p. 146.
"Edgewood, N. GA Conf." *SCA*, 10-28-1874, p. 170.
"A Visit to Clayton." *SCA*, 9-1-1875, p. 138.
"Nacoochee, N. GA Conf." *SCA*, 9-29-1875, p. 154; 10-20-1875, p. 167.
"Dahlonega Dist. Conf." *SCA*, 7-25-1876, p. 118.

Brannon, Franklin M. T.
"Grantville Cir., N. GA Conf." *SCA*, 8-14-1877, p. 130.

Brantley, Franklin L.
"Bethel Mission, GA." *SCA*, 4-29-1853, p. 118.
"Troup Cir., GA Conf." *SCA*, 10-16-1856, p. 79.
"Clinton Cir., GA Conf." *SCA*, 6-11-1857, p. 7.
"A Solemn Warning." *SCA*, 8-31-1866, p. 2.

Breedlove, Benjamin F.
m/11-8-1859, Annie Murrell (2-22-1840 - 9-26-1877), grad. Wesleyan 1858;
b/ SC; d. Bethany, Jefferson Co., GA.

"Ellaville Cir., GA Conf." *SCA*, 10-30-1862, p. 166; 9-24-1863, bp.
"Magnolia Cir., S. GA Conf." *SCA*, 10-4-1867, p. 158.
"Dawson, GA." *SCA*, 9-24-1869, p. 155.
"Fort Valley, S. GA Conf." *SCA*, 10-4-1871, p. 158.
"Cuthbert, S. GA Conf." *SCA*, 10-29-1873, p. 168.
"Bethany Cir., S. GA Conf." *SCA*, 8-8-1876, p. 126; 10-3-1876, p. 158.

Breedlove, J. H.   (1806 - 1-7-1870)   MECS
d. Drew Co., AR; father of B.F. Breedlove.

(L) GA CONF.

Breedlove, William M.   (3-4-1795 - 3-9-1867)
b. VA; moved as a child to Hancock Co., GA. m/1821, the widow Warren;
moved 1843 to Tallapoosa Co., AL; m2/ 1852, M.A. Rape (Lucy Stembridge),
d. 1852; He d. by the fall of a tree "with his own hands."

Brett, Andrew M.
(L) on Waresboro Cir.

Brewer, William M.
bur. Mt. Zion, Forsyth Co., GA. m2/ Martha L. Maness (1843 - 3-24-1902).

"Gainesville Cir., GA Conf." *SCA*, 11-4-1858, p. 90.

Brewton, Winfield C.
bur. McRae, GA.

Brice, Samuel J.
"Ellijay Cir., GA Conf." *SCA,* 11-10-1859, p. 303.

Bright, George
"Clinton, GA." *SCA,* 9-11-1846, p. 55.
"What Constitutes Atonement." serial. *SCA,* 4-2-1847 - 9-17-1847.
"Dahlonega Circuit, GA." *SCA,* 11-29-1850, p. 103.
"Modification of our Itinerancy Calmly Considered." serial. *SCA,* 4-10-1856
    - 5-22-1856.
"The Fall of Man." (series). *SCA,* 5-5-1859, fp.
"Modifications of Itinerancy Calmly Considered." *SCA,* 6-26-1856, pp. 14-15.
"Letter." *SCA,* 12-4-1868, p. 194.
"Letters from Missouri." (series). *SCA,* 3-5-1869, p. 38.

Bright, John M.
"Oakmulgee Mis., GA Conf." *SCA,* 6-22-1849, p. 10.
"Culloden Cir., GA Conf." *SCA,* 11-30-1866, fp.
"McDonough, GA." *SCA,* 8-16-1867, p. 130.

Brooks, Wyatt H.
served Wesley Chapel Mis. in 1852, when it originated. (Columbus).

"Chattahoochee Mission, GA Conf." (series of 12 articles appearing from
    1848-52), *SCA,* 5-26-1848, p. 202; 8-18-1848, p. 42; 11-3-1848,
    p. 86; 1-5-1849, p. 122; 4-27-1849, p. 186; 10-5-1849, p. 70;
    1-11-1850, p. 126; 6-26-1850, p. 14; 1-10-1851, p. 126; 6-13-1851,
    p. 6; 12-19-1851, p. 114; 7-23-1852, p. 30.
"Columbus Factory Mission, GA." *SCA,* 4-22-1853, p. 190.
"Flint River Mission, GA Conf." *SCA,* 12-16-1858, p. 115; 12-29-1859,
    p. 330; 12-17-1857, p. 115; 6-11-1857, p. 7.

Brotherton, Levi
in Dalton, GA, 1860.

"A Condensed Sketch of the Methodist Church in N. GA & Lower E. TN,
Beginning in the Year, 1835." ca 1887. See:SpCl. Woodruff; Reg. Lib.,
Dalton, GA. Printed in *Milestones,* June, 1989.

Brown, Elisha   (1778 - 1867)
b. Columbia Co., VA; d. Whitesville Cir., N. GA.

Brown, Jackeriah
10-26-1829, recom. to conf. for traveling connection, Washington Cir., Milledgeville Dist. (Wof.).

Bruner, Anthony C.
"Newton Cir., GA Conf." *SCA*, 12-25-1846, p. 115.
"Gadsden Mis., FL." *SCA*, 9-18-1840, p. 54; 12-25-1840, p. 110.
"Leon Mis., FL." *SCA*, 5-21-1841, p. 194; 7-16-1841, p. 18; 12-24-1841, p. 110.
"Warrior Mis., GA Conf." *SCA*, 8-18-1843, p. 38.

Bryan, A. J.   (2-2-1836 - 12-21-1874)   MPC   MECS
d. Chattooga Co., GA; moved there in 1868; ordained Coweta Co., GA.
Tribute of Respect, Summerville Cir., N. GA Conf. 3-13-1875.

Bryan, James S.
"Education in Georgia." *SCA*, 9-30-1837, p. 34.
"Letter on Wesley Manual Labor School, Houston Co., GA." *SCA*, 11-9-1838, p. 82.
"Report on Wesley Manual Labor School, Houston Co., GA." *SCA*, 12-27-1839, p. 110-111.

Bryan, James Sidney
m/ 6-17-1874, Ella Pope, dau. of Cadesman Pope of Pike Co., GA.

"Pike Cir., N. GA Conf." *SCA*, 8-28-1872, p. 134.

Bryan, Robert B.
"Black Creek Church." *SCA*, 8-28-1872, p. 134.
"Savannah Dist. Conf." *SCA*, 6-20-1876, p. 98.
"Davisboro Cir., S. GA Conf." *SCA*, 8-14-1877, p. 130.

Bryant, W. C.   (1-28-1806 - 12-23-1872)
(L) b.Wilkes Co., GA; d. Greene Co., GA.

Bunch, John
1-22-1833, Letter to conf. asking for a location; 1-11-1835, missionary report for N & S Santee Mis. (Wof.).

Burch, Edwin J. (1-26-1845 - 11-13-1920)
b. Dodge Co., GA; d. Richland Co., GA. CSA. dau. Alice, d.10-1-1934.

"St. Mary's, GA, SS Celebration." *SCA*, 9-2-1870, p. 138.
"Darien & McIntosh Cir., S. GA Conf." *SCA*, 11-29-1871, p. 190.
"Bethel Cir., S. GA Conf." *SCA*, 10-1-1873, p. 154; 8-26-1874, p. 130.
"Louisville Cir., S. GA Conf." *SCA*, 8-8-1876, p. 126; 6-27-1876, p. 102.

Burdge, Michael
1-24-1815, letter to Wm. McKendree re charges against Hilliard Judge. (Wof.).

Burke, John W.
A Life of Robert Emmett. uv.
"Canton Cir., GA Conf." *SCA*, 8-2-1855, p. 35.
"Lights & Shadows of a Tract Agent." series. *SCA*, 6-3-1858, p. 3; 6-24-1858, p. 14; 3-4-1858, p. 159.
"Sunday School Celebration at Butler." *SCA*, 7-21-1859, p. 238.
"Lawrenceville Cir., GA Conf." *SCA*, 9-11-1856, p. 59.

Burke, William
"The Origin, Nature & Power of the Methodist Episcopacy, General Superintendency & General Conference." *SCA*, 4-25-1845, p. 181; 5-2-1845, p. 185; 5-9-1845, p. 189.

Burkes, Napoleon T. (9-19-1852 - 8-5-1885)
b. Henderson, TX; d. Willis Point, TX, of typho-malarial fever. bur. GA. Grad. 1874, Emory College. m/ Mary M. Palmer, dau. of Jas. E. Palmer, prof. of Emory College; lost wife & 2 chrn. while in GA. m2/ 1883, Maria Weaver, dau. of W.M. Weaver of Greensboro, GA.

Burkhalter, D.N. (d.4-12-1876)
(L). See: Buckhalter. d. Buena Vista Cir.

Burtz, Michael T. (b. 3-10-1841)
bur. Mt. Bethel, Cobb Co., GA.

Bussey, Hezekiah T.
son of Nathan Bussey & Susannah Dowsing who m/3-4-1811, Lincoln Co. & had 7 chrn. m/12-9-1836, Lincoln Co., GA.

Bussey, William D.
son of Nathan Bussey & Susannah Dowsing; m/11-3-1839, Bulloch Co., GA. served Buckhorn in 1873.

"Ogeechee Mission, GA." *SCA,* 5-21-1841, p. 194; 7-16-1841, p. 18; 12-10-1841, p. 102.

Butler, William O.
"City Mis., Atlanta, GA." *SCA,* 6-24-1874, p. 98.
"Douglasville Cir., N. GA Conf." *SCA,* 10-30-1877, p. 174.
"Quincy, FL." *SCA,* 2-12-1878, p. 22.

Caldwell, Andrew W. (1814 - 1902)
son of Garland Caldwell & Elizabeth Matthews.

Caldwell, Charles M.
son of Garland Caldwell & Elizabeth Matthews.
tf to MEC(N) in 1867.

Caldwell, John Hollis (6-41820 -3-11-1899)   (MEC)(N)
                                                    (MPC)
b. Spartanburg, SC; son of Garland Caldwell & Elizabeth Matthews.
Oct. 1832, joined MEC; cvt. Aug. 1836; 7-11-1842 LE.
was never Pres. of Wesleyan FC but was one of the founders and early professors at Andrew FC. d. Dover, DE; bur. Lakeside Cem., Dover.

m/1-2-1849, Elizabeth Thurston Hodnett, dau. of Mjr. John Hodnett & Elizabeth Tignor of Meriwether Co., GA. chrn. William Lane, 10-18-1849; Julia Andrew, 9-26-1851; Frank Hollis, 9-30-1853; Robinson Jackson (2-26-1857 - 4-10-1857); Elizabeth Jane, 3-14-1858; James Hope, 9-25-1860; Mary Rebecca Charles, 8-26-1863; John Hodnett, 2-9-1865; Lillie Belle (8-16-1869 - 2-9-1870).

1856 - tried to raise money for Andrew FC through conducting a lottery, which angered many, especially Rev. E.H. Myers, ed. of the *SCA.* 1868-70, served in GA Legislature; 1870, delegate, National Republican Convention; 1871, apptd. judge of 37th Judicial Dist. Ct. (Troup, Heard, Carrol cos.).

WILMINGTON CONFERENCE, MEC(N): 1872-74 Still Pond, MD; 1875-77 Dover, DE; 1878-80 St. Paul's, Wilmington, DE; 1881-83 Dover, DE; 1884-84 PE, Easton Dist.; 1885-88 Pres. Deleware College; 1888-91 Frederica, DE.

Reminiscences of the Reconstruction of Church & State in GA. (Wilmington, DE: J.Miller Thomas, 1895).

Slavery & Southern Methodism: Two Sermons Preached In the Methodist Church In Newnan, GA. (New York: printed by author, 1865).

The Mysterious Messenger: Founded on Fact by a Member of the GA Conference; A Temperance Story. (Nashville, TN: for author by J.B. McFerrin, 1860).

The Thurstons of the Old Palmetto State; or, *Varieties of Southern Life Illustrated in the Fortunes of a Distinguished Family of South Carolina.* (New York: Joseph Russell, publisher, 1861).

A Sermon on the Centenary of American Methodism. (Griffin, GA: 1866).

"Relations of the Colored People in the Methodist Episcopal Church, South." *MQR,* July, 1866.

The Georgia Question Before the Judiciary Committee of the United States Senate: Arguments of Hon. J.H. Caldwell & Hon. J.E. Bryant. (Washington, DC: Gibson bros., printers, 1870).

"The Rev. J.H. Caldwell of GA." *SCA,* 10-5-1865, np.

Stowell, Daniel W. "The Failure of Religious Reconstruction: The MEC in Georgia, 1865-1871)." (MA thesis). UGA, 1988.

Stowell, Daniel W. "We Have Sinned and God Has Smitten Us: John H. Caldwell and the Religious Meaning of Confederate Defeat." *GHQ,* Summer, 1994.

Caldwell, Willis T.
"Gainesville Cir., GA Conf." *SCA,* 8-31-1866, fp.
"Hancock Cir., N. GA Conf." *SCA,* 10-2-1868, p. 158.

Calhoun, David W.
"Sylvania Cir., GA Conf." *SCA,* 9-30-1858, p. 71; 10-28-1858, p. 86.

Callaway, Morgan
son of Jesse & Mary Wootten Callaway; admitted to GA Bar; CSA Capt., Cutt's Btn.; Chap. Co. B., 11th GA Artillery Btn.; attended school Athens, GA; admitted to GA bar; bur. Rest Haven, Washington, GA; D.D., Emory; m/ Margaret Hinton (not Winton); m2/ 6-24-1868, Georgia Frances Ficklen. Wrote: "The Education of Women." uv. See: Boring, Jesse entry re letters to Callaway at Paine College.

"Washington, GA." *SCA,* 10-5-1866, p. 5.

Camp, Hiram (12-23-1806 - 5-19-1874)
b. Jackson Co., GA; d. Coweta Co., GA; cvt. Aug. 1828 Walton
Campmeeting; m/ 10-5-1828, Peninah Reynolds; 1830 moved to Coweta
Co., GA.

(L) GA CONF. 1841 le, Mt. Horeb; lp & Deacon, 9-15-1848; Chap. of
United Friends of Temperance; Tribute of Respect, Grantville & Pierce Cirs.

Camp, Hosea (1-21-1775 - 4-30-1857)
b. NC; d. Cedartown, GA; bur. on James Everett Plantation, Antioch, GA.
A tax collector in Jackson/Gwinnett counties from 1800-1850.

Campbell, John (d.1826)
d. Amite Co., MS.

Campbell, Thomas J.
"Columbia Mis., AL Conf." *SCA*, 7-23-1847, p. 26.

Campbell, William H. (9-12-1811 - 1-17-1869)   MECS
b. Madison, GA; d. Oxford, GA; son of Charter Campbell.

(L) GA. CONF. 1847, deacon

Candler, Warren A.
Grad. 1857, Emory College; Gen. Conf. Delegate 1886, 1890; mv 11-21-
1877, Nettie Cartwright of LaGrange, GA; Candler College, Havannah, Cuba,
named for him; chrn. Annie Florence, John C., Samuel Covington, Warren A.,
Emory (d. inf.).

Young J. Allen, The Man Who Seeded China. Cokesbury, Nashville, 1931.
"The Pierces, Father And Son." *WCA*, v100, n35, 9-4-1936, p. 10.
"The Proposed Plan of Unification." *WCA*, v100, n16, 4-17-1936, p. 10, 18.
"The Athens Dist. Conf." *SCA*, 8-21-1877, p. 134.
"Watkinsville Cir., N. GA Conf." *SCA*, 10-23-1877, p. 170.

Cantrell, Anderson C.
bur. New Smyrna Cem., Cobb Co., GA; Laura C. Cholson, b. 2-22-1862.

Capel, Britton
He left the MEC and joined those who were called Reformed Methodists.
Years later he made the statement, "It is too late for me to retrace my steps
and come back." See: Travis, Joseph. *Autobiography*, p. 60.

Capers, Benjamin H.
2-10-1835, letter to conf. asking for a change of work; 11-10-1858, letter to Mrs. Bass. (Wof.).

Capers, Samuel W.
"Camden, SC." *CA*, 9-9-1831, p. 6.

Capers, Thomas H.
Chap. 18th AL Reg. CSA; Mason

"Letter from LaFayette, AL." *SCA*, 9-7-1838, p. 46.
"Tuskegee Cir., AL." *SCA*, 11-22-1839, p. 91.
"Mobile, AL." *SCA*, 10-8-1841, p. 66.

Capers, William
11-8-1821, Articles of agreement between Bishops & SC Conf. and the Chiefs of the Creek Nation in Council; 1828, Autograph Album; 1828, 6 letters to editor of *Charleston Observer* vindicating the sermon of Bishop Soule against a review; 1839, letter to conf. at Cheraw; 12-24-1836, letter to *SCA* & Cokesbury School; 12-6-1817, letter to SC Conf.; 12-7-1817, recom. to SC Conf. from Georgetown QC; 2-20-1834, letter to Henry Bass; 1-1-1839, 2 letters to SC Conf. & bookstore. (Wof.).

"The Rule of Ardent Spirits." *SCA*, 12-20-1839, p. 106.
"Letters on Southern Domestic Missions." *SCA*, 4-1-1842, p. 166; 4-8-1842, p. 170.
"Funeral Sermon of Mrs. Andrew." *SCA*, 10-21-1842, f. & p. 75.
"Charleston District." *CA*, 11-19-1830, p. 46.
"Athens, GA, Revival." *CA*, 7-1-1831, p. 174.

Sampley, Ethelene. "William Capers, A Second-Generation Methodist In America." *HH*, v2, n2, Dec. 1972.

Carpenter, Alfred G.
dv. 9-21-1871.

"Cumming Cir., N. GA Conf." *SCA*, 11-18-1870, p. 182.

Carroll, Jesse W.
m/ 12-9-1819, Ann Hodge (7-14-1798 - 3-15-1870), dau. of Rev. James Hodge, b. Oglethorpe Co., GA; d. near Conyers, Newton Co., GA.

"Carnesville Cir., GA Conf." *SCA*, 11-13-1846, p. 91.

Carruth, James L. (1-27-1842 - 1-9-1862)   MECS
b. Madison, FL; d. Fernandina; cvt. 1857.

1859 OT, LP. FLORIDA CONFERENCE: 1860 Brunswick (St. Mary's);
1861 Marion (Tampa); 1862 CSA. Record incomplete.

Carson, Addison C. (12-27-1819 - 1-13-1893)
b. TN; d. Cullman Co., AL; bur. Old Bethel Cem., Cullman Co., AL.
with wife. chrn. Nancy J. , b. ca 1843; Sarah Elizabeth (1-17-1846 -
8-21-1917); Martha J., b. ca 1849; Margaret M., b. Apr. 1860.

"Cooper's Creek Sabbath School (Fannin Co., GA)." *SCA*, 12-2-1858,
      p. 106.
"Morganton Mis., GA Conf." *SCA*, 9-17-1863, bp.

Carter, Benjamin
bur. Harris MH, Washington Co., GA.

Carter, George W.
12-26-1829, recom. to itineracy from Little River Cir. (Wof.).

Carter, John Collier   (1801 - 6-16-1874)
b. Wilkes Co., GA; d. Russell Co., AL; m/ 1822, Ann H. White of
Columbia Co., GA.

Carter, William C.
"Veni Creator." (poem). *SCA*, 7-28-1875, fp.
"God a Refuge." (poem). *SCA*, 5-28-1878, fp.

Carter, William L.
"On Predestination." (pamphlet, 1889). in *WCA*, 1889.

Cary, Clement C.
"Morganton Cir., N. GA Conf." *SCA*, 11-12-1873, p. 175.
"Norcross Cir., N. GA Conf." *SCA*, 9-23-1874, p. 150.
"N. Lincoln Cir., N. GA Conf." *SCA*, 9-1-1875, p. 138.
"Winterville, N. GA Conf." *SCA*, 10-17-1876, p. 166; 11-13-1877, p.182.

Cary, S. F.
"Morven, S. GA Conf." *SCA,* 9-12-1876, p. 146.

Cassels, William Henry (9-22-1797 - Sept. 1857)   MEC,
MECS
b. Liberty Co., GA, son of Elias & Sarah Jones Cassels; bapt. 10-8-1797; labored as a Meth. minister in vicinity of Bainbridge, GA & Gadsden, Leon, Jefferson, Madison & Sewannee counties, FL. bur. Chester Church Cem., Decatur Co., GA.

"Bainbridge Cir., GA." *SCA,* 8-28-1840, p. 42.

Causey, W. J.
1908, served New Hope MPC.

Chambers, Joseph
"Murphy Mis., GA Conf." *SCA,* 8-30-1855, p. 51.
"Duck Town Mis., GA Conf." *SCA,* 3-27-1856, p. 171.
"Jefferson Cir., GA Conf." *SCA,* 9-15-1864, np.

Chandler, John
listed as Chap. 88th GA Reg. CSA. (No such unit existed).

Chandler, William B.
38th GA Reg., CSA.

Chappell, George A. (d. 7-23-1838)

Chappell, John B.
wife, Margaret (1791 - 12-30-1868), b. Wilkes Co., GA; d. Oglethorpe Co., GA; she had m1/ 1814, Silas Griffin who d. 1841; m/ 1845, J.B. Chappell.

"Broad River Mission, GA." *SCA,* 8-19-1842, p. 39.

Chappell, John D.
12-26-1829, recom. to itineracy from Sparta QC, Milledgeville Dist. (Wof.).

Chase, Thomas G. (10-22-1850 - 2-10-1908)
m/10-25-1870, Isabella D. Founts Osborne (2-23-1842 - Jan. 1881), dau. of Wm. P. & Jane Adeline Wild Founts. bur. Oak Hill Cem., Gilmer Co., GA. m2/5-11-1881, Sophia Harris (9-4-1849 - 8-13-1925), bur. w/ him Ft. Hill Cem., Cleveland, TN. 4 chrn. in 1880 Gilmer Co. Census:

Henry Theodore (2-13-1872 - 10-29-1913); William Dean (8-18-1873 - 5-12-1960); Emma (8-5-1875 - 1-16-1960); T. Robert (1-13-1879 - 8-10-1950).

Served following appts. in HOLSTON CONFERENCE: Tellico Cir., 3 yrs; N. Athens Cir., 1 yr; Cleveland Cir., 5 yrs. Helpless for 3 yrs. with a stroke.

Childs, Seaborn J.
"Waresboro Cir., S. GA Conf." *SCA,* 10-11-1867, p. 162.
"Davisboro Cir., S. GA Conf." *SCA,* 10-22-1869, p. 171.
"Washington & Gibson Mis., S. GA Conf." *SCA,* 12-9-1870, p. 192.

Choice, William
"St. Mary's Dist., GA." *SCA,* 10-7-1837, p. 62; 10-19-1838, p. 70.
"Revival in Telfair Co., GA." *SCA,* 3-29-1839, p. 162.
"Leon Cir., FL." *SCA,* 6-11-1841, p. 206.
"Tallahassee, FL." *SCA,* 10-21-1842, pp. 74-75.
"Jeffersonville, Twiggs Co., GA." *SCA,* 11-9-1838, p. 82.
"Leon Mis. to Blacks, FL." *SCA,* 7-31-1846, p. 30; 5-28-1847, p. 206.
"Tallahassee Mis., FL." *SCA,* 8-27-1847, p. 46.
"Leon Mis., FL. Conf." *SCA,* 10-29-1847, p. 82.
"Wakulla Mis., FL." *SCA,* 5-27-1853, p. 210; 8-19-1853, p. 46.

Christenbury, David Fields (8-9-1793 - 1870)
See: nv/ Daniel F. m/ 11-23-1822, Lincoln Co., NC, Susan Wells (9-25-1793 - 6-18-1846) b. Mecklenburg Co., NC, bur. Old Bethesda Cem., Huntersville, NC. chrn. A.B. (male); Reuben Fletcher; Ann Wilmuth; Joseph B., Thomas Columbus, Fannie, Joshua, 2 others. See: Brigance, Albert, H. *Christenberry / Christenbury Genealogy,* 1988.

Christian, Abda
son of John & Mary Christian.

Christian, Elam
son of Elisha Clement Bennett Christian & Phoebe Winter.

Christian, Gabriel (1774 - by 1834)
b. Madison Co., FL, son of John & Mary Christian; m/ 1808, Harrison Blair Gilmer, dau. of John Blair Gilmer of Goosepond section, Oglethorpe Co., GA. child, Julia (1812 - 1883). Harrison B.G. Christian m2/ 1834, Whitson J. Hines.

Christian was a man "whom scarcely anyone ever heard from inclination the second time. Though he was wanting in powers to persuade others to become Christian, he followed faithfully the straight and narrow path himself." Gilmer, George R., *Early Settlers of Upper GA*, pp. 24-25.

2-21-1825, copy of letter to from SC Conf., Wilmington, in regard to Elder's Orders; 12-1-1824, letter to bishops written from Oglethorpe, GA. (Wof.).

Christian, Heyden C.
b. Newon Co., GA; son of Presley Franklin Christian & Elizabeth O. Sappington; g.son of Isaac Christian (1787 - 1807) and Mildred White. m1/ 4-17-1867, Susan V. Baldwin (1848 - ca 1881), dau. of William Lawson Baldwin, Sr., & Martha Warren. Chrn. Lena, b. 1868; Laura, b. 1877; Hayden, b. 1879. m2/ Kate O'Donnelly (1858 - 1900); Chrn. John O., b. 1883; Thornton G., b. 1888. m3/ Lizzie ?, b. 1855. No issue.

"Dallas Cir., N. GA Conf." *SCA*, 11-6-1872, p. 174; 1-29-1873, p. 14.
"Lafayette Cir., N. GA Conf." *SCA*, 6-24-1874, p. 98.
"McLemore's Cove Cir., N. GA Conf." *SCA*, 9-15-1875, p. 146;
    10-17-1876, p. 166.
"Dalton Dist. Conf." *SCA*, 6-6-1876, p. 90; 6-5-1877, p. 90;
    10-16-1877, p. 166.

Christian, Thomas J.
wife, Margaret E. (1868 - 1927).

Christian, Thomas T.
son of Elisha Clement Bennett Christian & Phoebe Winter. wife Lucy Morton (12-30-1838 - 4-29-1919) bur. College Pk., GA.

"Cave Spring Cir., GA." *SCA*, 8-30-1855, p. 51.
"Dahlonega Cir., GA Conf." *SCA*, 9-30-1858, p. 71; 10-7-1858, p. 75.
"Wilkes Cir., GA Conf." *SCA*, 8-18-1859, p. 254; 7-28-1859, p. 242.
"Subligna Cir., GA Conf." *SCA*, 7-31-1856, p. 35; 8-21-1856, p.47.
"Clarkesville Cir., GA Conf." *SCA*, 3-26-1857, p. 171; 4-2-1857,
    p. 175; 7-30-1857, p. 37; 10-8-1857, p. 75.
"Hancock Cir., GA Conf." *SCA*, 10-30-1862, p. 166; 11-6-1862, p. 171.
"Columbus Dist., S. GA Conf." *SCA*, 8-23-1871, p. 134; 6-17-1870, p. 94;
    10-14-1870, p. 162.
"Macon, First Street." *SCA*, 6-9-1864, np.
"Terrell Cir., GA Conf." *SCA*, 11-2-1866, fp.

"Dawson Cir., S. GA Conf." *SCA*, 8-16-1867, p. 130; 9-13-1867, p. 146;
    10-11-1867, p. 162; 8-28-1868, p. 138; 9-25-1868, p. 154.
"A Narrow Escape - Answer to Prayer." *SCA*, 2-28-1868, fp.
"Columbus Dist. SS Convention." *SCA*, 2-12-1869, p. 26.
"Talbotton, GA." *SCA*, 7-16-1869, p. 114.
"Wesley Chapel, Columbus, GA." *SCA*, 7-10-1872, p. 109.
"Revival in Columbus." *SCA*, 4-9-1873, p. 54.
"Americus, S. GA Conf." *SCA*, 6-17-1874, p. 95.
"Revivals in Americus." *SCA.*, 10-14-1874, p. 162.
"Make Haste Slowly." *SCA*, 11-27-1877, fp.

Clark, Archibald
"Jesup Cir., S. GA Conf." *SCA*, 10-16-1872, p. 162; 8-25-1875, p. 134.
"Wayne Mis., S. GA Conf." *SCA*, 8-1-1876, p. 122.

Clark, Charles
nv Clarke

"Isle of Hope & Skidaway Mis., GA." *SCA*, 6-2-1843, p. 200.

Clark, J.H.
"Jefferson Mis., GA." *SCA*, 6-27-1851, p. 14; 1-2-1852, p. 122.

Clark, James O.A.
Adams, A. Ray. "The Life & Work of J.O.A. Clark (1827-1894)." *HH*, v9, n2,
    Dec. 1979, pp. 7-10.
"Emory College." *SCA*, 1-1-1863, p. 2.
"Washington, GA, Revival/ Bereavement." *SCA*, 6-11-1857, p. 7.
"The Destruction of Mt. Zion Church, Glascock Co." *SCA*, 6-23-1875, p. 98.
"The Spiritual Power of the MEC." *SCA*, 8-11-1875, p. 126.
"Mt. Moriah Campmeeting." *SCA*, 9-29-1875, p. 154.
"The Presiding Eldership." *SCA*, 5-29-1877, fp.
"The Modern Campmeeting." *SCA*, 8-28-1877, fp.

Clark, John
ref. in Jenkins, James, *Experiences*, etc. pp. 59-62.

Clark, John D.
m/ 11-1-1874, Sarah F. McKinnon.

"Our Old Sewing Machine." *SCA*, 6-5-1877, p. 90.

Clarke, Benjamin W. (d. 9-11-1868)
le Muscogee Co., GA.

Clarke, George Citizen
m/ Martha H. Wilson, 7 chrn. bur. Oaklawn Cem., Ft. Valley, GA.
Travis, Joseph. *Autobiography.* pp. 204-205.

"Americus Dist., GA Conf." *SCA,* 5-15-1856, pp. 198-99; 9-3-1857, p. 55.
"A Chapter of Calamities." *SCA,* 6-2-1859, p. 211.
"An Explanation." *SCA,* 6-19-1856, p. 11.
"Perry Cir., GA Conf." *SCA,* 9-18-1862, p. 143.
"Bainbridge Dist., S. GA Conf." *SCA,* 9-11-1868, p. 146; 8-30-1871, p. 138.
"Dawson, GA." *SCA,* 7-31-1872, p. 118; 12-2-1874, p. 190.

Clarke, William Henry
lp 1833; 10th GA State Guard Cavalry, CSA.

Clecker, Richard C.
"The Flashlight From Calhoun Darktown." *WCA,* v99, n42, 10-25-1935, p. 13.

Clements, Stephen D.
m2/ 11-11-1869, Fredonia C. Dozier.

Cliffs, Thomas. (d. 11-13-1865)
moved to GA from Colleton Dist., SC.

Clontz, Michael A.
m/ Rachel A. Stover (9-23-1830 - 7-13-1867), b. Habersham Co., GA;
Ocala, FL; dau. of Jeremiah & Ann Stover. He went to the Baptist Church.
See: Burke, John B. *Autobiography,* p. 103.

"Clayton Mis., GA Conf." *SCA,* 12-22-1848, p. 114.
"Murphy Mis., GA." *SCA,* 4-27-1849, p. 186; 10-12-1849, p. 74.
"Blairsville Mis.," *SCA,* 5-16-1851, p. 198.
"Forsyth Cir., GA Conf." *SCA,* 9-16-1858, p. 63; 10-14-1858, p. 78.
"The Christian Index," *SCA,* 9-30-1858, fp.
"Ft. Valley, GA Conf." *SCA,* 4-28-1859, p. 191; 9-22-1859, p. 275.

Clontz, William P.
"Fayetteville Cir., GA Conf." *SCA,* 10-2-1856, pp. 70-71.
"Franklin, GA Conf." *SCA,* 10-8-1857, p. 75.

Cobb, Howell
"Public Meeting In Perry, GA." *SCA*, 7-12-1844, p. 19.

Coburn, John Robert
"Santee Mis., SC." *SCA*, 9-9-1837, p. 46.
"S. Santee Mis., SC." *SCA*, 11-15-1839, pp. 86-87.
"Combahee & Ashepoo Missions, SC." *SCA*, 11-27-1840, p. 94; 5-19-1843,
        p. 192; 8-11-1843, p. 34; 11-19-1841, p. 90.
"Combahee Mis., SC." *SCA*, 10-2-1846, p. 66; 5-26-1848, p.202.
"Beaufort Mis. Report." *SCA*, 7-5-1855, p. 19; 5-25-1855, p. 203.

Cofer, Merritt J.
"Hall Cir., N. GA Conf." *SCA*, 9-18-1877, p. 150.

Cohron, Joseph
nv Joseph Choram, Cohran. bur. Jonesville City Cem.

Coleman, Thomas C.
wife Frances (1813 - 12-31-1873).

"Letter from Perry Cir., GA. *SCA*, 10-5-1838, p. 62.
"Tazewell Cir., Ft. Gaines Dist., GA Conf." *SCA*, 8-6-1841, p. 30.
"Ft. Valley Mission to People of Color." *SCA*, 9-25-1846, p. 62; 6-18-12847,
        p. 6; 10-8-1847, p. 70; 12-31-1847, p. 118; 7-14-1848, p. 22; 10-6-
        1848, p. 70; 1-19-1849, p. 130; 8-31-1849, p. 50; 8-15-1851, p. 42.
"Milford Mission, FL Conf." *SCA*, 6-7-1855, p. 3.
"Morgan Mission, FL Conf." *SCA*, 11-19-1857, p. 99.

Coley, James M.
prob. Jesse M.

"Payne Chapel, Atlanta, GA." *SCA*, 2-11-1872, p. 22.
"Fulton Cir., N. GA Conf." *SCA*, 9-11-1877, p. 146; 10-16-1877, p.166.

Collier, George
10-24-1929, rec. to itinerancy. (Wof.).

Collier, William E.
9-2-1837, rec. to itinerancy from Sharon, Cokesbury QC. (Wof.).

Collinsworth, John
m/ 1816, Mildred L. Scarborough (7-20-1797 - 11-29-1873) b. Burke Co., GA; d. Eatonton, GA.

Collinsworth, William
letter complaining of his actions in regard to a horse lent to him by Mr. Finch and never returned. (Wof.).

Colquitt, Alfered Holt (4-20-1824 - 3-26-1894)   MECS
b. Walton Co., GA; d. Washington, DC; bur. Rose Hill, Macon, GA; grad. Princeton, 1844; GA Attorney 1845; Mjr. Mexican War; m/ May 1848, Dorothy Tarver; m2/ Sarah Tarver; 1852 US Congress; 1859 GA Legislature; CSA Capt., Co 8, 6th GA Reg.; Mjr. Gen.; GA Governor, 1876-82; 1882 US Senate; Trustee, Emory College.

(L) No Conference Record.

Conaway, Curtis A.
nv Conoway, Connoway. joined CMC later in life.

"Monroe Cir., N. GA Conf." *SCA*, 11-25-1870, p. 185.
"Winterville Cir., N. GA Conf." *SCA*, 10-15-1873, p. 163; 8-12-1874, p. 126; 11-4-1874, p. 174; 9-29-1875, p. 154.

Cone, William H.C.
Chap. 19th GA Reg. d. hosp. Richmond, VA.
See: 1860 Census, Heard Co., GA.

"Factory Mis., GA." *SCA*, 7-15-1853, p. 26; 12-23-1853, p. 118.
"Elberton Cir., GA Conf." *SCA*, 7-3-1856, p. 19.

Conley, R. J.
"Pulaski & Wilcox Mis., S. GA Conf." *SCA*, 11-25-1874, p. 186.

Conley, William F.
wife Francina E. Smith (7-10-1842 - 5-21-1873)

"Subligna Cir., GA." *SCA*, 8-30-1855, p. 51; 9-20-1855, p. 68.
"Reidsville Cir., GA Conf." *SCA*, 7-15-1858, p. 27; 5-23-1858, p. 207.
"Springfield Cir., GA Conf." *SCA*, 7-28-1859, p. 242; 9-22-1859, p.275.
"Roswell Cir., GA Conf." *SCA*, 9-11-1856, p. 59.

"Summerville Cir., GA Conf." *SCA*, 9-24-1857, p. 67.
"Jacksonville Cir., S. GA Conf." *SCA*, 9-2-1874, p. 138.

Conley, William M. C.
"Bryan Mis., S. GA Conf." *SCA*, 10-9-1872, p. 158.

Connor, Robert A.
"Andrew Chapel Colored Charge." *SCA*, 6-27-1851, p. 14.
"Talbot Cir., GA Conf." *SCA*, 11-20-1856, p. 99.

Connor, William G.
"Letter from LaGrange, GA." *SCA*, 5-29-1856, p. 207.
"Spartanburg FC." *SCA*, 7-30-1863, bp.
"In Texas." *SCA*, 3-19-1869, p. 46.

Connors, Charles H.
"Starkville Mis., GA Conf." *SCA*, 10-1-1863, bp.

Cook, Francis
bv. Kershaw Dist., SC; son of Wm. Cook & Jemimah Flake who moved from
VA to Anson Co., NC, to Kershaw Dist., SC; g.son of Rev. Isaac Smith.
joined MEC 8-21-1808 in the home of Rev. Isaac Smith, Camden, SC; cvt.
6-1-1811 at camp-meeting two m. from where he was born on Sanders Ck.
near Camden, Kershaw, SC; class leader at Camden SC 1823 apptd. by
Reuben Tucker; le 4-1-1834, Mt. Zion, Harris Co., GA; LP 9-7-1834 by QC;
trustee of Mulberry Grove CG, Harris Co., GA; lp 1836; Deacon (E) Dec. 1839;
moved to Culloden, GA, 1840; Ord. Deacon by J.O. Andrew at Wesleyan
7-16-1840; moved in 1870s to Marietta. dv 5-10-1872. bur. Old City Cem.,
Marietta, GA.

(**Fam. data expanded, inclusive of vol.**). m1/ Elizabeth Heath
(1801 - 7-18-1827) bur. Quaker Cem., Camden, SC. chrn. Henry M.
(1820-1871); Sarah Jemima Flake (Nov. 1822 - 6-10-1822); William
Thomas (6-17-1825 - 10-9-1826). m2/ Margaret Milligan Ellison, bur.
City Cem., Marietta, GA. chrn. Susan Elizabeth (5-16-1829 - 8-5-1847);
John Ellison (12-6-1830 - 1-22-1890); William Francis (11-20-1832 -
12-19-1902); Sarah Jane bd; Samuel Kennedy (b. 1836); James Osgood
Andrew (8-23-1838 - 9-7-1919); Jane Milligan (Jennie) (b. 1840); Julia B.
(b. 1842); Susan (b. 1848); Winfield (6-21-1850 - 9-15-1855).

Cook, James O.A.
"From Gen. Lee's Army." *SCA*, 2-25-1864, np.
"Upson Cir., GA Conf." *SCA*, 9-7-1866, fp.
"Cuthbert, GA Conf." *SCA*, 3-8-1867, p. 38.
"Reconstruction of Circuits," *SCA*, 4-26-1867, fp.
"A Church Burned." (Cuthbert). *SCA*, 9-11-1868, p. 146.
"Cuthbert, S. GA Conf." *SCA*, 9-17-1869, p. 150.
"Letter From Brunswick, GA." *SCA*, 1-24-1872, p. 10.
"Brunswick, S. GA Conf." *SCA*, 6-11-1873, p. 90.
"Taylor's Ck. Campmeeting." *SCA*, 11-11-1874, p. 178.
"Thomasville, S. GA Conf." *SCA*, 9-8-1875, p. 142; 9-5-1876, p. 142.
"Spring Hill Cir., S. GA Conf." *SCA*, 9-25-1877, p. 154.

Cook, John Wesley   (1-20-1817 - 3-6-1892)
bur. Jasper Co., GA, fam. cem. m/ Mary Parnel, b. 1816, SC. Chrn. John
Wesley, Jr., 1853; Benjamin W., 1841; Nathail Greene, 1848; Mary A., 1851.

Cook, Jones E.
"Rome Cir., GA." *SCA*, 12-6-1850, p. 107.

Cook, Osgood F.
mv m/1-4-1894, Gussie Mallard

Cook, William F.
(Fam. data expanded, inclusive of vol.).
son of Francis Cook & Margaret Milligan Ellison; bur. Newnan, GA; m/
Louisa Jane Richards (10-26-1836 - 7-11-1898), dau. of Alexander Richards &
Elizabeth Gamble. chrn. James Glenn (11-27-1858 - 5-9-1862); Ellison
Richards, b. 1862; Mary Lou \(2-4-1863 - 10-17-1953); Edmund Francis
b.1-24-1867; Emma Florrie, b. 6-3-1868; Margaret Melinda (3-1-1870 -
6-26-1958); Bessie Sawrie (8-6-1871 - 6-28-1872).

"Culloden Cir., GA Conf." *SCA*, 9-2-1858, pp. 54-55.
"Forsyth, GA Conf." *SCA*, 9-25-1862, p. 147.
"Griffin Dist., GA Conf." *SCA*, 11-2-1865, np.
"Marietta, GA." *SCA*, 5-17-1867, p. 78.
"Our Sunday School." (series) see: *SCA*, 9-23-1870, fp.
"Rome, N. GA Conf." *SCA*, 10-28-1870, p. 170.
"Exitus Acta probat." *SCA*, 11-1-1871, fp.
"Sunday School Conventions." *SCA*, 6-12-1872, p. 90.
"Rome Dist., N. GA Conf." *SCA*, 9-9-1874, p. 139.

"The Temperance Question." *SCA*, 10-21-1874, fp.
"Wesleyan Female College." *SCA*, 9-1-1875, p. 138.

Cooper, Charles P.
"The Gen. Conf. & the Bishops." *SCA*, 11-11-1874, fp.
"Sketches of Methodism in Jacksonville, FL. (series). *SCA*, 11-25-1874, fp.

Cooper, Stephen H. (7-1-1812 - 6-20-1873)
b. Liberty Co., GA; d. Clinch Co., GA.

"Ogeechee Mis., GA." *SCA*, 7-28-1843, p. 26; 1-5-1844, p. 118.
"Buena Vista, GA Conf." *SCA*, 4-24-1856, p. 187.

Cooper, Thomas W.
1834 wrote of Connection between Geology & Peutateuch.

"Telfair Cir., GA." *SCA*, 9-13-1839, pp. 50-51; 12-6-1839, p. 99.
"Newnansville Cir., FL." *SCA*, 10-2-1846, p. 67.
"Tampa Dist., FL Conf." *SCA*, 9-23-1858, p. 66; 6-30-1859, p. 229; 10-15-1857, p. 79.
"E. FL Seminary." *SCA*, 7-23-1857, p. 31.

Copelen, A. H. ?
wife Lucretia (2-15-1803 - 9-19-1877); b. Greenville Dist., SC; d. Gwinnett Co., GA.

Corley, Robert J.
"The Discipline In Our Sunday Schools." *SCA*, 8-23-1871, fp.
"Talbotton Cir., S. GA. Conf." *SCA*, 3-5-1869, p. 38.
"Talbot Cir., S. GA Conf." *SCA*, 11-26-1869, p.190.
"Letter From Albany." *SCA*, 10-11-1871,
"Columbus, GA." *SCA*, 5-5-1875, p. 70; 5-19-1875, p. 78; 10-13-1875, p. 162; 9-12-1876, p. 146.

Cotter, Robert N.
"Jacksonville Cir., GA Conf." *SCA*, 9-11-1856, p. 59.
"The Church's Compromises." *SCA*, 8-6-1857, fp.

Cotter, William J.
"Blairsville Mis., GA Conf." *SCA*, 10-23-1846, p. 78; 12-25-1846, p. 114.
Warren Cir., GA." *SCA*, 9-20-1855, p. 68; 11-20-1856, p. 99.

"Waynesboro Cir., GA Conf." *SCA*, 6-24-1858, p. 15; 4-15-1858, p. 183;
    5-23-1858, p. 207.
"Greensboro Cir., GA Conf." *SCA*, 11-20-1862, p. 179; 9-11-1862, p. 138.
"Forsyth Cir., GA Conf." *SCA*, 10-26-1865, np.
"From Fort Valley." *SCA*, 3-30-1866, fp.
"A Terrible Failure - A Glorious Success." *SCA*, 1-11-1867, fp.
"Whitesville Cir., N. GA Conf." *SCA*, 4-19-1867, p. 62; 10-18-1867, fp;
    9-11-1868, p. 146; 9-18-1868, p. 151.
"Sabbath School Celebration at Whitesville, Harris Co., GA." *SCA*,
    8-23-1867, p. 134; SS Aniversary, 8-14-1868, p.130.
"Grantville Cir., N. GA Conf." *SCA*, 8-20-1869, p. 134; 9-2-1874, p. 138
    9-22-1875, p. 152; 10-20-1875, p. 166; 9-12-1876, p. 142.
"LaGrange FC." *SCA*, 5-13-1870, p. 75.
"Troup Cir., N. GA Conf." *SCA*, 9-9-1870, p. 143; 9-16-1870, p. 146;
    10-7-1870, p. 153; 3-13-1872, p. 38; 10-9-1872, p. 158.
"Elberton, N. GA Conf." *SCA*, 2-13-1877, p. 26; 8-14-1877, p. 130.
"The Presiding Elder Question." *SCA*, 6-12-1877, fp.
Memoir of his parents. *SCA*, 11-15-1871, fp.

Cotton, James G.
reared in Putnam Co., GA; taught school in Forsyth & Harris cos., GA.
(L) 1835.

Cotton, Smith
RS, Ensign in SC Militia; Ensign, Hancock Co. Reg. of Militia, 1799; will
in Bk. 2, p. 73, Hamilton, GA. Preached at Rehoboth, Harris Co., GA.

Cotton, Stephen G.
"Northwestern Texas." *SCA*, 4-16-1869, fp.
"Northeastern Texas." *SCA*, 4-23-1869, fp.

Cowart, Robert J.
"Marietta Circuit, GA." *SCA*, 9-1-1843, p. 47.

Cowles, Samuel
Travis, Joseph. *Autobiography.* pp. 207-220.

Cox, Cary (7-28-1795 - 1-12-1878)
b. Edgefield Dist., SC; d. Monroe Co., GA; moved to Jones Co., GA age 8.
probable (L) of Monroe Co., GA.
m/ Sarah W. ? (10-19-1795 - 6-21-1870.

Cox, Daniel D.
m2/ Emily Luckie, d. 8-23-1867; m3/ 10-1-1868, dau. of Judge O.A. Bell.

"Jeffersonville Dist., GA." *SCA*, 9-27-1855, p. 67.
"Dahlonega Dist., GA Conf." *SCA*, 11-11-1858, p. 94; 7-31-1856, p. 35;
    9-25-1856, p. 67; 9-24-1857, p. 67.
"Whitesville Cir., GA Conf." *SCA*, 11-20-1862, p. 179; 9-18-1862, p. 143.
"Asbury & Trinity Mis., Augusta, GA." *SCA*, 7-23-1863, bp.
"Asbury Church, Augusta." *SCA*, 10-26-1865, np; 11-9-1865, np; 7-27-1866,
    p. 5; 11-23-1866, p. 5.
"A Good Meeting." (Macon Cir.). *SCA*, 9-13-1867, p. 138.
"Atlanta, GA." *SCA*, 11-13-1872, p. 179.
"Forsyth, N. GA Conf." *SCA*, 12-8-1875, p. 194.
"Gainesville, N. GA Conf." *SCA*, 9-19-1876, p. 150; 11-21-1876, p. 186.

Crandle, Smith
dv 2-18-1840 (headstone). bur. Canton UMC Cem.

Cranford, Henry
"Clayton Mis., GA Conf." *SCA*, 7-24-1846, p. 26; 11-13-1846, p. 90.
"Murphy Mis., GA Conf." *SCA*, 6-18-1847, p. 6; 10-1-1847, p. 66.
"Factory Mis., GA." *SCA*, 5-2-1851, p. 190; 8-1-1851, p. 34; 8-13-1852,
    p. 42; 4-30-1852, p. 190.
"Kingston Mis., GA." *SCA*, 11-28-1851, p. 102; 7-22-1853, p. 30.
"Broad River Mis., GA." *SCA*, 7-28-1854, p. 30; 8-28-1856, p. 51.
"Broad River Col. Mis., GA." *SCA*, 11-1-1855, p. 87.
"Factory Mis., Clarke Co., GA." *SCA*, 5-21-1857, p. 203.

Craven, Isaac Newton
son of Rev. John Craven & bro. to Thos. W. Craven below. d. in TX;
chrn. Carolyn, 1828; Eliza, 1830; Arnold, 1834; Richard, 1837; Margaret,
1842; Charles, 1846; James, 1848. Family researched by Thurman N.
Palmer, Tacoma, WA.

"Ocilla Mis., FL Conf." *SCA*, 9-18-1846, p. 58.

Craven, Thomas W.
wife Phoby C. ? (1-15-1798 - 3-20-1872), b.NC; d. Polk Co., GA.

Crawford, Hinton   (12-27-1798 - 2-22-1868)
b. Greene Co., GA; d. State Asylum, Milledgeville, GA; cvt. 1827;
deacon 12-17-1837. (not the same as Wm. H. Crawford).
wife Harriett ? (1796 - 1872) d. near Fork Chapel, Greene Co., GA.

"Watkinsville, GA." *SCA*, 11-11-1842, p. 85.

Crawford, William
"Thomaston Cir., GA." *SCA*, 11-13-1840, p. 86.
"Thomaston Cir., GA Conf." *SCA*, 10-25-1850, p. 79.

Crenshaw, David
m2/ Jane S. Reid (4-5-1813 - 2-24-1875); b. Scotland; d. Terrell Co., GA.

"Reidsville Cir., GA Conf." *SCA*, 10-2-1846, p. 67.
"Americus Cir., GA Conf." *SCA*, 9-30-1858, p. 71.
"Ft. Gaines Cir., GA Conf." *SCA*, 8-6-1857, p. 39; 8-27-1857, p. 51;
      9-24-1857, p. 67.
"Sandy Springs CG." *SCA*, 11-5-1873, p. 171.

Crook, William
m/ 1-7-1830, Mary E. ? (1-11-1816 - 10-22-1870); b. Wilmington, NC;
d. & bur. near Yorkville, SC.

"Santee Cir., SC." *SCA*, 10-21-1837, p. 70; 12-8-1837, p. 98.
"Lincolnton Dist., SC." *SCA*, 9-23-1842, p. 59; 10-14-1842, p. 71.
"Sharon Camp-Meeting, Cokesbury Cir. SC." *SCA*, 9-1-1843, p. 47.
"Camp-Meeting at Smyrna, Cokesbury Cir. SC." *SCA*, 11-10-1843, p. 87.
"Cokesbury Cir., SC Conf." *SCA*, 11-1-1844, p. 83.
"Black Swamp Cir.," *CA*, 8-26-1831, p. 206.
"Marion, SC Qtrly. Meeting." *SCA*, 9-15-1848, p. 58.

Crowell, Churchwell A.
son of John Crowell & Isabella McWilliams; g.son of Simon & Elizabeth
Crowell of Union Co., NC.

"Greenville Cir., SC." *SCA*, 10-7-1837, p. 62.
"Santee Cir., SC." *SCA*, 8-16-1839, p. 34.
"Sumpterville, SC." *SCA*, 9-13-1839, p. 50.
"Orangeburg Cir., SC Conf." *SCA*, 10-23-1846, p. 79.
"Cokesbury, SC, Revival." *SCA*, 9-15-1848, p. 58.

Crowell, Josiah F.   (Oct. 1826 - 5-30-1901)
same as James F., text, p. 129.
b. Mecklenburg Co., NC; d. Carroll Co., GA; son of Benjamin Crowell; g.son of Simon Crowell. pvt. Co. C., 1st GA Cav. CSA; one child by wife Leah, Sophia Janette, b. Mar. 1854; m/2 Mamie ?, b. May, 1873. son, Samuel (7-30-1898 - 2-14-1899) bur. County Line Cem., Center Point MC, Temple, GA.

See: 1870 Census, Carroll Co., GA for J.F., 1828; Leah, 1830; Janetta, 1864.

Crum, Earnest
"Tornado in SE GA." *SCA,* 5-3-1871, p. 70.

Crumley, William M.
"Satilla Mis., GA." *SCA,* 12-10-1841, p. 102.
"Rome, GA Conf." *SCA,* 9-23-1858, p. 67.
"Augusta, GA." *SCA,* 10-16-1856, p. 79; 6-19-1856, p. 11.

Crumpler, Pleasant H.
m2/ 6-25-1894; bur. Ashburn, GA.

"Spring Hill Cir., S. GA Conf." *SCA,* 9-9-1874, p. 139.
"Washington Cir., S. GA Conf." *SCA,* 10-20-1875, p. 166.
"Stewart Cir., S. GA Conf." *SCA,* 9-26-1876, p. 154.
"Florence, Stewart Co., GA." *SCA,* 11-7-1876, p. 178.
"Ellaville Cir., S. GA Conf." *SCA,* 10-16-1877, p. 166.

Culpepper, John B.
"Davisboro Cir., S. GA Conf." *SCA,* 9-22-1875, p. 152; 11-3-1875, p. 175; 11-17-1875, p. 182.
"Crawford Cir., S. GA Conf." *SCA,* 11-20-1877, p. 186.

Cummings, J.
"Fairburn Cir., N. GA Conf." *SCA,* 9-17-1873, p. 146.

Cunyus, William   (7-21-1828 - 6-17-1876)
b. Houston Co., GA; d. Bartow Co., GA; cvt. age 14; grad. Emory 1850 m/ 12-12-1850, Celestia A. Jennings of Wetumpka, AL.

le Covington Cir. 5-7-1850; lp Perry Cir. 10-31-1854; supplied Van Wert Mis. 1872; taught school 7 yrs.

Curry, Daniel (b. 11-26-1809)

1837 Grad. Wesleyan Univ., Middleton, CT; 1839, Prof., Wesleyan, Macon, GA; founded NY EAST CONFERENCE; 1884 Book Ed. of MEC. Ed. following: *The History of American Methodism, The Life of Wyckliff, The Metropolitan City of America, Life of Bishop Davis W. Clark.*

"The Work of God in Georgia." *SCA,* 11-19-1841, p. 90.

Curtis, Julius T.

m/ Lou Bell (Phillips) Applewhite who was b. 9-30-1876.

"Mississippi Correspondence." *SCA,* 5-24-1871, p. 82.
"Senoia Cir., N. GA Conf." *SCA,* 8-28-1877, p. 138; 9-4-1877,
    p. 142; 9-18-1877, p. 150.

Danforth, Jacob R. (4-23-1816 - 2-4-1873)

b. Saratoga Co., NY; d. Macon, GA; cvt. St. John's, Augusta, age 18. went to Episcopal Church. See: John B. Burke, *Autobiography,* pp. 106-107.

Daniel, Jephthah H. (d. 6-10-1894)

Danneley, James

1825, Account w/ Book Concern. (Wof.).

Darsey, Lowndes A.

m/ 7-7-1871, Saphronia A. Ponder (10-10-1855 - 2-28-1874), b. Burke Co., GA; d. Jasper, Hamilton Co., FL; dau. of Ephriam & Axallna Ponder.

"Millen Mis." *SCA,* 10-15-1869, p. 166.

Davenport, James T.

"Acworth Cir., N. GA Conf." *SCA,* 8-19-1874, p. 131; 11-18-1874, p. 182; 11-24-1875, p. 186.

Davenport, Smith

"Letter from Key West, FL." *SCA,* 3-26-1873, p. 46.

Davenport, Thomas E.

1884, grad. Emory College; 1888, attended Drew Seminary.

"The Sad Case of Achan Clem." *WCA,* v100, n42, 10-23-1936, p. 13.

"The Gates of Glory." (poem). *American Voices,* 1935, Avon House, NY. also in *WCA,* v100, n8, 2-21-1936, p. 13.

Davenport, Wilson L.
lived at Clem, Carroll Co., GA; preached at Shiloh CG.

"Etowah Mis., N. GA Conf." *SCA,* 1-10-1868, p. 6.

Davidson, Frederick (d.1832)
bur. Mossy Ck. MC; gave land for Mossy Ck. church; pastor in Habersham Co., 1820-32.

Davies, Francis B.
"Forsyth Cir., N. GA Conf." *SCA,* 9-11-1868, p. 146; 10-8-1869, p. 162.

"Monticello Cir., N. GA Conf." *SCA,* 10-21-1870, p. 166.

"Decatur Cir., N. GA Conf." *SCA,* 10-30-1872, p. 170; 8—26-1874, p. 130.

"Oxford, GA." *SCA,* 4-28-1875, p. 66.

"Social Circle, N. GA Conf." *SCA,* 6-9-1875, p. 90.

"Warrenton, GA." *SCA,* 2-27-1877, p. 34; 11-13-1877, p. 182.

Davies, Lewis J.
"Scriven Mis., GA." *SCA,* 5-18-1849, p. 198; 10-19-1849, p. 78; 10-25-1850, p. 84.

"Augusta GA Colored Charge." *SCA,* 5-23-1851, p. 202.

"Cassville, GA Conf." *SCA,* 9-23-1858, p. 67; 10-29-1857, p. 87.

"Lumpkin, GA." *SCA,* 9-24-1863, bp.

"Items from Lumpkin Dist., GA Conf." *SCA,* 7-13-1866, fp.

"LaGrange Dist., N. GA Conf." *SCA,* 11-6-1868, p. 178; 6-18-1869, p. 98.

"Asbury Church, Augusta, GA." *SCA,* 10-11-1871, p. 162.

Davies, William J.
b. Savannah, GA; m2/ 1859, Kate Wightman of Palatka, FL.

Davis, Amos
cvt. & joined MEC 1854; lp 1854;

FL CONF. OT 1855 Isabella Mis.; 1856 Green Bay Cir.; 1857 Alapha Mis.; 1858 Flint River Cir.; 1859 Troupville Cir.; 1860 Hamilton Cir.; 1861 Taylor Mis. (left due to absence of support); 1862-63 Liberty Cir.

Davis, John B.
"Savannah Black River Mis.," *SCA*, 8-12-1837, p. 30.

Davis, John W.
m/ 1-31-1872, Mrs. Mary Davis of Carroll Co., GA.

Davis, William C. (1850 - 10-4-1944)
son of Capt. R.T. Davis of Eatonton, GA; bur. West View, Atlanta.

Dawson, Thomas H. (1809 - 1873)
M.D., b. Greene Co., GA; d. Glennville Sta.

Day, Elijah
"Isle of Hope & Skidaway Mis., GA." *SCA*, 7-2-1841, p. 10; 12-17-1841,
        p. 106; 5-13-1842, p. 190; 8-26-1842, p. 42.

Dean, Alvin J. (d. 7-20-1877)
bv Gwinnett Co., GA; dv Perry, GA; in 1853; son of Charles &
Abbie Rilla Dean.

lp 1853; served Decatur (DeKalb) Cir.;

"Burke Cir., GA Conf." *SCA*, 9-18-1856, p. 63.
"Hamilton Cir., GA Conf." *SCA*, 10-13-1864, np; 10-26-1866, p. 5
        11-1-1867, p. 174.
"Something That Explains Itself." *SCA*, 3-2-1866, fp.
"Dedication of Prospect MEC, Hamilton Cir., GA." *SCA*, 3-23-1866, fp.
"A Member of the GA Conf. on Change." *SCA*, 3-30-1866, bp.
"From Western GA." *SCA*, 8-23-1867, p. 134.
"Letter from Southern GA." *SCA*, 4-17-1868, p. 62.
"Lower GA." *SCA*, 6-26-1868, p. 102.
"Modern Preaching Ineffective." *SCA*, 10-30-1868, fp.
"Revival in Bainbridge." *SCA*, 4-23-1869, p. 66.
"Bainbridge Dist. Meeting." *SCA*, 4-30-1869, p. 71; 4-29-1870, p. 66.
"Primary Ground for Giving." *SCA*, 11-12-1869, fp.
"The Mimpriss System." *SCA*, 2-18-1870, p. 26.
"Our Church Literature." *SCA*, 5-13-1870, p. 75.
"The Prominence of Faith." *SCA*, 4-10-1872, fp.
"Perry, S. GA Conf." *SCA*, 9-4-1872, p. 138.
"Drifting Away From God." *SCA*, 3-12-1873, fp.
"Errors of Human Philosophy." (series). *SCA*, 5-14-1873, fp.

"Americus Dist." *SCA*, 4-22-1874, p. 62.
"Lumpkin, S. GA Conf." *SCA*, 9-16-1874, p. 146; 5-5-1875, p. 70.
"The Lumpkin SS." *SCA*, 1-13-1875, p. 6.
"Church Fairs." *SCA*, 2-18-1874, fp.

Dean, Emory F.
Bailey, Eloise Y. "Emory Franklin Dean." *HH*, v15, n2, Dec. 1985, pp. 39-42.

Deavours, Andrew J.
"Broad River Mis., GA." *SCA*, 9-24-1852, p. 66; 12-7-1852, p. 118; 6-24-
1853, p. 14; 8-26-1853, p. 50; 11-25-1853, p. 102; 12-23-1853,
p. 118.
"Worth Mis., GA." *SCA*, 4-28-1854, p. 190.
"Clayton Mis., GA." *SCA*, 4-6-1849, p. 173; 7-20-1849, p. 26; 1-11-1850,
p. 126.
"Tampa Bay & Chicachatta Mis., FL." *SCA*, 5-26-1843, p. 196; 8-11-1843,
p. 34.

Dempsey, Alvin G.
bur. Old Smyrna Cem., Cobb Co., GA; 18th GA Reg., CSA.
m/ Martha E. Waters (11-5-1833 - 11-3-1895).

"Acworth Mis., N. GA Conf." *SCA*, 9-18-1868, p. 151.
"Stone Mountain Cir., N. GA Conf." *SCA*, 9-18-1872, p. 146.
"Glorious Times at Shiloh." (Cobb Co.). *SCA*, 9-26-1876, p. 154.
"A Trip to the Mountains." *SCA*, 10-10-1876, p. 162.
"East Point Cir." *SCA*, 7-29-1874, p. 118.

Dempsey, Elam F.
"Christ Our King Eternal." *WCA*, v100, n42, 4-23-1937, p. 9.

Densmore, Samuel P.   (3-22-1809 - 1873)
b. Buncombe Co., NC; (L) on Cleveland Cir.

1809 Buncombe Co., NC; 1873 White Co., GA.

Derrick, David
"German Mis., Charleston, SC." *SCA*, 7-14-1848, p. 22; 10-20-1848, p. 78.
"Recollections of Geo. Dougherty." *SCA*, 3-3-1859, fp.
"Recollections of an Itinerant." (series). *SCA*, 9-8-1859, fp.
"Visiting The Churches." *SCA*, 11-10-1859, p. 303.
"A Thank Offering From Boon Hill." *SCA*, 10-23-1856, p. 83.

"The SC Conference." *SCA*, 10-8-1857, p. 75.
"Visit to Spartanburg." *SCA*, 11-5-1857, p. 91.

Dickey, James M.
"Louisville, GA." *SCA*, 5-28-1857, p. 207.
"Warren Cir., GA Conf." *SCA*, 9-20-1867, p. 150.

Dickinson, John F.   (8-8-1828 - Mar. 1870)
b. Henry Co., GA; d. Pike Co., AL; son of John P. & Elvirah E.
Dickinson. cvt. 1843; class leader Himilton, GA; taught school in
AL. 1848-50. m/ Nov. 1852, Martha J. Norton, dau. of Rev. John W.
Norton of Barbour Co., AL. lp 1856, Abbeville Cir.

AL CONF. 1857 Abbeville; 1858-59 Union Cir.; 1860-61 Troy Cir.;
1862-63 Union Cir.; 1864-66 Perote Cir; 1867 Brundidge Cir; 1868-69
Troy & Bethel; 1870 Rocky Mt. Cir. d. member MONTGOMERY CONF.

Dickinson, John P.
d. Troy, AL.

10-15-1825, Recom. to SC Conf. Athens Dist. Conf. (Wof.).

"Greenville Cir., GA Conf." *SCA*, 10-23-1846, p. 79.
"Clinton Cir., GA." *SCA*, 9-23-1837, p. 54; 10-21-1837, p. 70.
"Letter from Forsyth Cir., GA." *SCA*, 9-7-1838, p. 46; 9-28-1838, p. 58.
"Ft. Valley, Perry Cir., GA." *SCA*, 9-3-1841, p. 47.
"Union Cir., FL Conf." *SCA*, 11-5-1863, bp.

Dillard, Miles H.
This man's father, Fielding Dillard, when a young boy was taken in at age
10 and reared by Miles Hill in Wolfskin Dist., Oglethorpe Co., GA. In
later years, after the death of the Hills, he named his son in honor of a man
who gave him a home and a start while a child.

Dimon, Stephen H.
wife died in Atlanta, GA, 2-27-1935.

Dixon, Robert M.
"Talbotton, GA." *SCA*, 10-23-1868, p. 170.
"From Talbotton, S. GA Conf." *SCA*, 6-12-1872, p. 90.

Dixon, Robert W.
"Cuthbert, S. GA Conf." *SCA*, 6-2-1875, p. 86.

Dodd, Jacob E.
Chap., 5th GA Reg., CSA.

Dodge, William A.
Chap., 23rd GA Reg., CSA.
wife Henrietta H. Williams (1-25-1844 - 4-12-1868), dau. of Robt. L. &
A.L. Williams; b. Oxford, GA; d. DeKalb Co., GA.

"Atlanta City Mis." *SCA*, 10-1-1869, p. 159.
"Dahlonega, GA." *SCA*, 8-11-1871, p. 179
"St. Paul's, Atlanta, GA." *SCA*, 5-26-1875, p. 82.

Dodson, James
le 1848; lp 1852.

Domingoes, John W.
m/ Gibson, GA, 10-1-1874, H. A. Lassiter of Warren Co., GA;

"A Good Meeting - Snow Springs." *SCA*, 8-1-1876, p. 122.
"From Vienna." *SCA*, 11-21-1876, p. 186.
"Jeffersonville, S. GA Conf." *SCA*, 9-18-1877, p. 150; 10-16-1877, p. 166.
"Dancing." *SCA*, 3-5-1878, p. 34.
"Stewart Cir., S. GA Conf." *SCA*, 11-3-1875, p. 175.

Donnan, Hanover (d. 1822)
nv Donon. m/ Lucy ? (3-31-1779 - 1-5-1870) b. Louisa Co., VA; d. Talbot
Co., GA, in home of son-in-law, John M. Lumpkin.

Joseph Travis, *Autobiography*, p. 211.

Dorman, Alfred
"Zebulon Cir., GA." *SCA*, 10-7-1837, p. 62.
"Perry Cir., GA." *SCA*, 8-19-1842, p. 39.

Dorris, John M.
wife (1806 - 1-26-1873); b. Jackson Co., GA; d. Douglas Co., GA.

Dougherty, George

A native of SC and notable preacher. His influence on Benjamin Wofford was responsible for the benefaction which founded Wofford College at Spartanburg, SC. F. Asbury has a letter to Dougherty dated 1-8-1800; In 1801 at Cumberland St., Charleston, SC, he was dragged through the streets and punished by a mob due to the Gen. Conf. of 1800 which called for the south to free their slaves. See: James Jenkins, *Experiences,* etc. pp. 102-103; Jos. Travis, *Autobiography,* pp. 86-87. John B. Burke, *Autobiography,* pp. 79-80.

1802 Letter, SC Dist. *SCA,* 8-21-1846, p. 41.
"Letter to Lewis Myers." 1806. *SCA,* 10-28-1837, p. 75.
"Recollections of Geo. Dougherty." (D. Derrick). *SCA,* 3-3-1859, fp.

Dougherty, Thomas

Burke, John B., *Autobiography,* pp. 79-80.

Douthet, James

Travis, Joseph. *Autobiography,* pp. 210-211.

Dowling, Zaccheus

"Dog River Mis., AL." *SCA,* 9-24-1852, p. 66.
"Pea River Mis., AL." *SCA,* 6-24-1853, p. 14; 11-25-1853, p. 102.
"Columbia Mis., AL Conf." *SCA,* 2-5-1847, p. 138.
"Pea River Mis.," *SCA,* 6-16-1848, p.6; 9-1-1848, p. 50.
"White Water Mis., AL Conf." *SCA,* 6-7-1850, p.?; 8-30-1850, p. 50; 12-27-1850, p. 118.

Dowman, Charles E.

"Tallahassee Dist. Conf." *SCA,* 4-7-1875, p. 54.
"Quincy, FL." *SCA,* 4-28-1875, p. 66; 6-13-1876, p. 94.
"Live Oak Dist., FL Conf." *SCA,* 4-23-1878, p. 62.

DuBose, Horace M.

Educated Waynesboro Academy, Emory & Henry College; interested in archeology and instrumental in uncovering the site of Shechem in Palestine.

"Papers on Russellism." (Series). *WCA,* v76, n31, 8-2-1912.

Duncan, John P.

"Washington, Wilkes Co., GA." *SCA,* 9-49-1846, p. 51.
"Waynesboro Cir., GA." *SCA,* 7-9-1847, p. 19.

"Madison, GA." *SCA*, 7-16-1841, p. 19.
"Eatonton Cir., GA." *SCA*, 11-15-1839, p. 86.
"Letter from Lincoln Cir., GA." *SCA*, 8-31-1838, p. 42.
"Letter from Warrenton Cir., GA." *SCA*, 6-24-1837, p. 2; 11-10-1837, p. 82.
"Americus Cir., GA Conf." *SCA*, 12-29-1859, p. 330.
"The Meeting in Cuthbert." *SCA*, 10-18-1867, fp.
"Reminiscences of Macon, GA." *SCA*, 10-25-1867, p. 170.
"A Visit to Athens." *SCA*, 12-6-1867, p. 194.
"Visit to the Clinton Cir." *SCA*, 7-3-1868, p. 106.
"The Rome Dist. Meeting." *SCA*, 7-9-1869, p. 110.
"Dalton, GA." *SCA*, 12-10-1869, p. 198.
"Barnesville, N. GA Conf." *SCA*, 9-20-1871, p. 150.
"Dedication at Forsyth." *SCA*, 2-21-1872, p. 26.
"A Blind Man's Jitters." *SCA*, 2-24-1875, p. 30.

Duncan, William McKendree (3-1-1818 - 7-20-1914)
son of Charles Duncan (1775 - 1865) and Mary Ford (1774 - 1858); joined US Army in Mar., 1838 and served 3 mo. to help remove Indians from GA. Pvt. GA Militia. m/9-18-1845, Macon Co., NC, Sara Ann Elizabeth Gillespie (3-19-1828 - 10-7-1902; chrn. Mary Lavonia (7-19-1846 - 5-4-1934); Cornelia Silvanis (Nellie) (8-27-1854 - Nov. 1940).

Dunlap, William C.
Chap., 8th GA Reg. CSA.

"Religion In The Army." *SCA*, 3-12-1863, p. 40.
"Revivals In The Army." *SCA*, 4-16-1863, p. 58.
"Summerville, GA." *SCA*, 8-23-1871, p. 134.
"Carrollton Cir., GA Conf." *SCA*, 8-24-1866, p. 5; 9-20-1867, p. 150; 10-25-1867, p. 170.
"Manasses & Carroll Cirs." *SCA*, 10-5-1866, p. 5.
"A Great Work (Carrollton Cir.)." *SCA*, 10-12-1866, p. 5.
"Manasses & Kingston Cirs." *SCA*, 7-17-1868, p. 114.
"Kingston Mis., N. GA Conf." *SCA*, 8-28-1868, p. 138.
"Kingston Cir., N. GA Conf." *SCA*, 10-2-1868, p. 158.
"To TX and Back." (series). *SCA*, 5-7-1869, p. 74; 6-18-1869, p. 98; 7-23-1869, p. 118.
"Payne Chapel, Atlanta." *SCA*, 9-3-1869, p. 142; 9-24-1869, p. 155; 9-9-1870, p. 143; 9-16-1870, p. 146; 10-21-1870, p. 166.
"Baptismal Demonstrations." *SCA*, 11-25-1870, fp.
"Trion Factory, GA." *SCA*, 4-5-1871, p. 54.
"Summerville, N. GA Conf." *SCA*, 4-12-1871, p. 58; 4-26-1871, p. 66.

"Letter from Summerville Cir." *SCA*, 7-3-1872, p. 102.
"Carrollton & Bowdon Cir., N. GA Conf." *SCA*, 9-17-1873, p. 146.
"Letter from Carrollton & Bowdon, N. GA Conf." *SCA*, 10-22-1873, p. 164.
"Letter from Atlanta, GA." *SCA*, 1-13-1875, p. 6.
"The Mode of John's Baptism." *SCA*, 8-18-1875, p. 130; 1-26-1876, fp.
"Evan's Chapel, Atlanta." *SCA*, 9-19-1876, p. 150.
"Atlanta - Thomson." *SCA*, 2-20-1877, p. 30.
"Thomson, N. GA Conf." *SCA*, 9-25-1877, p. 154.
"Atlanta, GA." *SCA*, 9-5-1876, p. 142.

Dunn, John H. (12-20-1848 - 3-11-1914)

bv Ducktown, Polk Co., TN; lived in Gilmer & Pickens cos., GA; d.
Tallapoosa, AL; bur. Hollywood Cem., Tallapoosa; son of James Dunn &
Susan Wilke; Co. A., lst Btn. GA Inf., the only GA unit in the Union Army;
suffered measles & smallpox while in Army. m1/ 12-18-1866, Trissie Ann
Page (d. 5-8-1904), dau. of Gazaway & Nancy Page of Gilmer Co., GA.
chrn. Jesse Louise (10-3-1867 - 1-25-1932); James G., b. 3-1-1869;
Samuel N.; William A. (b. 12-22-1872); Maggie (2-6-1870 - 1960s).
m2/ 8-14-1904, Mettie Dodd of Dublin, GA.

In 1870 census he was working as a blacksmith, In 1897, after the
Ellijay, GA, seminary burned down, he and his followers moved to Fighting
town CG in Fannin Co., GA and created a new school at the town now
known as Epworth. They called it the Attala Seminary at first, but it
and the town later went by the name of Epworth.

ALABAMA CONFERENCE: 1903 Admitted; 11-30-1905 Readmitted;
1906 St. Paul's, Anniston; 1907 Dist. Supt. Anniston Dist.; 1912 retd.; 1912,
SS Missionary, Gulf Dist.; 1912 retd. to GA.

Dunn, John S.

The founder of Dunn's Chapel in Columbia Co., GA. In Asbury's, *Journal,* he
records a visit to Thos. Dunn on 12-12-1800 which is in the same location of
the chapel John S. Dunn later built. Most likely, Thos. Dunn had a society
there out of which came Dunn's Chapel.

cvt. 1839; lp 1844; a State Rep.

"Columbia Mis., GA Conf." *SCA*, 4-21-1848, p. 182; 10-20-1848, p. 78;
7-27-1849, p. 30.

Dunn, Levi

"Baker Mis., GA." *SCA*, 8-30-1839, p. 42.

Dunwoody, James

wife Sarah Sutton (1-30-1798 - 1-2-1867), b. Edgefield Dist., SC; dau. of Benj. Sutton; moved to Twiggs Co., GA, 1822; son Rev. Samuel Dunwoody.

"Ocmulgee Mis., GA Conf." *SCA*, 8-14-1846, p. 38.
"McDonough Cir., GA." *SCA*, 8-19-1837, p. 34.
"Zebulon & Fayette Cir., GA." *SCA*, 11-9-1838, p. 82.
"Ft. Valley & Flint River Mis., GA." *SCA*, 7-17-1840, p.18; 10-23-1840,
    p. 74; 2-12-1841, p.137; 11-19-1841, p. 90; 4-5-1844, p. 170.
"Thoughts on Methodism." *SCA*, 8-2-1867, fp.
"Causes of Declension in the Church." *SCA*, 8-23-1867, fp.
"Dusultory Remarks." *SCA*, 5-22-1872, fp.

Hemphill, Robt. D., *Dunwoodys of Faggs Manor, PA & Scriven Co., GA.*

Dunwoody, Samuel H.

dv. 6-9-1854, bur. Tabernacle Cem., Greenwood Co., SC. son of Mary Creswell, bro. of James. m/ Lavinia ? (5-27-1788 - 2-10-1873), b. Edgefield Dist., SC; d. Cokesbury, SC.

6-10-1827, Sermon on Baptism preached in Wesley Chapel, Savannah, printed at Conf. of 1834. 1846, sermon preached at Sharon Campmeeting, Cokesbury Cir.; 11-9-1850, letter to Conf. re superannuation; 10-30-1847, recom. from Newberry QC to Conf.; 1837, examination of sermon on slavery. (Wof.).

"Fairfield Dist., SC." *CA*, 10-8-1830, p. 22.
"Letter, Columbia, SC." *CA*, 7-1-1831, p. 174.
"Cypress Cir.," *SCA*, 8-26-1837, p. 38.
"Cokesbury Cir., SC." *SCA*, 9-28-1838, p. 58.
"Edgefield Cir., SC." *SCA*, 9-16-1842, p. 55.
"Mt. Vernon Campmeeting, Edgefield Circuit, SC." *SCA*, 9-1-1843, p. 47.

Smith, Whitefoord. "Samuel Dunwoody." *SCA*, 6-7-1871, fp.
Hemphill, Robt. D., *Dunwoodys of Faggs Manor, PA & Scriven Co., GA.*
See: "Short Sketches of SC Preachers." *SCA*, 11-13-1862, fp.

Dutton, Mann

of the VA Conf. m/ 1828, Elizabeth ? (12-17-1792 - 1-24-1870); She b. Effingham Co., GA; d. Bainbridge, GA; lived in Scriven, Bulloch & Decatur cos., GA.

Duval, William J. (1811 - 1869)
b. NY; cvt. age 14; joined NY Conf. 1845; moved to VA and was appt. Agt. for State Bible Soc.; moved to NC in 1845; moved to FL and was Chap. in 3rd FL Reg. CSA 1863-64; moved to Lake City, FL and entered a merchandise business until his death.

"Key West Station, FL Conf." *SCA*, 10-21-1858, p. 82.
"A Mission To Africa." *SCA*, 9-15-1859, p. 271.
"Leon Cir., FL Conf." *SCA*, 8-28-1856, p. 51.

Eakes, Marion H.
"Blairsville Mis., N. GA Conf." *SCA*, 11-29-1871, p. 190; 11-6-1872, p. 174.
"Carnesville & Franklin Springs Mis." *SCA*, 12-10-1873, p. 191.
"Duluth Cir., N. GA Conf." *SCA*, 2-11-1874, p. 22.
"Duluth Cir., N. GA Conf." *SCA*, 9-22-1875, p. 152.

Eakes, Robert A.
b. Gainesville, GA; son of Henderson & Milly Eakes. cvt. age 4, Holbrook's CG, Forsyth Co., GA; bur. Oxford Cem., Oxford, GA. sons J.H., Robt. F. & Geo. M. were Meth. preachers, N.GA Conf. Other chrn. Wm. J., Mather M., Mrs. C.E. Rogers.

Early, John
"Savannah River Mis.." *SCA*, 5-15-1856, p. 198.

Earnest, John Barrett   (MEC(N)) (CMC)
1910 - Pleasant Hill.

Eason, William   (1771 - 1831)
Eason, Lillian & Cain, Martha T., "Fading Footprints but Continuing Impact, The Reverend William Eason, 1771-1831." *HH*, v17, n2, Fall, 1987, pp. 15-23.

Easterling, W. F.
"Tallahassee Dist., FL Conf." *SCA*, 9-25-1868, p. 154.
"The Preacher's Obligation." (series). *SCA*, 6-18-1869, fp.

Edwards, George R.
Chap., Co. D., 23rd Reg., GA Vol., CSA

Edwards, Marcus H.
"Lafayette Cir., N. GA Conf." *SCA*, 10-28-1874, p. 170.

Edwards, Robert L.
1-20-1825, Letter to Conference. (Wof.).

Edwards, Thomas J.
"Blairsville Mis., N. GA Conf." *SCA*, 9-9-1874, p. 139; 10-14-1874,
    p. 162; 9-5-1876, p. 142.

Ellington, Lewis D. (4-14-1846 - 5-15-1927)
m/ 12-4-1888, Lydia S. Stiger. bur. Glenmore UMC; gave land
for the church.

Elliott, Abram B.
of Jasper Co., GA. m/ 12-31-1838, Mrs. Lucinda Young of Augusta, GA.

"Lexington Cir., GA." *SCA*, 11-2-1838, p. 78.
"Wetumpka, AL." *SCA*, 11-12-1841, p. 87.

Ellis, Cyrus H.
Manasses Cir., GA Conf." *SCA*, 9-7-1866, fp.
"Homer Cir., GA Conf." *SCA*, 4-12-1867, p. 58.
"Revival in Homer Cir., GA Conf." *SCA*, 8-2-1867, p. 123.
"Homer Cir., N. GA Conf." *SCA*, 9-18-1868, p. 151.
"Batesville, AR." *SCA*, 2-4-1870, p. 18.
"Letter from Arkansas." *SCA*, 9-23-1870, p. 150; 2-28-1872, p. 30.

Ellis, Frederick R.C.
"Troupville Cir., FL Conf." *SCA*, 8-2-1855, p. 35.
"Waukenan, FL Conf." *SCA*, 9-30-1858, p. 71.

Ellis, Henry J.
m/ 12-9-1875, Susie Smith of Oak Bowery, AL.

"Dublin Cir., S. GA Conf." *SCA*, 10-2-1872, p. 154.
"The Hinesville Dist. Conf." *SCA*, 11-6-1872, p. 174.
"Atlanta Dist. Conf." *SCA*, 8-11-1875, p. 126.
"Troup Cir., N. GA Conf." *SCA*, 10-24-1876, p. 170.

Ellis, Isaac
d. Girard, AL.

Ellis, Stephen
bur. Pine Log Church, Bartow Co., GA. m/ Phoebe Moss (1793 - 1872).
1827 deacon; 1853 elder; lived in Houston Co., GA.

Ellis, Thomas D.
son of Thomas James Ellis and Rebecca Gray; wrote first draft of the Plan for
Union and Declaration of Union.

Ellis, Thomas W.
"Lowndes Colored Mis., FL Conf." *SCA*, 6-16-1859, p. 219.

Ellis, Thomas Winans (d. 12-28-1943)
father & g.father were preachers; grad. Emory College; Prof. of Gk., Wofford
College, Sptbg. SC; d. Macon, GA; bur. Clinton, GA; 2 dau. by m1/ Mrs.
H.M. Frankfort, Mrs. J.V. KcKey. m2/ Sallie Barron; 1 dau. Mrs. E.N.
Whitman.

Ellison, John Francis (6-1-1833 - 12-9-1868)
b. LaGrange, GA; d. Clayton, AL., consumption; son of Rev. Wm. H.
Ellison; lp Enon Cir., 1862.

Ellison, William
preached in Gilmer Co., GA, 1832. son of David Ellison. chrn. William II
(1st pastor of Cartacay MC, Gilmer, Co.); J.F., d. 9-2-1851.

Ellison, William H.
"Dist. Meeting, Eufaula, AL." *SCA*, 10-19-1866, p. 2; 11-1-1867, p. 174.

Embry, George T.
Chap. 27th GA Reg., CSA.

"Jonesboro Cir., GA Conf." *SCA*, 8-31-1866, fp; 8-30-1867, p. 138;
        10-18-1867, fp.
"Buena Vista, S. GA Conf." *SCA*, 10-1-1869, p. 158.
"Terrell Cir., S. GA Conf." *SCA*, 11-25-1870, p. 185.
"Vienna Cir., S. GA Conf." *SCA*, 11-4-1874, p. 174.

Embry, James S.
m/ 2-19-1873, Mary E. Mays of Warren Co., GA.

"Loganville Cir., N. GA Conf." *SCA,* 10-16-1877, p. 166.

Embry, Thomas J.
lp 11-24-1855.

"Troup Cir., GA Conf." *SCA,* 9-10-1863, bp.

England, James E.
bur. Jonesboro, GA, cem.

"Sermon." p. 21-23. (found by preachers in the Centennial Anniversary of
    Mt. Pleasant MC, Oglethorpe Co., GA, 1920, Atlanta, GA, by
    C.C. Cary.
"Flat Shoals Cir., N. GA Conf." *SCA,* 9-29-1875, p. 154; 11-17-1875, p. 182.

England, Sherman R.
"Origin and History of the Church." (with a song written and sung by SRE,
    pp. 48-51 found by preachers in the Centennial Anniversary of the
    Mt. Pleasant MC, Oglethorpe Co., GA, 1920, Atlanta, GA , by
    C.C. Cary.

English, Bond
"Black Swamp Cir., SC Conf." *SCA,* 9-25-1846, p. 63.

Entriken, David D.
bur. Mt. Zion UMC, Carroll Co., GA. 1880-81 Ass't. teacher Mt. Zion
Seminary.

Epps, G. W.
wife Elizabeth H. ?, d. Harris Co., GA. 1868, age 74.

Erwin, John P.
"The Supreme Authority of Jesus Christ." *WCA,* v101, n34, 2-25-1938, p.7.

Evans, Charles W.
"Turtle River Mis., GA." *SCA,* 8-7-1840, p. 30; 12-25-1840, p. 110.

Evans, Clement A.
1853, LL.B. Tracy Gould's Law School, Augusta, GA.

"Manassas Cir., GA Conf." *SCA*, 11-16-1866, fp.
"Cartersville, N. GA Conf." *SCA*, 10-18-1867, fp.
"Athens, N. GA Conf." *SCA*, 10-29-1869, p. 175.
"Revival at Trinity Church, Atlanta." *SCA*, 8-13-1873, p. 126.
"Trinity & Pierce Chapel, Atlanta, GA." *SCA*, 10-14-1874, p. 162.
"Augusta, GA." *SCA*, 3-31-1875, p. 50.
"St. John's, Augusta." *SCA*, 3-22-1876, p. 46.

Military History of Georgia. uv.

Evans, James E.
Missionary to Ewell's Corp, Army of N. VA, CSA.

"Sanctification by Rev. J.H. Baxter." *WCA*, v50, n44, 4-7-1886, p. 5.
"Letter from Savannah." *SCA*, 8-12-1837, p. 30.
"Missionary Meeting in Savannah." *SCA*, 9-16-1837, p. 50.
"Dry Pond Campmeeting, Jackson Co., GA." *SCA*, 10-2-1840, p. 62.
"Augusta Dist., GA." *SCA*, 8-18-1843, p. 39; 12-1-1843, p. 99.
"Revival in Macon, GA." *SCA*, 5-30-1851, p. 207.
"Revival, LaGrange, GA." *SCA*, 5-6-1858, p. 195.
"Macon, GA." *SCA*, 5-14-1857, p. 199.
"The GA Conference Against Censor." *SCA*, 5-28-1857, fp.
"Rehoboth Association." (series). see: *SCA*, 3-11-1858, fp.
"From Gen. Lee's Army." *SCA*, 8-18-1863, bp.
"The Gen. Conf. & the Colored People." *SCA*, 6-1-1866, p. 2.
"The MECS & the Colored People." (series). *SCA*, 6-15-1866, p. 2.
"Revival in Columbus, GA." *SCA*, 8-10-1866, p. 4.
"The Epochs of the Church." *SCA*, 11-1-1867, fp.
"High Church Claims Examined." (series). *SCA*, 7-3-1868, fp.
"Church Union - Rev. James E. Evans." (J.M. Wright). *SCA*,
    6-19-1868, p. 98.
"St. Luke's, Columbus, GA." *SCA*, 1-15-1869, p. 10.
"Church Unity." (series). *SCA*, 3-5-1869, fp.
"Savannah, GA." *SCA*, 4-15-1870, p. 58.
"The Churches in Savannah." *SCA*, 5-6-1870, p. 70.
"Short Method With High Church Men." (pamphlet) uv.
"To the Colored People of the MECS." (series). *SCA*, 6-10-1870, fp.
"The Plan of Separation of 1844." (series). *SCA*, 9-4-1872, fp.

"Atlanta Dist." *SCA*, 6-30-1875, p. 102; 10-13-1875, p. 162.
"Dedication of Trinity Church, Atlanta." *SCA*, 1-16-1877, p. 10.

Evans, Lewellen
1818, letter concerning his debt to bro. McGehee. (Wof.).

Evans, Lucius G.
wife Susannah C. ? (12-2-1824 - 3-9-1872); d. Crawford Co., GA.

Evans, Robert F.
1894, withdrew and surrendered credentials because the church was, to his mind,
under the doom of the "abomination of desolation."

"Ocklocknee Mis., S. GA Conf." *SCA*, 9-18-1868, p. 151.
"Louisville Cir., S. GA Conf." *SCA*, 10-15-1869, p. 166.
"All Consecration." *SCA*, 6-17-1870, fp.

Evans, William H.
founded Evans Chapel in Atlanta, GA.

"Revivals in Covington & Monroe Cir., GA." *SCA*, 11-25-1842, p. 93.
"Lawrenceville Cir., GA." *SCA*, 8-28-1846, p. 47; 11-20-1846, p. 95.
"Greensboro Cir., GA Conf." *SCA*, 11-3-1848, p. 86.
"Revival in LaGrange F.C." *SCA*, 4-28-1859, p. 191.
"Newnan Cir., GA Conf." *SCA*, 10-16-1856, p. 79.
"Rome Station, GA Conf." *SCA*, 5-7-1857, p. 195.
"Newton Co., GA." *SCA*, 8-24-1866, p. 5.
"Troup Cir., N. GA Conf." *SCA*, 9-24-1869, p. 155.
poem abt. his death by M.W. Arnold. see: *SCA*, 11-25-1870, fp.

Fagg, George W.
"Albany, FL Conf." *SCA*, 10-21-1858, p. 82.
"Apalachicola, FL Conf." *SCA*, 10-30-1856, p. 87.

Farabee, George W.
"Burke Mis., GA." *SCA*, 11-13-1840, p. 86.

Fariss, Dewit C.
nv. Farriss. The above is the correct spelling of the name acc. to relative,
Mary A. Hunt, of Barnesville, GA. Fariss was her husband's g.father.

Farmer, John W.
"Burke Mis., GA." *SCA*, 5-10-1844, p. 190; 10-18-1844, p. 71.

Farr, Givens W.
bur. Roswell Meth. Cem. m/Minerva Turner (1861 - 1936).

Farrar, Gaston
nv Farrer.

"Sandersville, GA." *SCA*, 7-20-1838, p. 18; 10-21-1837, p. 70.
"Taloola Mis., GA." *SCA*, 9-13-1839, p. 50; 11-29-1839, p. 94.

Farris, Benjamin F.
m/ 1-13-1871, Lydia E. Norman, dau. of Rev. G.G. Norman of Wilkes Co., GA.

"Richmond Cir., N. GA Conf." *SCA*, 10-21-1874, p. 167.
"Revival at Berlin, Richmond Co., GA." *SCA*, 9-29-1875, p. 154.
"Appling Cir., N. GA Conf." *SCA*, 6-27-1876, p. 102; 8-22-1876, p. 134.

Fears, Thomas J.
"Troup Cir., GA." *SCA*, 8-21-1840, p. 38.

Felder, Hamlin R.
"Montezuma, S. GA Conf." *SCA*, 6-2-1875, p. 86.
"Albany, GA." *SCA*, 6-26-1877, p. 102.

Felder, J. Rufus
"A Revival in Dooly Co." *SCA*, 8-21-1872, p. 130.
"Montezuma, S. GA Conf." *SCA*, 9-3-1873, p. 139.

Fentress, Henry C.
mv/ 2-24-1870, A.S. Sessions, dau. of Rev. J.J. Sessions

Few, Ignatius A.
1-6-1830, letter from stewards of Lexington, GA, concerning his conduct and that of Thos. L. Wynn. (Wof.).

"A Divine Call to the Ministry." *SCA*, 6-19-1846, p. 5.
"Savannah, GA." *CA*, 9-16-1831, p. 10.

Travis, Joseph. *Autobiography*, pp. 127-129.

Few, J.N.
"Letter from Macon, GA, 9-1-1830." *CA,* 10-1-1830, p. 18.

Fincher, William M. (5-10-1794 - 9-28-1874)
b. Mecklenburg Co., NC; moved to Jasper Co., GA 1817; m/ 1818 Mrs. Diodema McClendon Graves, dau. of Isaac McClendon; moved to Troup Co., GA.

1822 class leader; 1827 le; 1830 lp; 1840 Deacon.

Fisher, Charles
lost his fortunes by accident, fire & the sudden liberation of his slaves.

Fitzgerald, Oscar P.
grad. Oak Grove Academy, Rockingham, NC; wrote for textbook firm in Macon, GA. See: Simmons, J.C. *Pacific Coast.* 1886.

"To Those Who Think of Emigrating to Mexico." *SCA.* 6-1-1866, fp.

Flanders, Frederick W.
"Irwinton Cir., S. GA Conf." *SCA,* 11-6-1872, p. 175.

Flanders, John T.
"Emanuel Mis., GA Conf." *SCA,* 6-12-1846, p. 2.
"Kingston Mis., GA." *SCA,* 5-18-1849, p. 198; 9-14-1849, p. 58.
"Putnam Mis., GA Conf." *SCA,* 6-7-1850, p. ?; 11-1-1850, p. 86.
"Dublin Mis., GA Conf." *SCA,* 5-12-1848, p. 194.

Flanders, William J.
"Mt. Vernon Cir. & Mis., S. GA Conf." *SCA,* 3-26-1878, p. 46.

Flewellen, A. H.
Georgetown, S. GA Conf." *SCA,* 9-2-1870, p. 138.

Flintroy, John T. (d. 5-1-1880)
bur. Jesup, GA.

Florence, William A.
'Madison, GA." *SCA,* 10-28-1870, p. 170.

Floyd, Moses
joined the Presbyterian Church. See: Jenkins, James. *Experiences*, etc. p. 92f.

Folsom, Jeremiah W.
"Personalities of Satan." *SCA*, 3-26-1878, fp.

Fondren, William H.
correct spelling of name. See text, p. 188, for listing.

Foote, William R.
"Sparta, GA Conf." *SCA*, 10-1-1857, p. 73.
"Morgan Cir., N. GA Conf." *SCA*, 10-29-1869, p. 175.

Foote, William R. Jr.
"Baldwin Cir., N. GA Conf." *SCA*, 9-26-1876, p. 154.

Forster, Francis X.
"Culloden Cir., GA Conf." *SCA*, 7-9-1857, p. 23.

Foster, Anthony E. (b. 1814)
Circuit rider in Hall Co., GA, 1820-30. son of Archillis nv Arkillis Foster.
Other siblings: Simpson Caswell; William E., 1812; Polly G., 1818; Isaac T.,
1820; J.F., 1823; Riley Bidemous, 1825; Edmund Bobo, 1827; Joel M. 1829;
H.L., 1831.

Foster, Samuel B.
"Jacksonville Dist., GA Conf." *SCA*, 11-20-1840, p. 90.
"Waresboro Mis., St. Mary's Dist. GA." *SCA*, 10-22-1841, p 74; 12-24-1841,
    p. 110.

Fowler, Thomas (d. 1860-61)
son of Rev. Joel F. Fowler who moved from Greenville, SC, to DeKalb Co.,
GA & had 4 sons who became preachers. m/Caroline Brown. He was
unpopular in his ministry due to his opposition to slavery. He had 4 sons
and 3 daughters by 2nd wife; 1 son by 1st wife. He was the father of James
Lowrey Fowler. See: Robb, R.H. *Life of Fowler.* pp. 9-12f.

"Van Wert Mis., GA Conf." *SCA*, 11-27-1846, p. 98.
"Marietta Cir., GA." *SCA*, 8-27-1841, p. 43.

Franklin, Benjamin C. (1-21-1830 - 10-7-1872)
b. Glynn Co., GA; d. Brunswick, GA; (L) Elder; lp age 18; received appts. in FL CONF.

"Brunswick Cir., FL Conf." *SCA*, 5-12-1864, np.
"The Brunswick Cir. Again." *SCA*, 6-22-1866, fp; 5-31-1867, p. 87.
"Should the Rules as Set Forth in the Discipline be Enforced?" *SCA*, 3-11-1870, p. 38.

Franklin, Osborn R.
"Ochesee Mis., AL Conf." *SCA*, 7-11-1851, p. 22.

Fraser, Benjamin F.
bur. Sardis, Gwinnett Co., GA. (was Hall Co.).

Fraser, Simon (7-8-1801 - 5-10-1881)
bur. Roswell Meth. Cem. m/ Matilda H. Bradford (7-17-1815 - 7-21-1884), b. Jackson Co., GA.

Fulton, William A. J.
description of him given in full under:
"An Imposter At Large." *SCA*, 1-26-1865, np.

Fulwood, Charles A.
Chap., 48th GA Reg., CSA.

"Andrew Chapel, GA Conf." *SCA*, 6-30-1848, p. 14; 1-5-1849, p. 122.
"Perry Cir., GA Conf." *SCA*, 10-28-1858, p. 87; 5-7-1857, p. 195; 9-17-1857, p. 63.
"Waynesboro Cir., GA Conf." *SCA*, 8-25-1859, p. 259.
"Burke Cir., GA Conf." *SCA*, 9-22-1859, p. 275; 10-13-1859, p. 286.
"Forsyth Cir., GA Conf." *SCA*, 9-11-1856, p. 59; 11-6-1856, p. 91.
"Revival at Milledgeville, GA." *SCA*, 10-29-1863, bp.
"Griffin, GA." *SCA*, 8-17-1866, p. 5.
"Letter from Griffin, GA." *SCA*, 11-9-1866, p. 5.
"Talbot Cir., S. GA Conf." *SCA*, 8-23-1867, p. 134.
"Brunswick, S. GA Conf." *SCA*, 3-25-1870, p. 46; 10-14-1870, p. 162.
"Letter from Key West." *SCA*, 7-3-1872, p. 102.
"Spanish Mission in Key West." *SCA*, 11-6-1872, p. 174.

"Key West, FL." *SCA,* 4-23-1873, p. 62; 11-5-1875, p. 171;
     9-15-1875, p. 146; 10-27-1875, p. 170; 1-12-1876, p. 6;
     9-12-1876, p. 146; 10-24-1876, p. 170.
"Tallahassee Dist., FL Conf." *SCA,* 10-30-1877, p. 174; 3-26-1878, p. 46.

Gable, Joseph M.
bur. Campground Meth. Cem., Cobb Co., GA; m/ Matilda D. (11-2-1839 -
3-4-1904).

Gaines, Edmund P.
dv. 2-23-1881; bur. Mt. Bethel, Cobb Co., GA.

Gaines, James M.
le 1842; lp 1852.

Gaines, John R.
lp 1859.

"Alpharetta, N. GA Conf." *SCA,* 8-23-1867, p. 134.

Gamble, James
wife Mary (2-11-1796 - 7-7-1866); b. Scriven Co., GA; d. Dooly Co., GA.

Gardner, George E.
m/ 11-14-1871, Mary R. Bell, in Cumming, GA.

"Gainesville Cir., N. GA Conf." *SCA,* 10-25-1871, p. 170.
"Dahlonega Cir., N. GA Conf." *SCA,* 11-13-1872, p. 179.
"Fayetteville Cir., N. GA Conf." *SCA,* 9-30-1874, p. 155.

Gardner, Julius   (8-31-1837 - 3-22-1875)
d. Butler, GA; cvt. Turner's Chapel 1853; lp 1868

Gardner, Sterling
m/ 8-24-1855, Emma ? (11-25-1838 - 10-30-1877), b. Upson Co., GA.

"Leon Cir., FL Conf." *SCA,* 3-19-1863, p. 45.
"To the Methodists of the FL Conf." *SCA,* 10-1-1863, fp.
"Decatur Cir., FL Conf." *SCA,* 9-24-1863, bp; 7-9-1863, bp.
"Key West, FL Conf." *SCA,* 12-7-1866, fp; 10-22-1869, p. 170;
     4-26-1871, p. 66.
"Micanopy Cir., FL Conf." *SCA,* 9-11-1872, p. 142; 4-17-1872, p. 58.

Gardner, T.N.
"Bainbridge Cir., FL Conf." *SCA*, 9-20-1855, pp. 67-68.
"St. Mary's Dist.." *SCA*, 8-14-1856, p. 43; 10-16-1856, p. 79; 5-6-1858,
    p. 195.

Garrison, Jedediah (1740-50 - 1828)

Garrison, Levi
12-29-1806 Conference, SC: Levi Garrison had left his work with Lewis
Myers at Charleston in mid-year for fear of yellow fever. So Geo. Dougherty
(himself in fast falling health) moved to dismiss from the rolls of the
Confernce any preacher who deserted his work for fear of an epidemic. A
great debate followed, motion carried 15-14.

12-30-1831, letter to SC Conf. re episcopacy. (Wof.).

Gartman, Daniel (8-20-1796 - 3-20-1870)
b. SC; d. Cave Spring, GA; deacon 1-8-1832; lived in Habersham Co., GA;
moved to AL; moved back to GA before death.

Gartrell, William J. (8-5-1827 - 4-13-1867)
b. Columbia Co., GA, son of Col. H. Gartrell. cvt. 1844; le 1848; lp 1852;
moved from Resaca, GA to Marion Co., FL in 1864.

Gay, Silas C.
bur. Charleston, GA.

Gentry, Robert D.
"Oconee Cir., S. GA Conf." *SCA*, 9-25-1872, p. 150.
"Fruitland Mis., FL Conf." *SCA*, 8-4-1875, p. 122.
"Waldo Cir., FL Conf." *SCA*, 8-15-1876, p. 130.

George, Enoch
Jenkins, James. *Experiences,* etc. pp. 82-83.
Travis, Joseph. *Autobiography,* p. 96.

George, J. W. (?)
wife Winnie S. Hightower (1-31-1838 - 5-21-1877), dau. of Raliegh &
Elizabeth Hightower of Henry Co., GA.

Gibson, James L.
"Montezuma, GA." *SCA*, 5-26-1875, p. 82.

Gibson, Tobias
son of Jordan Gibson and Mary Middleton; bur. fam. cem. SE of Vicksburg, MS; body moved 1935 to Crawford St. Church. unmarried.

Jenkins, James. *Experiences,* etc. pp. 36-37.

Gilbert, S. G.   (3-30-1838 - July 1877)
b. & d. Jackson Co., GA; member, Mulberry Cir., QC; "a preacher for 5 years, not as popular as some." 7 chrn.

Giles, Jessie J.
"Irwin Mis., FL Conf." *SCA*, 9-16-1858, p. 63.
"Valdosta Cir., S. GA Conf." *SCA*, 6-26-1868, p. 102.
"Decatur Cir., S. GA Conf." *SCA,* 10-25-1871, p. 170.

Glenn, James E.
wife Elizabeth, d. 1867.

1822, letter re Salem Academy in GA; Feb. 1822, letter to SC Conf. concerning the establishing of a seminary of learning near Abbeville. (Wof.).

Travis, Joseph. *Autobiography.* pp. 139-140.
See: "Short Sketches of SC Preachers." *SCA*, 11-27-1862, fp.

Glenn, John Bolles   (4-6-1786 - 8-9-1869)
bv Chester Dist., SC; d. Auburn, AL; son of James Glenn. In 1820 he farmed in Jones Co., GA; 1828 moved to Meriwether Co., GA; 1837 to Barbour Co., AL; 1847 Auburn, AL. Trustee, E. AL College. did not marry Bishop Capers' sister. Thomas Davenport Glenn m/ Sarah Capers.

Glenn, John W.
m/ 1-15-1874, Fannie Stevens of Baldwin Co., GA.

"Scarboro Cir., N. GA Conf." *SCA,* 10-9-1872, p. 158.

Glenn, John Walker
"Watkinsville Cir., GA." *SCA,* 9-2-1837, p. 42; 10-14-1837, p. 66.
"Letter from Cherokee Dist., GA." *SCA,* 11-16-1838, p. 86; 6-4-1841, p. 202.
"Athens Dist., GA." *SCA,* 11-4-1842, p. 81.

"Clarkesville Cir., GA Conf." *SCA*, 10-18-1844, p. 73.
"Carnesville Cir., GA Conf." *SCA*, 9-27-1844, p. 61; 10-1-1844, p. 65.

Glenn, Joshua N.
12-4-1828, letter to Conf. asking for location. (Wof.).

Temple, Robert M., Jr. *Florida Flame.* pp. 32-34.
Fain, Mrs. J.E. "J.N. Glenn: Pioneer Methodist Preacher in Florida." *HH,*
    v6, n2, Dec. 1976, pp. 41-44; diary excerpt in same issue, pp. 36-40.

"The Old & The New." *SCA*, 7-12-1871, fp.
"Old Times & New." *SCA*, 8-23-1871, fp; 5-17-1871, fp.
"Long Beards & the Gospel." *SCA*, 10-11-1871, fp.
"The Beard Question Again." *SCA*, 11-22-1871, fp.

Glenn, Nicholas Z.
"Brooksville Cir., FL Conf." *SCA*, 4-30-1878, p. 66.

Glenn, Thomas Davenport
m/ Sarah Capers

12-23-1809. The case of Thos. Glenn was deliberated in a conference meeting.
Asbury states: "Thomas Glenn's case is a serious one; he is suspended for
imprudence but not for gross immorality."

Glenn, Wilbur F.
"Old and New." *SCA*, 3-19-1869, p. 46.
"Marietta, GA." *SCA*, 10-14-1874, p. 162.
"Baptized Children." *SCA*, 11-27-1877, fp.

Glenn, William   (1790 - 7-1-1871)
(L) b. VA; d. Anderson Co., SC; lived in Elbert Co., GA.

Glenn, William C.
bur. Decatur, GA.

Glisson, Dennis
LP Sept. 1860; wounded Malvern Hill; d. pneumonia.
wife Lizzie E. Brown (8-27-1837 - 11-12-1870) dau. of Eben Brown of
Jefferson Co., GA.

Glover, Jasper K. (6-29-1829 - 11-22-1862)
b. Twiggs Co., GA; d. Waukeehah, FL.

"Newnansville Cir., FL Conf." *SCA*, 3-12-1857, p. 163; 9-10-1857, p. 59;

11-19-1857, p. 99.

Godfrey, James E.
was given resolutions for valor and devotion to his charge during a yellow
fever epidemic in Savannah in the 1850s. He was the collector of the Savannah
Port in the 1840s, the top federal job in GA. He helped establish Andrew
Chapel MC (black) in the 1840s and was one of the 4 whites and 20 blacks
who built its first sanctuary. He bacame its full-time pastor in the late 50s
with 500 members by lantern light at night. His wife and daughter are bur.
Oakland Cem., Atlanta, GA. He located in Cuthbert, GA, and was an
insurance agent. He and 2nd wife are bur. in Meth. cem., Lumpkin, GA.
m/ Agnes M. Taylor (10-2-1813 - 1873), dau. of Capt. Jas. Taylor, USN.
His sister, Anna, m/ Rev. Chas. Betts.

Chap., 54th GA Reg., CSA.

"Savannah Black River Mis.." *SCA*, 8-12-1837, p. 30; 1-8-1841, p. 118.
"Atlanta, GA (Wesley Chapel)." *SCA*, 9-18-1868, p. 151.
"Letter from Marion, SC." *SCA*, 3-5-1869, p. 38.
"Decatur Cir., N. GA Conf." *SCA*, 5-26-1875, p. 82.

Golden, Francis G.
bur. Cokes Chapel, Coweta Co., GA.

Gordon, Alexander (1785 - 1-4-1863)
"Ogeechee Mis., GA." *SCA*, 7-10-1840, p. 14.
"Cherokee Mis., GA." *SCA*, 5-14-1841, p. 190.
"Emanuel Mis., GA Conf." *SCA*, 11-26-1847, p. 98; 8-18-1848, p. 42;
        7-20-1849, p. 26; 7-12-1850, p. 22.

"Fairhaven Mis., GA." *SCA*, 7-18-1851, p. 26.

Gordon, Frederick M. (8-14-1864 - 1-24-1928)
bur. Citizens Cem., Cobb Co., GA.

Gordon, Thomas B.
M.D.; wife Jane E. Tooke, d. 8-6-1873, dau. of James & Elizabeth Tooke; d. Union Co., AR, formerly of Talbot Co., GA.

Graham, Alexander
"State of the ME Church in FL." *SCA*, 9-26-1851, p. 61; 10-17-1851, p. 75; 8-15-1851, p. 43.
"Letter from California." *SCA*, 10-29-1852, p. 85; 3-18-1853, p. 169.
"The ME Church Edifice at Jacksonville." *SCA*, 11-17-1848, p. 94.
"Leon Cir." *SCA*, 8-30-1850, p. 51.

Graham, William Harper   (d. 5-28-1893)
b. GA; bap. 1818; cvt. Rehoboth CG; m1/ 2-11-1837Miss P.J.Osmore (8-19-1819 - 11-23-1873), d. Monroe Co., GA; 12 chrn; m2/ 1874, Temperance Rebekah Olive. 1852 organized 1st CMC in GA in Monroe Co., GA with others. lived near Milner, GA. On 5-28-1893, both he and his wife were killed by the Nancy Hanks train as they walked the tracks home from a Baptist Church meeting. Funeral at Fredonia Church, Monroe Co., bur. there. 14th GA Reg., CSA.

"Pike Cir., N. GA Conf." *SCA*, 11-1-1871, p. 174.
"Upson Cir., N. GA Conf." *SCA*, 11-5-1873, p. 171.

Graham, Windsor P.
"Newton & Walton Cir., GA." *SCA*, 11-15-1839, p. 86.
"Lawrenceville Cir., GA." *SCA*, 11-12-1841, p. 87.
"Troup Cir., GA." *SCA*, 10-21-1842, p. 75.
"State Line Mis., GA." *SCA*, 8-13-1852, p. 42; 11-5-1852, p. 94.
"Ellijay Mis., GA." *SCA*, 10-21-1853, p. 82.
"Lafayette Cir., GA Conf." *SCA*, 10-25-1850, p. 79.
"Jacksonboro Cir. & Scriven Mis., GA Conf." *SCA*, 6-19-1846, p. 4; 4-30-1847, p. 186; 10-22-1847, p. 78.
"Scriven Mis." *SCA*, 11-20-1846, p. 94; 12-10-1847, p. 106.

Gramling, William Andrew   (11-21-1783 - 1874)
d. Cherokee Co., GA; joined church 11-17-1806; class-leader 4-25-1808; deacon 12-25-1812. SC CONF. 1810 OT; 1810 Laurens Cir.; 1811 Rutherford Cir.

m/ 11-10-1811, Rebecca Foster (10-18-1794 - 1874), dau. of John & Sidney Foster of SC.

12-9-1818, letter to Camden Conf. asserting his belief. (Wof.).

Grantham, William M. (1790 - 1-23-1868)
b. GA; d. Kirbytown, AL. son of John William Grantham and Rhoda/Elinor ? bur. McFarland Cem., Marshall, AL. moved 1982 to Vaughn Cem., Jackson Co., AL. m/ Susannah Richardson (1800 - 2-23-1873), b. Buncome Co., NC; d. Wichita, KS. bur. Highland Cem., Tract 8, Sec. 1, KS. chrn. Rebecca, 12-3-1820; John Wesley, 1823; Matthew Mathias, 1827; Jesse Richardson, 6-8-1833; William.

Gray, Albert
"Decatur Cir., GA." *SCA,* 9-20-1855, p. 68.
"McDonough Cir., GA Conf." *SCA,* 10-7-1858, p. 75; 11-5-1857, p. 91.
"Capers' Chapel (black church), N. GA Conf." *SCA,* 11-8-1867, fp.
"Conyers Cir., N. GA Conf." *SCA,* 9-17-1869, p. 151; 10-21-1870, p. 166.
"Social Circle SS." *SCA,* 1-25-1871, p. 15.
"Monticello, N. GA Conf." *SCA,* 9-8-1875, p. 142; 10-9-1877, p. 162.

Gray, Edward A.
"S. Lincoln Cir., N. GA Conf." *SCA,* 8-18-1875, p. 130.

Gray, John D.
"Pessimism, A Word to Croakers." (sermon). 1883. uv.
"Hampton Cir., N. GA Conf." *SCA,* 9-30-1874, p. 154; 10-21-1874, p. 166; 10-20-1875, p. 167; 11-10-1875, p. 178.
"Conyers Cir., N. GA Conf." *SCA,* 10-16-1877, p. 166.
"Eatonton, GA." *SCA,* 4-16-1878, p. 58; 4-23-1878, p. 62.

Green, A.J.
"Savannah River Mis." *SCA,* 6-19-1846, p. 4.

Green, Henry Davis (10-5-1791 - 4-19-1871)
b. Georgetown, SC; d. Sumter Co., SC. Tribute from Sumter Cir.

Green, James (9-15-1805 - 5-11-1874)
lp 1844; 185 jr. preacher of Marietta Cir. Tribute by Villa Rica Cir.

"Sandtown Mis., N. GA Conf." *SCA,* 9-11-1872, p. 142.

Green, Thomas (b. ca 1777)
(L), Wayne Co., GA in 1850. m/ Lucy Leigh Altman, b. 1790, SC, dau. of Lionell Leigh of Liberty Co., GA.

Green, William A.
m/ 11-7-1871, Carrie M. Gardner of Taylor Co., GA.

Greene, Myles (6-26-1767 - 1-31-1853)
b. Brunswick Co., VA; bapt. 7-26-1787, Surry, Albemarle Parish, VA; bur. Salem MC, Monroe Co., GA, where he served; will same co. 2-14-1850; son of Peter Greene & Judith Love. m1/ 10-15-1789m Elizabeth Hunt (1769 - 1809), dau. of Daniel D. Hunt & Joyce Green Sutton. chrn. Raleigh, 1797; John H., 1792; Miles, Jr., 6-6-1801; Peter B.; Lucy Ann; Elizabeth W.E. m2/ 6-7-1810, Nancy Bass; m3/ Mary McGehee. left 2p. biography.

11-20-1816, letter to conf. asking for elder's orders. (Wof.).

Greene, Raleigh
dv. April 1858. son of Rev. Myles Greene & Elizabeth Hunt. m/ Elizabeth Floyd, b. 1800, dau. of John Floyd. chrn. Sarah E., 1826; John Myles Stewart, Feb. 1832; Martha R., 1834.

"Factory Mis., Columbus, GA." *SCA*, 6-12-1856, p. 7; 11-27-1856, p. 103.

Grice, Q. C.
no record that he was a minister.

"Fairburn, N. GA Conf." *SCA*, 10-14-1874, p. 162.

Griffeths, George J.
m/ 10-28-1875, Anna W. Wightman, dau. of Rev. John Wesley Wightman of the KY Conf.

"Blackshear Sta., S. GA Conf." *SCA*, 2-6-1877, p. 22.

Griffin, James
*see: Griffith, James (below).
wife Sarah A. Johnson, d. 12-13-1860, Butler, GA.

Griffin, Smith H.

m/ Martha ? chrn. Lucinda, Marietta, Henry L., Charlie S., Walter J., Willie A., John H. Griffin owned property in the 1850s near Hampton, GA. His home, Oaklea Manor, still stands and is now on the Nat. Reg. of Hist. Places. He named the town of Hampton in 1873, formerly called Bear Ck. Station.

Griffin, William (1785 - 1868)

b. Henry Co., GA. m/ Mary Booker Barnett. dau. Caroline Matilda. See: first Wm. on p. 216 of text.

Griffin, William W.

wife Ann Cole Veal (7-28-1815 - 1873)

"Turtle River Mis., GA." *SCA,* 12-25-1840, p. 110.
"Aucilla Mis., FL Conf." *SCA,* 3-27-1856, p. 171.

Griffith, James (d. 11-20-1871)

d. Butler, GA.

"SS Celebration at Reynolds, GA." *SCA,* 5-31-1867, p. 86.

Griffith, William Leon

not Wm. LeRoy. (p. 217 of text). bur. Rose Hill Cem., Columbus, GA.

Griner, John C.

bur. Springfield, GA.

Grist, John (b. 1821)

b. Spartanburg, SC; m1/ Louisa Hazelwood; m2/ 5-29-1887, Paulding Co., GA, Sarah Zebedee.

Grogan, John H.

1868, 1st trustee of Flatwoods Academy, Elbert Co., GA, near Fortsonia.

"Richmond Cir., GA Conf." *SCA,* 11-10-1859, p. 303.
"Lincolnton Cir., GA Conf." *SCA,* 11-13-1856, p. 95.
"Elberton Cir., GA Conf." *SCA,* 9-18-1862, p. 43.

Groover, Peter

bur. Holly Springs Cem., Cobb Co., GA.
wife ? Mauldin (7-14-1837 - 3-21-1873). b. Elbert Co., GA; d. Cobb Co., GA; dau. of F.P. & Eliza Mauldin.

Groves, John J. (4-4-1800 - 3-14-1885)
d. Selma, AL. m/ Mary Harvey. (**Note:** Mrs. Mary L. Groves, widow of
Rev. J.T. Groves of Covington, GA, d. Atl. 7-3-1887, age 81.).

"Palmetto Cir., GA Conf." *SCA,* 9-24-1857, p. 67.

Guest, John P.
15th GA Reg., CSA.

Gunnels, Joel D.
wife Martha Eliza Parks was dau. of Rev. Wm. J. Parks. Both bur. New
Salem Church, Banks Co., GA.

Hair, Malcolm
wife Jennetta Bledsoe (5-13-1833 - 1-24-1869), b. Muscogee Co., GA;
d. Buena Vista, Marion Co., GA., dau. of John & Catharine Bledsoe.
m2/ 11-25-1869, Sue McMichael of Marion Co., GA. 51st GA. Reg., CSA.

Haisten, John M. (3-8-1802 - 5-22-1877)
b. Edgefield Dist., SC; d. Whitesburg, GA; 1847 le; 1848 lp; lived in Greene,
Fayette 1827, Coweta 1834, Carroll 1868. His motto: "Never sleep before
prayer."

Hall, Willis
"Altamaha Cir., GA." *SCA,* 10-25-1839, p. 75.
"Meeting at Albany, GA." *SCA,* 8-8-1844, p. 31.
"Altamaha Mis., FL Conf." *SCA,* 6-26-1856, p. 15.

Hamby, William T.
"Young Harris College, Its Glorious Heritage." *WCA,*
        v100, n30, 7-24-1936, pp. 4-5.

Hamilton, A. L.
m1/ Martha James Herring, d. 9-1-1874; dau. of James & Mary Herring of
LaGrange, GA, grad. Southern FC, LaGrange 1845; m2/1866; bur. Macon.

Hamilton, Moses
bv. 4-21-1795; son of Robert Hamilton

Hamilton, Wiley T.
"Lafayette Cir., GA Conf." *SCA*, 9-7-1866, fp.

Hamlin, Robert B. (6-19-1862 - 3-20-1937)
1st pastor of Molena, Pike Co., GA; bur. Fredonia Cem., Lamar Co., GA; m/ 12-26-1889, Sarah Frances Means. Chrn. Adelle, 1-19-1891; Elizabeth, 1893; Francis Asbury, 8-17-1895; Ruth, 7-29-1898; William Anderson, 7-5-1900; Lee, 7-4-1902; Irene, 6-17-1905.

Hammill, Andrew
"Columbus, GA." *CA*, 9-16-1831, p. 10.

Hammond, John D.
was Pres. of Centenary College, MO; Wesleyan College, Macon, GA; was Gen. Sec. of Bd. of Ed. of MECS; lived in Islip, Long Isl. NY.

"Roswell Cir., N. GA Conf." *SCA*, 8-28-1872, p. 134.
"The Dahlonega Dist. Conf." *SCA*, 8-28-1877, p. 138.

Hanson, J.B. (1-10-1814 - Jan. 1885)
m/ 9-25-1836, Permilla Freeman.

Hanson, W. G.
"Jackson Cir., N. GA Conf." *SCA*, 9-13-1871, p. 146.
"Canton Cir., N. GA Conf." *SCA*, 8-19-1874, p. 131.

Haralson, Henderson (12-25-1796 - 1869)
m/ 5-21-1821, Elizabeth (11-29-1794 - 8-21-1868). She m1/ Isaac L. Patterson; lived in Greene Co., GA 10 yrs; moved to Troup Co., GA for 20 yrs; then to Tallapoosa, AL in 1857 where she died.

(L) for 28 years.

Harbin, Tyre B.
"Ellijay Mis., GA Conf." *SCA*, 7-26-1855, p. 31.
"Cave Spring Cir., GA Conf." *SCA*, 9-18-1856, p. 63; 8-20-1857,
        p. 47; 9-17-1857, p. 63; 9-24-1857, p. 67; 10-8-1857, p. 75.
"From the Army of N. VA, Dole's Brigade." *SCA*, 5-19-1864, np.
"The GA Soldier's Resolve." *SCA*, 4-13-1865, bp.
"From Illinois." *SCA*, 2-12-1869, p. 26.
"Letter from IL." *SCA*, 4-5-1876, p. 58.

Harden, William
wife Mary Clifton (5-6-1810 - 1-22-1889), dau. of Ezekiel & Elizabeth Clifton, b. Tattnall Co., GA.

Hardin, Joseph M.
"Cherokee Cir., N. GA Conf." *SCA*, 9-18-1872, p. 146; 10-23-1872, p. 166.

Hardy, George A.
LP, bur. Coke's Chapel, Coweta Co., GA.

Hardy, Charles W.
1823, account of his birth, conversion & license to preach; 7-18-1827, letter from Wm. Stone. (Wof.).

"Cullodenville, GA." *SCA*, 10-21-1837. p. 70.

Hardy, William M.
wife Mary V. Lockhart, (1803 - 10-21-1872); d. Henry Co., GA.

Harkins, James S.
"Calhoun, GA." *SCA*, 8-24-1866, p. 4.

Harp, Mosie E. (4-17-1819 - 9-4-1874)
b. Jones Co., GA; cvt. Mt. Zion CG 1841; le 1843; lp 1847; Deacon 12-19-1852; Elder 8-25-1867; d. Fayette Co., GA.

m/ Fayette Co., GA, Sarah Hill, b. 1821 SC; chrn. Martha E., 1841; Nancy L., 1843; Ellen L. 1847 - 1886; Wm. Nathan Tally, 1849 - 1905; James R., 1852 - 1935; Sarah E., 1856; Mary Francis, 1856 - 1924; Louise, 1863 - 1864.

Harris, Aaron W.
"Irwin Mis., GA." *SCA*, 8-15-1851, p. 42.
"Alapaha Mis., FL Conf." *SCA*, 9-30-1858, p. 71.

Harris, Frank
mentioned as a LP on the Canton Cir. by J.W. Burke, *Autobiography*, p. 28. Invested money in a mine in the area and lost it.

Harris, J. B.
"South Western Georgia." *SCA*, 10-7-1858, p. 74.

Harris, James J.

m/ Exter W. Turner (11-7-1825 - 4-15-1867); bur. Smith Chapel, Catoosa Co., GA.

"Montezuma Cir., S. GA Conf." *SCA,* 11-18-1870, p. 182.
"Stewart Cir., S. GA Conf." *SCA,* 11-1-1871, p. 174.

Harris, Jesse J.

"Jasper Cir., N. GA Conf." *SCA,* 4-8-1874, p. 54; 9-30-1874, p. 154;
    11-11-1874, p. 178; 9-1-1875, p. 138; 11-17-1875, p. 182.
"Alpharetta Cir., N. GA Conf." *SCA,* 2-23-1876, p. 30; 10-3-1876, p. 158;
    8-28-1877, p. 138; 10-16-1877, p. 166.

Harris, James W.

located in Cartersville, GA. m1/ ? Hamilton from Athens, GA; m2/ Julia Florence Candler of Villa Rica, GA.

Harris, John H.

"McDonough Cir., N. GA Conf." *SCA,* 8-20-1869, p. 134; 9-3-1869, p. 142;
    10-1-1869, p. 158; 8-26-1870, p. 134; 10-21-1870, p. 166;
    6-14-1871, p. 94; 10-4-1871, p. 159; 9-25-1872, p. 150.
"Newton Cir., N. GA Conf." *SCA,* 9-24-1873, p. 151; 10-1-1873, p. 155.
"Evan & Oakland, N. GA Conf." *SCA,* 5-19-1785, p. 78.

Harris, Matthew   (3-20-1754 - 10-7-1806)

bur. 2 & 1/2 m. from Sandersville Ct.house on the Linton Rd. on the r., 200 yds. off the rd. Harris Church dedicated in May of 1952 is across the road. The church came from Harris MH. m/ Angelica (1753 - 5-13-1803). See: Washington Co. Grant Bk. C., p. 22 re 200 a. on Buffalo Ck. See: LL, 1805.

Bateman, Osgood & Frances, "Harris Meetinghouse." *HH,* v18, n2, Fall, 1988, p. 14.

Harris, Philemon C.

Stewart Cir., GA Conf." *SCA,* 8-18-1859, p. 254.
"Springfield Cir., GA Conf." *SCA,* 11-5-1857, fp.

Harris, Thomas P.

m/ 11-13-1867, Walker Co., GA, Jane Lenard.

Harris, William Evans
a preacher on the Marietta Circuit in 1843.

Harris, William Franklin   (5-3-1823 - 8-6-1871)
b. Rockingham, NC; d. Atlanta, GA; grad. Emory & Henry College, VA; prof. of FC in Knoxville; lp early in life; moved to Atlanta before the war. No record.

Harrison, Nathan
preached at Bethlehem, GA; bur. Smyrna Church, Walton Co., GA. G.father b. in VA ca 1760-70 of Irish descent. 5 chrn. Samuel (lp); John, b. NC 1812; Abraham Pickens (1815 - 1861); Peggy; ? See: Harrison, H.M., "Pioneer Methodism." *WCA*, v83, n49, 12-5-1919, p. 15. (Henry M. Harrison was g.son of Nathan Harrison).

Harrison, William P.
"Difficult Passages of Scripture." (series). *SCA*, 2-15-1867, fp.
"Bishops & Presiding Elders." *SCA*, 3-5-1869, p. 38.
"Presiding Elders." *SCA*, 5-28-1869, fp.
"The Four Witnesses." (series). *SCA*, 11-20-1872, fp.
"The Wine of Scripture." *SCA*, 10-7-1874, fp.
"That Scene in Fulton Co. Jail." *SCA*, 8-18-1875, p. 130.
"Forgiveness of Injuries." *SCA*, 10-20-1875, fp.

Hartsell, J. C.
"Chesterfield Cir., S. GA Conf." *SCA*, 10-1-1869, p. 158.

Harwell, Richard J.
bur. Jonesboro, GA. m/ Harriett Isabella Middleton, d. 1877.

"Chatham Mis., GA." *SCA*, 9-20-1855, p. 68.
"Dedication of a New Mission Chapel at Fair Haven, Burke Co., GA." *SCA*, 7-15-1858, p. 27; 7-29-1858, p. 34.
"Burke Colored Charge." *SCA*, 5-14-1857, p. 199.
"Watkinsville Cir., N. GA Conf." *SCA*, 11-19-1869, p. 185.
"Palmetto, GA." *SCA*, 8-18-1875, p. 130.

Harwell, Samuel   (1-17-1805 - 1-1-1878)
b. Sparta, GA; d. Opelika, AL; cvt. 1828; m/ 2-12-1832, Emily Frances Slaughter; moved 1846 AL.

"Thomaston Cir., GA." *SCA*, 7-23-1841, p. 23.

Harwell, Theophilus S. L.
bur. Jonesboro, GA.

"Meth. Churches New & Old, LaGrange, GA." *SCA*, 10-11-1855, p. 75.
"Springfield Cir., GA Conf." *SCA*, 11-6-1856, p. 91.
"Rev. Asbury Morgan, Olivet Church, Liberty Co., GA." *SCA*, 4-16-1857, fp.
"Starkville Cir., GA Conf." *SCA*, 6-30-1864, np; 9-8-1864, np.
"Troup Cir., N. GA Conf." *SCA*, 7-26-1867, p. 118; 8-28-1868, p. 138.
"Whitesville Cir., N. GA Conf." *SCA*, 9-24-1869, p. 154; 9-9-1870, p. 143;
    10-25-1871, p. 170.
"Acworth Cir., N. GA Conf." *SCA*, 10-21-1874, p. 166.

Hauser, William
"Louisville Cir., GA Conf." *SCA*, 10-5-1866, p. 5.

Hayes, Charles L.
"Letter from Forsyth Cir., GA." *SCA*, 9-7-1838, p. 46.
"Perry Cir., GA." *SCA*, 9-2-1837, p. 42.

Hayes, Charles R.H. (7-16-1832 - 6-8-1874)
d. Butler, GA; son of Rev. Charles Hayes. cvt. 1852; lp 1865;
Tribute by Butler Cir. (L).

Hayes, William M.
m/ 4-23-1869, Laura E. Hebberd of Darien, GA.

"Darien, S. GA Conf." *SCA*, 11-6-1868, p. 178.
"From Brunswick, GA." *SCA*, 10-3-1876, p. 158.

Haygood, Atticus G.
1858 LE; Chaplain, 15th GA Reg. CSA. (his father, Greene B. (1-22-1811 -
12-24-1862) was born on Barber's Ck., near Watkinsville, GA & d. in Atlanta.
He was the son of William Haygood & Polly Stroud of NC). m/ 3-11-1838,
Martha A. Askew, dau. of Rev. Josiah Askew.

Cry of One Half Million of Georgia's Children. Constitution Pub. Co., 1888.
"The Good & The Bad." (Thanksgiving Sermon, Emory College, Oxford,
    11-25-1886), *WCA*, v50, n48, 12-1-1888, p. 1.
"Revivals on the Watkinsville Cir." *SCA*, 10-16-1862, p. 159.
"From Gen. Longstreet's Army." *SCA*, 3-24-1864, np.
"Atlanta, The Gate City Again." *SCA*, 12-15-1864, np.
"Revivals in Rome Dist." *SCA*, 10-18-1867, p. 166.

"Memoir of Rev. John Walker Glenn." *SCA*, 7-17-1868, fp.
"Our Ended Work & the Rome Dist. in 1868." *SCA*, 11-27-1868, p. 190.
"Thanksgiving for a Demijohn of Whiskey." *SCA*, 7-23-1869, p. 118.
"The Atlanta Dist." *SCA*, 9-24-1869, p. 154.
"The Orphan's Home." *SCA*, 3-18-1870, p. 42.
"The Gen. Conf., What Will It Do For Our Sunday Schools." *SCA*, 4-22-1870, p. 62.
"The Christian Church & the Education of the People." *SCA*, 8-5-1874, fp.
"The Mission Field." (series). *SCA*, 10-21-1874, fp.
"The Proposed Unification." *SCA*, 2-10-1875, fp.

Hayle, Thomas   (1802 - 8-3-1871)
a refugee from TN to Dawson, GA during the war; d. at the home of his son, L.C. Hayle. Prob. (L).

Hayles, William A.   (6-13-1819 - 7-11-1877)
d. Jefferson Co., GA; le.

Hays, William   (10-8-1795 - 7-16-1874)
b. VA; bur. Terrell Co., GA; cvt. 1821; lp 1822 in Morgan Co., GA; 1839 moved to Randolph Co., GA.

Heard, Peter A.
"Covington, GA." *SCA*, 6-5-1868, p. 90; 9-24-1869, p. 154.
"Atlanta Dist. Meeting." *SCA*, 8-20-1869, p. 134.
"Augusta Dist. Conf." *SCA*, 8-19-1870, p. 130.
"Athens, GA." *SCA*, 4-28-1875, p. 66.

Hearn, Thomas   (1781 - 1852)
a minister and medical doctor; bur. Bethlehem Ch. cem., Elbert Co., GA.

9-5-1829, Recom. to itinerancy by Montgomery Cir., Lincolnton Dist. (Wof.).

Heath, William D.
later joined the Presb. Church.

"Spring Place Cir., N. GA Conf." *SCA*, 10-4-1867, p. 158; 11-1-1867, p. 174.
"Ringgold Cir., N. GA Conf." *SCA*, 7-31-1868, p. 122.
"Alpharetta Cir., N. GA Conf." *SCA*, 8-13-1873, p. 126.
"Monroe Cir., N. GA Conf." *SCA*, 10-28-1874, p. 170.

Hebbard, Melatiah H.
"Covington Cir., GA Conf." *SCA*, 10-25-1850, p. 79.
"Morgan Cir., GA Conf." *SCA*, 10-21-1858, p. 82.
"Factory Mis., GA Conf." *SCA*, 10-20-1859, p. 291.
"Bethel Colored Mis., GA Conf." *SCA*, 6-5-1856, p. 3.

Heidt, John W.
"Cave Spring Cir., N. GA Conf." *SCA*, 10-18-1867, fp.
"Broad River Cir., N. GA Conf." *SCA*, 9-11-1868, p. 146; 10-15-1869, p. 166.
"Athens Dist. Conf." *SCA*, 9-9-1870, p. 142.
"Griffin, GA." *SCA*, 10-25-1871, p. 170; 9-25-1872, p. 150; 9-30-1874, p. 154.
"The Griffin Dist. Conf." *SCA*, 7-2-1873, p. 98.
"LaGrange Dist., N. GA Conf." *SCA*, 9-8-1875, p. 142; 2-9-1876, p. 22; 5-23-1876, p. 82.

Henderson, John
1827 joined MEC, class leader.

Hendrick, R.J.B.
local preacher on Broad River Circuit; son of James H. Hendrick & wife Sarah A. (4-27-1825 - 7-4-1885) who was b. in Warren Co., GA & m/8-26-1851. She is bur. at Independence UMC, Tignall, GA. R.J.B. was a brother to Elisha T. Hendrick.

Hendrix, J. C.
"Payne's Chapel, Atlanta." *SCA*, 8-30-1871, p. 139.
"Lumpkin Campmeeting." *SCA*, 9-17-1873, p. 146.

Hendry, John M.
"Newnansville Cir., FL." *SCA*, 11-8-1850, p. 91.
"Revival in Madison, FL." *SCA*, 7-5-1871, p. 107.
"Convention of the FL Conf. to Provide for the Education of Orphans of Confederate Soldiers." *SCA*, 9-8-1864, fp.
"Quitman, S. GA Conf." *SCA*, 6-12-1868, p. 94.

Henry, Edward H.
"Jackson Cir., GA Conf." *SCA*, 8-20-1863, bp; 10-10-1863, bp.

Herbert, George E.   (1843 - 9-6-1872)
came from MI in 1869; taught school; joined MECS in 1870 having been confirmed in the Protestant Episcopal Church. cvt. 1871; m/ Nov. 1871,

Fannie J. Beardin (1849 - 9-15-1872), dau. of John C. Beardin. lp 1872; d. Putnam Co., GA.

Hewitt, Ashley
Travis, Joseph. *Autobiography,* pp. 213-215.

Hicks, William W.
engaged in politics, twice married; encouraged FL blacks against white population. Burke, J.W., *Autobiography,* pp. 172-173. Located from MECS and joined MEC in FL as pastor of Trinity, Jacksonville.

Hickson, Seaborn   (June, 1799 - 5-6-1871)
b. Georgetown, SC; d. Sumter Co., SC.

Hill, Christian G.
1-4-1840, letter to Conf. asking superannuated relation. (Wof.).

"Santee Mis., SC." *CA,* 7-13-1832, p. 182.

Hill, James
Travis, Joseph. *Autobiography,* pp. 212-213.

Hill, Whitman C.
1-21-1829, letter to SC Conf.; 1-4-1830, letter of experiences in York Cir. (Wof.).

Hilliard, David
1822, Com. to investigate charges; 11-7-1839, location cert. & conf. letter. (Wof.).

Hilliard, Henry W.
b. Fayetteville, NC; grad. SC College; 1829 admitted to Bar; practiced law in Athens, GA, 1824-31; Prof. of AL Univ.; 1842-44 appt. l'affaires to Belgium by Pres. Tyler; US House of Rep. from AL; CSA Gen.; 1877-81, US Minister to Brazil; author of 5 books; Prof. of Wesleyan FC, Tuscaloosa, AL; practiced law in Atlanta, GA; d. Atlanta, GA.

"Letter from Long Branch." *SCA,* 8-30-1871, p. 138.
"Correspondence with Stewards of St. John's MEC." *SCA,* 10-15-1863, bp.
"Donation to St. John's Church." *SCA,* 7-7-1864, np.
"The Dignity of Man." *SCA,* 9-27-1871, fp.
"Columbus Dist. Conf." *SCA,* 9-12-1876, fp.

Hines, Carolin C.

"Louisville Cir., S. GA Conf." *SCA*, 11-20-1872, p. 182.
"Glen Alta Cir. & Mis., S. GA Conf." *SCA*, 11-26-1873, p. 183.
"Dublin Dist. Conf." *SCA*, 9-26-1876, fp.
"Mt. Vernon Cir., S. GA Conf." *SCA*, 9-26-1876, p. 154.
"The Dublin Dist. Conf." *SCA*, 9-25-1877, p. 154.

Hines, J. E.   (10-5-1859 - 7-24-1909)

bur. Bay Springs Church, Oconee, Washington Co., GA.

Hinton, James W.

"Columbus Dist., GA Conf." *SCA*, 9-22-1859, p. 275.
"General Conference Disciplinary Changes." (series). *SCA*, see: 12-13-1857, fp.
"Atlanta & Marietta." *SCA*, 6-22-1866, fp.
"Letter from Washington, GA - Sore Bereavements." *SCA*, 6-28-1867, p. 102.
"A Financial System Wanted - One Proposed (series). *SCA*, 10-11-1867, fp.
"Affairs of the Savannah Dist." *SCA*, 5-1-1868, p. 70; 3-1-1871, p. 34.
"Springfield Cir., S. GA Conf." *SCA*, 6-5-1868, p. 90.
"Preachers & Preaching." (series). *SCA*, 6-26-1868, fp.
"Savannah Dist. Meeting." *SCA*, 7-17-1868, p. 114.
"Letter from Savannah Dist." *SCA*, 8-21-1868, p. 134; 4-29-1870, p. 66.
"Affairs in Savannah Dist." *SCA*, 10-16-1868, p. 167; 9-24-1869, p. 154.
"The Savannah Dist. Missionary Collections." *SCA*, 10-7-1870, p. 153.
"Savannah Dist." *SCA*, 9-13-1871, p. 146.
"Ministerial Labors, Methodistic Operations." *SCA*, 1-17-1872, p. 6.
"Macon Dist., S. GA Conf." *SCA*, 9-18-1872, p. 146; 8-19-1874, p. 130;
      9-30-1874, p. 154.
"Action on the Liquor Question." *SCA*, 11-18-1874, fp.
"The Poetic Mind." (poem). *SCA*, 1-13-1875, fp.
"Affairs in the Macon Dist., S. GA Conf." *SCA*, 9-22-1875, p. 152.
"Americus Dist., S. GA Conf." *SCA*, 10-3-1876, p. 158.
"The Resurrection of Christ." (series). *SCA*, 10-30-1877, fp.

Hodge, James (2-5-1768 - 10-19-1841)

b. Wilkes Co., GA; d. Newton Co., GA. A trustee of the Starrsville Church
in Covington, GA & later trustee of Covington Church. prob. (L).
m/ Rachel Hullum (7-8-1766 - 11-26-1858), b. SC. Both are bur. at the
site of Old Lane MH off Dixie Rd. in Starrsville, GA. Chrn. John E, Andrew,
David, Ann, Stephen & Sally.

Hodges, Samuel K.
2-2-1818, letter to Rev. David L. White; 12-29-1829, letter to Conf.; 1823, memorandum c. Books on hand; 2-25-1824, receipts of notes; letter from Jesse Richardson re charges against Wiley Warwick, nd; 1821, acct. w/ Book Concern (Wof.).

"Columbus Dist., GA." *SCA*, 8-31-1838, p. 42; 11-8-1839, p. 82.
Poem attributed to his memory, *SCA*, 10-23-1840, p. 75.

Hodnett, George Tip
13th GA Reg., CSA.

Holland, Robert A.
Chap. Buford's Cavalry Brigade, CSA.

"Lectures Upon Jerusalem." uv 1869.

Holliday, William E.
12-19-1835, rec. to itinerancy by Cokesbury Cir., QC; 11-12-1842, rec. for readmission by Santee Conf. (Wof.).

Holly, James
Jenkins, James. *Experiences,* etc. pp. 59-62.

Holmes, Emory J.
"Cedar Spring Mis., S. GA Conf." *SCA*, 9-25-1877, p. 154.

Holmes, David T.
"Thomasville Station, FL Conf." *SCA*, 11-24-1859, p. 311.
"Famine in AR." *SCA*, 2-24-1875, p. 30.

Holmes, J.W. (8-4-1884 - 5-31-1909)
b. Gilmer Co., GA; d. Atlanta, GA; bur. Roswell, GA. m/ Isabell Allison (10-10-1883 - 3-24-1956).

Holmes, Joseph Callaway (1821 - 4-25-1894)
native of Fairfield Dist., SC; m/ Sara King, dau. of Littleberry King & Sara Davis Dillard. a son, Wadsworth King who m/ Mary Cade Akers. m2?/ 1873, Annie Floyd of Madison, GA.

Holmes, Robert
part of his will bequeathing the Meth. connection a grant of Oglethorpe Co., GA land. nd. (Wof.).

Holt, Abner F.
"Forsyth Cir., GA Conf." *SCA*, 10-11-1844, p. 69.

Honiker, Robert L.
m/ 11-12-1874, Mary Lelia Dougherty of Macon, GA.

"The Macon Dist. Conf." *SCA*, 8-14-1877, p. 130.

Hopkins, Isaac S.
scout, CSA.

"Savannah Dist. Meetings." *SCA*, 7-31-1868, fp.

Howard, Columbus W.
Capt., 8th GA Reg., CSA; bur. Greenville, GA.

Howard, J. W.
of Bibb Co. m/ 9-15-1868, Mrs. Annie E. Redding of Houston Co., GA.

Howard, John
6-28-1823, communication from N. Bangs & F. Mason on account between agents & committee of accounts of SC Conf.; 2-3-1825, letter to Conf. asking for location; 1-28-1828, letter to Conf. asking readmission. (Wof.).

"Milledgeville." *CA*, 10-14-1831, p. 21.

Howren, Robert H.
son of Rev. James C. Howren, FL Conf. who d. 7-18-1876, age 90.

"South Madison Mis., FL. Conf." *SCA*, 10-25-1850, p. 84
"Madison Dist., FL." *SCA*, 11-22-1855, p. 99.
"Leon Cir., FL Conf." *SCA*, 6-23-1859, p. 286.
"Centreville Cir., FL Conf." *SCA*, 9-22-1859, p. 275.
"Campmeetings." *SCA*, 8-9-1871, fp.
"Decatur Cir., FL Conf." *SCA*, 8-24-1866, p. 4.
"SS Celebration, Springfield Cir., S. GA Conf." *SCA*, 7-31-1868, p. 122.
"Sylvania Cir., S. GA Conf." *SCA*, 8-13-1869, p. 131; 11-12-1869, p. 183; 11-26-1869, p. 190.
"The General Conf." *SCA*, 1-21-1870, fp.
"Davisboro Cir., S. GA Conf." *SCA*, 8-19-1870, p. 130; 9-16-1870, p. 146.
"Keys of the Kingdom of Heaven." *SCA*, 11-4-1870, fp.
"Groversville Cir., S. GA Conf." *SCA*, 10-23-1872, p. 166.

"Spring Creek Mis., S. GA Conf." *SCA,* 10-1-1873, p. 155.
"Leon Cir. Past & Present." *SCA,* 4-8-1874, p. 55.
"FL Conf. Reminiscences." *SCA,* 1-20-1875, p. 10.
"Waukeenah Cir., FL Conf." *SCA,* 9-12-1876, p. 146; 9-19-1876, p. 150;
    9-4-1877, p. 142; 9-18-1877, p. 150.

Hubert, Robert W.
"Warrenton Cir., GA Conf." *SCA,* 10-21-1858, p. 82; 1-22-1869, p. 14;
    3-19-1869, p. 46.

Huckabee, Patton M. (d. 9-28-1862)
LP, 1861; Co. E. 11 Reg., GA Vol., CSA. d. typhoid, Fairburn, GA;
m/ 7-27-1858, Sarah Matilda Legg, dau. of Laton & Eliza M. Legg.

Hudson, James
LP, entered ministerial duties in 1813.

12-10-1829, cert. for Elder's orders. (Wof.).

Hudson, John H.
bv. 6-4-1849; cvt. 1872 during a revival at Salem Church, McDuffie Co., GA,
& bur. there. mv. dau. of Mrs. Hillery Langford. Following 1884, he went to
Green Cove, FL, for a month of rest and then to White Sulpher Springs as a
supply. 4 chrn.

Huff, James H.
"The Division of the Dalton Cir." *SCA,* 11-29-1871, fp.

Hughes, Andrew J.
wife Georgia C. Hines (1832 - 2-10-1870), b. Bryan Co., GA; d. Liberty Co.,
GA. m2/ 1-25-1871, M.A. Rogers of Liberty Co., GA.

"Spring Place Cir., N. GA Conf." *SCA,* 10-9-1877, p. 162.

Hughes, Francis G.
"Clarkesville Cir., GA Conf." *SCA,* 10-12-1866, p. 5; 7-12-1867, p. 110;
    9-25-1868, p. 154.
"Greenville Cir., N. GA Conf." *SCA,* 9-20-1867, p. 150.
"Andrew Male HS." *SCA,* 7-17-1872, p. 110.
"Elberton Cir." *SCA,* 9-16-1874, p. 146.
"Athens Dist. Conf." *SCA,* 8-25-18785, p. 134.
"Greensboro Cir., N. GA Conf." *SCA,* 10-6-1875, p. 158; 10-27-1875, p. 171.
"Elberton Dist. Meeting." *SCA,* 9-4-1868, p. 142.

Hughes, Goodman
"Dalton Cir., GA Conf." *SCA,* 12-2-1858, pp. 106-107.
"Carnesville Cir., GA Conf." *SCA,* 10-5-1866, p. 4.

Hughes, James M.
bur. Ebenezer UMC, Forsyth Co., GA.; wife Nancy E. Parks (10-28-1838
- 8-21-1914).

Hull, Hope
1818, letter to bishops at Conf. in Jan. (Wof.).

Travis, Joseph. *Autobiography,* pp. 125-126.

Hume, Benjamin L.
was Gen. Stonewall Jackson's chief scout and was with him the night he
was killed. He was scout because he had previously been a circuit rider in
the Shenandoah Valley.

wife Adaline, d. 9-3-1873; b. VA; d. Morgan Co., GA

Humphries, Joab
joined MEC 1841 at Harrison's Church, Murray Co., GA; cl Mt. Zion;
lp 1846.

Humphries, Thomas
story of preaching to the dancing master in Georgetown ref. Travis, Joseph,
Autobiography, pp. 87-88.

Hunnicut, Elijah Y. (d. 10-2-1840)
died of yellow fever in Jacksonboro, Scriven Co., GA. in the house of
Mr. Nunely.

"Clarkesville Cir., GA." *SCA,* 10-18-1839, p. 70.

Hunnicutt, James B.
bur. Turin, Coweta Co., GA.

"Senoia, GA.," *SCA,* 8-23-1871, p. 134.

Hunter, James (11-29-1785 - 12-10-1862)
of Meriwether Co., GA. LE 1806, Carroll's MH, Broad River Cir.
12-7-1808, deacon; 12-8-1810, elder; Liberty Chapel, GA.
m/ 9-8-1810, Elizabeth Tucker, (7-5-1789 - 9-4-1862).
Located, Jasper Co., GA; later moved w/ bro. John to AL.
d. Meriwether Co, GA.

"Jasper Co., GA." *CA*, 12-30-1831, p. 70.

Hunter, John
m2/ 5-18-1848, Chambers Co., AL, Eliza Spikes.

Ivey, James L.
"Knock and It Shall Be Opened Unto You." *WCA*, v50, n46,
    11-17-1886, p. 2.

Jackson, Crawford (9-28-1861 - 7-8-1929)
b. Cuthbert, GA; d. Atlanta, GA. son of James Bradley Jackson
& Electra Houghton. m/ Henrie O. Sherman (12-1-1864 - 9-8-1902),
b. Lunpkin, Stewart Co., GA & d. East Point, GA.

Near Nature's Heart. (poems). 1923.
"With the Mansfields on the Mountain." (poem) pvt. col.
"Letter from David McWilliams." pvt. col.

Jackson, J. W.
*pos. Jas. W. below

"Oglethorpe, N. GA Conf." *SCA*, 6-2-1875, p. 86.

Jackson, James B. (1813 - 2-18-1868)
Chap., CSA. father of Crawford Jackson. m/ Electra Houghton, b. 1825

Burke, John B. *Autobiography,* pp. 70-72.
"Campmeeting in Springfield Cir., GA." *SCA*, 10-21-1842, p. 75.
"Marietta Mis., GA." *SCA*, 5-15-1840, p. 190.

Jackson, James W.
"Columbia Cir., E. FL." *SCA*, 12-18-1868, p. 202.

Jackson, Jonathan
1814, letter to Conf. asking for location; 2-7-1820, explanation of his book account. (Wof.).

Travis, Joseph. *Autobiography,* pp. 208-210.

Jackson, William J.
"Camden, SC." *SCA,* 8-31-1838, p. 42.

Jacobs, General Harrison (11-29-1859 - 10-25-1937)
b. Robeson Co., NC; son of Wm. Jacobs & Rotha Grant; m/ 7-15-1883, Eliza Robinson (9-21-1866 - 12-4-1930), dau. of Noah Robinson & Harriet E. Clay. chrn. Charles Wesley, 7-9-1886; Vian Thurman, 8-1-1888; James Mitchell, 8-5-1890; William Harrison, 11-29-1892; Frederick S., 8-22-1894; Robert T., 1-27-1896; Ollie M., 10-4-1897; James F. 4-23-1900; Noah Curtis, 8-19-1902; Agnes Gertrude, 10-23-1906.

Jacobs served Bethel, Prospect, & Trader's Hill in Charlton Co., GA; St. George, Moniac, Macedonie, Verdie, Racepond & Glenmore in FL.

Jarrard, Josiah D.
"Mossy Creek Camp Meeting." *SCA,* 10-2-1868, p. 158.

Jarrell, Anderson J.
Chap. 19th GA Reg., CSA.

"Sparta, N. GA Conf." *SCA,* 9-17-1869, p. 151.

Jarrell, Charles C.
"A Revealing Revival." *WCA,* v99, n38, 1934, p. 6.

Jeffords, H.V.
"Waresboro Mis., GA." *SCA,* 10-11-1850, p. 74; 12-20-1850, p. 114.

Jenkins, J. H.
"Ft. Valley, GA Conf." *SCA,* 4-14-1859, p. 182.

Jenkins, James
Chreitzberg, A.M., "James Jenkins: A Pioneer of Southern Methodism." *MQR,* v15, n2, Jan. 1894, pp. 314-326.
"Letter on Campmeetings." *SCA,* 7-3-1840, pp. 10-11.

Jenkins, Samuel
1-5-1824, letter to Conf. cert. for Elder's orders. (Wof.).

Jewett, Charles R.
m1/ Martha Octavia Chester (1830 - 5-11-1853). inf. dau. Martha Octavia
d. 7-25-1853, age 4 mo. & 8 days. bur. Old City Cem., Marietta, GA.
m2/ Martha P. Plements (1-19-1835 - 12-22-1869), b. Meriwether Co.,
GA; di. Fort Valley, GA; grad. Wesleyan; dau. of Bishop & E.J. Clements.
m3/ 11-8-1870, Annie S. Howard, dau. of Ellis W. Howard of Bibb Co., GA.

"Griffin, GA Conf." *SCA*, 9-23-1858, p. 67; 7-9-1857, p. 23.
"Macon Dist., S. GA Conf." *SCA*, 10-30-1868, p. 174; 11-12-1869, p. 183.

Jerry, John L.
speaking of 1838 and comparing it with conditions of 1827 in FL he writes:
"We then had four temperance societies, numbering 300 members, and not one
grog-shop. Religion flourished, and peace and harmony prevailed; but her glory
is departed. Our temperance officers are now the first to take the bottle, and our
old gray-headed Methodists and Baptists drunk, drunk wallowing in their filth.
Whiskey shops are scattered over our once happy land! Go to the different posts
and your ears are saluted with the horrid yells of drunken men, and others are
gambling from morning to night."

"Tallahassee Dist., FL." *SCA*, 10-7-1837, p. 62.
"Alachua & Randolph Missions, FL." *SCA*, 10-9-1838, p. 70.
"Sad News From Florida," *SCA*, 11-2-1838, p. 79.
"Letter from Tallahassee Dist., FL." *SCA*, 11-16-1838, p. 86.
"Quincy Station Missionary Society," *SCA*, 6-14-1839, p. 206.
"Newnansville Dist., FL." *SCA*, 5-14-1841, p. 190; 12-31-1841, p. 114.
        6-18-1841, p. 2.

Temple, Robert M. *Florida Flame*. pp. 37-39.

Johnson, Aaron   (Jan. 1784 - 3-1-1870)
d. of mouth cancer, Warrenton, GA. 11 chrn.

Johnson, Amos   (11-3-1819 - 12-15-1873)
*dates vary in text
cvt. 9-18-1839; le 10-7-1840; lp 1-5-1841; Elder 1855; preached his last
sermon 11-13-1873 on text, "ask for the old paths." (L) Warrenton Cir.

"Warrenton Cir., GA Conf." *SCA*, 9-23-1858, p. 67.

Johnson, Benjamin J.
m/ 10-15-1863, Mary Frances Arnold (5-19-1835 - 6-29-1871), dau. of
Ev and Susan Arnold of Henry Co., GA. m2/ 10-1-1872, G. Josephine
Blankston of Fulton Co., GA.

"To the People of Florida." *SCA*, 5-14-1863, p. 66.
"Spring Place Cir., GA Conf." *SCA*, 7-27-1866, p. 5; 10-19-1866, p. 5.
"Whitfield Cir., N. GA Conf." *SCA*, 10-4-1867, p. 158.
"Lawrenceville Cir., N. GA Conf." *SCA*, 2-19-1869, p. 30.
"Fact In Place of Fiction." *SCA*, 5-14-1869, fp.
"Atlanta Cir., N. GA Conf." *SCA*, 9-14-1872, p. 138.
"Cumming, GA." *SCA*, 9-24-1873, p. 151.
"Culloden Cir., N. GA Conf." *SCA*, 6-24-1874, p. 98; 11-4-1874, p. 174.

Johnson, Charles G.
m2/ Margaret Ann Vinson, d. 9-1-1867, Twiggs Co., GA.
m3/ 1-2-1868, Martha D. Gibbs, Twiggs Co., GA.

Johnson, Daniel P.
bur. Munnerlin, GA.

Johnson, Francis A.
"Hernando Mis., FL." *SCA*, 7-23-1852, p. 30.

Johnson, George H.
"Letter from Schley." *SCA*, 9-27-1871, p. 154.

Johnson, John B.
"Isabella Mis., FL Conf." *SCA*, 8-28-1856, p. 51.

Johnson, John Calvin
Chap., CSA; wife Matilda Harrison, d. 5-3-1874, Watkinsville, GA.

Johnson, Luke G.
in 2 years in AR, he built 3 new churches.

Johnson, Marcus DeLafiette Clinton

Johnson, R. F.
"Atlanta Cir., N. GA Conf." *SCA*, 8-23-1871, p. 134.

Johnson, Robert A.
"Lumpkin Cir., GA." *SCA,* 9-10-1841, p. 50.

Johnson, Robert R.
m/ 7-1-1875, Mary L. West.

"Putnam Cir., N. GA Conf." *SCA,* 11-6-1868, p. 178.
"Villa Rica Cir., N. GA Conf." *SCA,* 10-8-1869, p. 163.
"Lawrenceville, N. GA Conf." *SCA,* 5-26-1875, p. 82.

Johnson, Russell Welborn (1810 - 1-18-1873)
d. Bartow, Jefferson Co., GA; Bethany Cir.

"Marietta Mis., GA." *SCA,* 7-18-1839, p. 18.

Johnson, Samuel C. (d. 10-2-1870)
(L) member of Dawsonville QC.

Johnson, William G. (1836 - 1886)
bur. Culloden, GA.

Johnston, George S.
"Spring Vale Cir., S. GA Conf." *SCA,* 10-15-1869, p. 166.
"Ellaville, S. GA Conf." *SCA,* 10-18-1871, p. 167.
"Oglethorpe, S. GA Conf." *SCA,* 9-18-1872, p. 146.
"Revival in Hamilton." *SCA,* 9-15-1875, p. 146.
"Hamilton Cir., S. GA Conf." *SCA,* 10-6-1875, p. 158; 2-23-1876, p. 30.
"Butler Cir., S. GA Conf." *SCA,* 8-21-1877, p. 134; 9-18-1877, p. 150.

Joiner, Hamilton W.
Alford, Mary Bance J., "The Reverend Hamilton Wynn Joiner." *HH,* v14,
    n2, Dec. 1984, pp. 45-47.

Jones, Charles Pickney
lived in Fayetteville, NC, in the early 1800s, a lead member of the NC Conf.;
Capt. of artillery in CSA; son Charles Octavius served at age 12 in his
company & became a preacher. m/ Sarah Ann McLaughlin. Jones lived in
Thomasville, GA. Obit. in *WCA,* 12-25-1936, p. 13.

Jones, Dabney P. (1792 - 3-8-1867)

d. Palmetto, GA; an apostle of Temperence; Mason, Oxford Lodge; Knights of Jerico.

"An Old Man's Opinion." *SCA*, 7-30-1863, fp.
"A Temperance Revival." *SCA*, 3-16-1866, fp.
"The Ladies Home." *SCA*, 9-7-1866, p. 5.

Jones, Edward W. (1803 - 9-22-1870)

b. Columbia Co., GA; grad. Med. College of Charleston.

"Cassville Cir. QC." *SCA*, 8-8-1844, p. 33.

Jones, Enoch W.

b. Fayette Co., GA; son of Enoch George Jones & Elizabeth Travis; 5 chrn., Margaret, Elizabeth, Elmer W., Leon T., R.E.

Jones, James

m/ Rhoda M. (2-18-1808 - 2-22-1874); b. Abbeville Dist. SC; d. Senoia, GA of pneumonia; mother of Rev. Robt. F. Jones. m2/ mv 10-17-1875 *SCA*.

"Elbert Cir., GA." *SCA*, 10-25-1839, p. 75.
"Warrenton Cir., GA." *SCA*, 10-8-1841, p. 66.
"Kingston Mis., GA." *SCA*, 6-30-1843, p. 10; 11-24-1843, p. 94.
"Ft. Valley Mis., GA." *SCA*, 5-25-1855, p. 203; 11-1-1855, p. 87.
"Hancock Mis., GA Conf." *SCA*, 6-12-1846, p. 2; 11-20-1846, p. 94;
    8-13-1847, p. 38.
"Hancock Mis. to Blacks." *SCA*, 9-18-1846, p. 58; 11-12-1847, p. 90;
    7-7-1848, p. 18.
"Sparta Mis., GA Conf." *SCA*, 9-29-1848, p. 66.
"Hancock Cir. & Mis." *SCA*, 10-7-1858, p. 75; 10-15-1857, p. 79.
"Burke Mis., GA Conf." *SCA*, 6-16-1859, p. 219.
"Zebulon Cir., GA Conf." *SCA*, 10-30-1856, p. 87.
"Hancock Colored Mis.." *SCA*, 3-19-1857, p. 167.
"Methodism - Past, Present & Future." *SCA*, 6-27-1871, fp.
"Bethel Church, GA Conf." *SCA*, 10-5-1866, p. 5.
"Campbellton Cir., N. GA Conf." *SCA*, 10-25-1867, p. 170.
"A Report from the Macon Mis." *SCA*, 5-1-1868, p. 70.
"Pray for the Spirit." *SCA*, 6-5-1868, fp.
"The Witness of the Spirit." *SCA*, 9-18-1868, fp.
"Prayer & Family Religion." *SCA*, 7-2-1869, fp.
"City Mis., Macon, GA." *SCA*, 7-1-1870, p. 102.
"Houston Cir., S. GA Conf." *SCA*, 10-11-1871, p. 162.

"Cuthbert, S. GA Conf." *SCA*, 4-24-1872, p. 62.
"Grantville Cir., N. GA Conf." *SCA*, 9-18-1872, p. 146.
"Chalybeate Springs Cir., N. GA Conf." *SCA*, 10-20-1875, p. 167.

Jones, James H. (9-8-1838 - 3-1-1926)
b. Elberton, GA; d. Gadsden, AL; M.D.; Surgeon, 22nd GA Reg., CSA.

Jones, John H.
"Elberton Dist. Conf." *SCA*, 8-28-1877, p. 138.

Jones, L. H.
"Norcross Cir., N. GA Conf." *SCA*, 9-11-1877, p. 146.

Jones, Robert Fraser
dv 6-27-1862. 38th GA Reg., CSA.
(L), bur. Cokes Chapel, Coweta Co., GA.

Jones, Robert Frazier (11-20-1828 - 1-17-1876)
m/ 12-3-1854, P.W. Sandeford (6-12-1836 - 4-5-1873), b. Burke Co., GA; d. Senoia, GA; dau. of Hill & Mary Sandeford. He grad. Emory 1850.

"Hancock Mis., GA." *SCA*, 6-13-1851, p. 6.

(Ed. note: The two R.F. Jones above are distinguished in MPG by Lawrence though they appear to have the same or similar names. There were obviously two separate persons, one local and one itinerant, though their relationship is unclear. According to gathered data, one is the son of a James; the other the son of a Rev. James).

Jones, Robert H.
"Acworth Cir., N. GA Conf." *SCA*, 9-29-1875, p. 154.

Jones, Russell H.
12-19-1829, rec. to Conf. for Itinerancy from Broad QC. (Wof.).

"Broad River Cir., GA." *CA*, 8-5-1831, p. 198; 8-12-1831, p. 198.

Jones, Samuel P.
"Van Wert Cir., N. GA Conf." *SCA*, 10-8-1873, p. 159; 7-15-1874, p. 110; 10-21-1874, p. 167.
"Rome Cir., N. GA Conf." *SCA*, 10-31-1876, p. 174.
"A New Church." (Desoto). *SCA*, 7-11-1876, p. 110.

Jones, W. L.
"Beaver Dam Cir." *SCA,* 6-26-1872, p. 94.

Jones, William Edward
"From The Army." *SCA,* 6-18-1863, p. 78.

Jones, William Fletcher (4-18-1810 - 1888)
b. Abbeville Co., SC; *SCA* mentions death of child, wife named Nancy and mother-in-law named Gillispie. d. Erath Co., TX.

11-15-1840, OT & ordained in Holston Conf. at Ellijay Mis., Gilmer Co., GA (then Cherokee territory). Pastored in 1850s Wesley Chapel, Gordon Co., GA; moved to Etoway Co., AL in 1867 & pastored Bristor's Cove (today called Sneed Mem.).

Jones, William P.
m/8-8-1860, Martha O. Prescott of Scriven Co., GA.

"Liberty Cir., FL Conf." *SCA,* 1-14-1870, p. 6.

Jones, William Parks (11-20-1826 - 6-7-1873)
*pos. same as above.
(L) son of Rev. James Jones; b. Newnan Co., GA.

Jordan, Elias
wife Lavenia C. Edwards (4-9-1798 - 5-2-1878), b. Washington Co., GA; d. Dooly Co., GA.

Jordan, Julian S.
m/ 2-11-1874, Tallulah G. Heidt, dau. of Rev. E. Heidt, Effingham Co., GA.

Jordan, Thomas H. (d. 7-19-1863)
Capt. of cavalry, Gen. Bragg's Army, CSA; Chap. Co. A., 2nd GA Bttn.

"Marietta, GA Conf." *SCA,* 11-4-1858, p. 90; 5-23-1858, p. 207.
"Savannah, GA." *SCA,* 5-7-1857, p. 195.

Jordan, William J.
m/ Margaret Holland (4-1-1825 - 2-18-1878), b. Sumter Dist. SC; d. Reidsville, Tatnall Co., GA.

"Bryan Mis., S. GA Conf." *SCA,* 11-3-1875, p. 175.

Jordan, Willis A. (11-8-1801 - 4-22-1877)
d. Spalding Co., GA; cvt. Rock Springs CG 1818; lp 1822.

Judge, Hilliard
1-24-1815, letter to Wm. McKendree re charges against Bro. Judge. (Wof.).

Travis, Joseph. *Autobiography*, pp. 217-218.

Kaigler, H. M.
*not a minister.

"Cedar Creek Cir., S. GA Conf." *SCA*, 8-20-1869, p. 134.

Kellett, Pinkney A.
"Address of Welcome" and personal mention found by preachers in the Centennial Anniversary of Mt. Pleasant MC, Oglethorpe Co., GA, 1920, Atlanta, GA by C.C. Cary, pp. 14-15, 71-80.

Kelly, John M.
8-18-1834, cert. of restoration as local deacon by Mayville Cir. QC; 10-19-1836, letter to Conf. re his standing. (Wof.).

Kelsey, Daniel
mv/1-16-1848, Elizabeth A. Townsley (3-29-1824 - 5-13-1876)
b. Sandersville, GA; d. Harlem, Columbia Co., GA; dau. of Lot & Sarah Townsley.

"Muscogee Cir., GA." *SCA*, 11-1-1850, p. 87.
"Monticello Cir., GA Conf." *SCA*, 10-30-1862, p. 166.
"Madison, GA Conf." *SCA*, 10-15-1857, p. 79.
"Monticello Cir., N. GA Conf." *SCA*, 10-11-1867, p. 162.
"Thomaston Cir., N. GA Conf." *SCA*, 9-4-1868, p. 142.

Kendall, Sandy
"Griffin Dist. Colored MECS." *SCA*, 7-16-1869, fp.

Kendall, Thomas R., Sr.
at age 15, ran away and joined CSA; was Capt. by age 17; wounded at Battle of Peachtree Ck. m/ 9-16-1869, Julia Thomas of Monroe Co., GA; chrn. Ruth, T.R. Jr., David W.

"Hampton, N. GA Conf." *SCA*, 10-9-1877, p. 162.

Kennedy, D.L.
"Madison Circuit, FL Conf." *SCA*, 6-11-1857, p. 7.

Kennedy, William M.
numerous letters: 4-30-1811, to Daniel Asbury; 1-18-1814, from SC Conf. to
Tarrant re neglected duties as a deacon; 1-18-1820, from Conf. restoring elder's
orders for someone; 2-9-1831, to H. Bass; 8-19-1812, report of com. to
examine historical letters. (Wof.).

"St. Mary's Dist., FL." *SCA*, 7-19-1855, p. 27.
"Revival in Brunswick, FL Conf." *SCA*, 7-26-1855, p. 31.
"Columbia, SC." *CA*, 12-30-1831, p. 70.
H.A.C.W., "An Humble Tribute." (poem to the memory of Kennedy and
that of Samuel K. Hodges). *SCA*, 10-23-1840, p. 75.
M.M., "Poem on the death of .." *SCA*, 3-6-1840, p. 150.
"Jacksonville Dist., FL Conf." *SCA*, 10-13-1859, p. 286.
"Bainbridge Dist., FL Conf." *SCA*, 9-11-1856, p. 59; 7-9-1857, p. 23.
"Concord, Gadsden Co., FL." *SCA*, 10-16-1862, fp.
"Micanopy, FL." *SCA*, 5-13-1858, p. 199.

Key, Benjamin W.
"St. Mary's GA." *SCA*, 11-7-1876, p. 178.

Key, Caleb W.
"Sparta Station, GA." *SCA*, 5-18-1855, p. 199.
"Wesley Chapel Charge, Atlanta, GA." *SCA*, 7-15-1858, p. 27; 6-18-1857,
    p. 11.
"Christian Baptism." *SCA*, 10-25-1850, p. 81; 11-1-1850, p. 85; 11-29-1850,
    p. 101; 12-6-1850, p. 105.
"Divorce of Georgia & the Grog Shops." *SCA*, 6-21-1839, p. 3.
"LaGrange, GA." *SCA*, 9-30-1842, p. 63.
E.G.B.S., "Poem on the Death of Mrs. Elizabeth J. Key." *SCA*, 7-22-1837,
    p. 1.
"Revival in Atlanta, GA." *SCA*, 10-21-1858, p. 82.
"Revival in Eatonton, GA." *SCA*, 6-2-1859, p. 211.
"Dedication of a New Church, Griffin, GA." *SCA*, 6-5-1856, p. 3.
"Griffin, GA Conf." *SCA*, 7-3-1856, p. 19.
"Collingsworth Institute." *SCA*, 7-28-1864, np.
"Americus, GA Conf." *SCA*, 11-9-1865, np.
"Asbury Charge, Augusta Dist." *SCA*, 9-13-1867, p. 138; 9-25-1868, p. 154;
    6-18-1869, p. 98; 10-7-1870, p. 153.

"Augusta Dist., N. GA Conf." *SCA*, 11-29-1871, p. 190; 4-2-1873, p. 50; 12-3-1873, p. 187.
"Great Revival of Religion in Augusta." *SCA*, 4-30-1873, p. 66.
"St. Luke's Mis., Augusta, GA." *SCA*, 9-29-1875, p. 154.

Key, Howard W.
m/ 12-22-1874, Ozella Biggers, dau. of James L. Biggers of Harris Co., GA.

"Cataula Cir., S. GA Conf." *SCA*, 10-6-1875, p. 158.

Key, Joseph S.
at the Gen. Conf. of 1866, Key introduced the idea of the Dist. Conf. to the MECS.

"Pearce Chapel Mis., Athens, GA." *SCA*, 7-6-1849, p. 18.
"Athens Colored Charge, GA." *SCA*, 12-28-1849, p. 118.

Kimball, Francis Asbury (8-25-1829 - 12-12-1878)
began in the TN Conf., son of Rev. Nathan Kimball of the VA Conf. chap. CSA.

"Preachers on the Battlefield." *SCA*, 2-26-1863, p. 32.
"Greenville Cir., N. GA Conf." *SCA*, 9-20-1867, p. 150; 10-25-1867, p. 170.
"Wesley Chapel, Atlanta." *SCA*, 10-9-1868, p. 162.
"Forsyth, N. GA Conf." *SCA*, 10-4-1870, p. 162.

King, Geraldus
1861 elder.

King, Hiram K. (d. 1883)
bur. Old Smyrna Cem., Cobb Co., GA. m/ Martha White (1818 - 1891)

King, James Alexander (12-10-1782 - 8-18-1827)
lp signed by Wm. M. Kennedy, PE; LP Town Creek, Brunswick Cir. on 6-11-1814.

m1/ 11-21-1802, Priscilla Campbell (1-9-1774 - 5-12-1830). chrn. Mary White, 6-13-1805; Drewcilla, 5-21-1807; Susan, 6-3-1809; Sarah, 8-8-1803. m2/ 2-20-1832, Sarah Harris (3-17-1782 - 6-7-1851) b. NC, d. AL. (Entry in text as wife of James King, d. 1797, in error, p. 299).

King, William W.
"Peedee Cir., SC." *CA*, 9-9-1831, p. 6.

Kirk, G. Robert (12-16-1854 - 11-23-1939)
bur. Roswell Meth. Cem. m/ Abi Weems (7-15-1852 - 1-24-1931)

Kirkpatrick, W. G.
"Dole's Chapel, Crawford Co., GA." *SCA*, 10-25-1867, p. 170.

Knight, John W.
"Putnam Cir., N. GA Conf." *SCA*, 10-25-1867, p. 170.

Knowles, Joshua (8-11-1811 - 3-25-1887)
b. E. Hampton, MA; d. Greensboro, GA; bur. Knowles Fam. Cem., Greene Co., GA; m/ Sarah Elizabeth (5-7-1833 - 9-28-1918), b. Warrenton, GA; d. Rome, GA.

"Andrew Chapel Mis. (Savannah)." *SCA*, 12-25-1846, p. 114.

Knox, Walter
"Sandersville Dist., GA Conf." *SCA*, 4-24-1856, p. 186; 5-1-1856, p. 191; 12-2-1858, p. 106; 9-18-1856, p. 63; 11-6-1856, p. 91; 4-30-1857, p. 191; 7-16-1857, p. 27.
"Pope's Chapel, Wilkes Co., GA." *SCA*, 9-27-1839, p. 59.
"The Training of Children." (series). see: *SCA*, 2-18-1858, fp.
"Perry, S. GA Conf." *SCA*, 8-30-1871, p. 139.
"Ministerial Study." (sermon)(series). *SCA*, 1-26-1866, np.
"The Tatnall Campmeeting." *SCA*, 12-6-1867, p. 199.
"Savannah Dist., S. GA Conf." *SCA*, 11-8-1867, p. 178.
"Perry, GA." *SCA*, 9-3-1869, p. 142.
"The General Rules of the MECS." (series). *SCA*, 8-10-1871, fp.
"The Mode of Baptism." (series). *SCA*, 11-15-1871, fp.
"Peter's Cluster of Christian Virtues." (series). *SCA*, 4-3-1872, fp.
"Formalism." (series). *SCA*, 5-8-1872, fp.
"Christian Union." (series). *SCA*, 6-18-1873, fp.
"Macon Dist. Conf." *SCA*, 8-13-1873, p. 126.
"The Lord's Prayer." (series). *SCA*, 7-14-1875, fp.
"Talbotton, GA." *SCA*, 8-25-1875, p. 134.
"The Ridge, near Darien." *SCA*, 11-14-1876, p. 182.

Kramer, George C.M.R.
Chap. 39th GA Reg., CSA.
"Cartersville & Brandon's Chapel, N. GA Conf." *SCA*, 8-28-1872, p. 134.
"Lawrenceville Cir., N. GA Conf." *SCA*, 10-8-1873, p. 159; 10-22-1873,
     p. 164.
"Resignation to the Divine Will." *SCA*, 4-8-1874, fp.

Kramer, William P.
m/ 5-26-1869, Janie F. Mobley, dau. of Samuel Mobley of Floyd Co., GA.
withdrew from MECS and applied for orders in Protestant Episcopal Church.

"Eatonton, N. GA Conf." *SCA*, 11-18-1870, p. 182.
"Rome Dist. Conf." *SCA*, 9-20-1871, p. 150.
"Oostanaula Cir., N. GA Conf." *SCA*, 11-1-1871, p. 174.
Letter re the charges against him. *SCA*, 5-1-1872, p. 66.

Laine, Wylie T.
"Norcross Cir., N. GA Conf." *SCA*, 9-29-1875, p. 154; 10-17-1876, p. 166.

Lambert, Jesse
m/ 5-15-1870, Aletha A. Langston of Floyd Co., GA.

Lampkin, Wallace W.
m/ 11-25-1875, Fannie M. Booker of Wilkes Co., GA.

"County Line Cir., N. GA Conf." *SCA*, 11-26-1873, p. 183.
"Watkinsville Cir., N. GA Conf." *SCA*, 8-19-1874, p. 131.
"Little River Cir., N. GA Conf." *SCA*, 9-29-1875, p. 154.
"LaFayette Cir., N. GA Conf." *SCA*, 10-3-1876, p. 158.
"Norcross Cir., N. GA Conf." *SCA*, 9-18-1877, p. 150.

Lane, Henry H. (b. 1789)
established a Lane's Chapel in Randolph Co., AL in 1852, after migrating
from GA. He was b. in GA and lived in Coweta and what is now Heard
counties.

Lane, James S.
"From the FL Camps." *SCA*, 4-7-1864, np.

Lane, Samuel

son of Richard Lane & Mary Flint; m/ Mary Matilda Carter, dau. of Jacob Carter & Charity Hamilton. chrn. Jefferson, d. 8-25-1853; Amanda; Marcus; Martha J.. 2-22-1811 (m/ 9-6-1835 Chambers Co., AL, Rev. Paul F. Stearns); Sarah; Mary; Matilda; Winifred; Balsora.

served in Jasper Co., GA 1820; Pike Co. 1830s; Heard Co. 1840s.

Lane, Wesley

bur. Screven Co., GA. m1/ Mary E. McKinnon (1843 - 7-7-1874); b. Thomas Co., GA; d. Ellaville, GA; dau. of Kenneth & Ann McKinnon.

"Ellijay Cir., GA Conf." *SCA*, 10-30-1862, p. 166; 9-4-1862, p. 132.
"Supreme Love to God." *SCA*, 8-9-1871, fp.
"Swainsboro Cir., GA Conf." *SCA*, 10-13-1864, np.
"Gibson Cir., GA Conf." *SCA*, 11-16-1866, fp.
"Fidelity of the Apostle Paul." *SCA*, 5-21-1869, fp.
"Spring Hill Cir., S. GA Conf." *SCA*, 8-20-1869, p. 134.
"Grooversville Cir., S. GA Conf." *SCA*, 11-12-1869, p. 183.
"The Love of the World." *SCA*, 4-22-1870, fp.
"Blessed are the Dead who Die in the Lord." *SCA*, 12-9-1870, fp.
"Evil Communications Corrupt Good Manners." *SCA*, 4-26-1871, fp.
"A Little Sermon." *SCA*, 5-24-1871, p. 84.
"Jacob's Dream" *SCA*, 11-22-1871, fp.
"Letter from Ellaville, GA." *SCA*, 11-4-1874, p. 174.
"Ellaville Cir., S. GA Conf." *SCA*, 11-3-1875, p. 174.
"Cairo Cir., S. GA Conf." *SCA*, 10-2-1877, p. 158.

Laney, J.W.

"Athens Cir., GA." *SCA*, 8-5-1842, p. 31.

Laney, Noah

"Perry Cir., GA." *SCA*, 9-9-1837, p. 46.
"Macon & Russell counties, AL." *SCA*, 11-23-1838, p. 90.
"Campmeeting in Russell Co., AL." *SCA*, 12-27-1839, p. 111.

Langford, Franklin P.

judged insane on 1-16-1894; sent to asylum.

Lanier, Thomas B.

"Springfield Cir., S. GA Conf." *SCA*, 7-29-1870, p. 118; 10-21-1870, p. 166.

Lanier, Walter (4-9-1819 - 11-18-1912)
bur. Elmwood Cem., Birmingham, AL.m/ Eliza Meade (1-26-1821 - 1-27-1881), bur. Clarke Co., GA, near Athens.

LaPrade, William H.
"Cedartown, N. GA Conf." *SCA*, 8-5-1874, p. 122.
"Rome Dist. Conf." *SCA*, 8-22-1876, fp.
"LaGrange, N. GA Conf." *SCA*, 3-5-1878, p. 34.
"Revival at Kirkwood, GA." *SCA*, 7-23-1873, p. 114.

Lasseter, Thomas A. (6-1-1814 - 9-2-1886)
(L) in Haralson Co., GA. No Record.

Lassiter, Jacob
LP of Wesley Chapel, DeKalb Co., GA.

Leak, M. A.
"Powder Springs Cir., GA Conf." *SCA*, 8-18-1859, p. 254.
"Atlanta Cir., GA Conf." *SCA*, 10-22-1863, bp.

Leake, John K. (b. 9-16-1833)

Leake, Sanford
m/ 7-13-1871, Nannie E. Smith of Catoosa Co., GA.

"Morganton Mission, GA Conf." *SCA*, 10-30-1862, p. 166.
"Rockspring Cir., N. GA Conf." *SCA*, 8-23-1871, p. 134.
"Spring Place Cir., GA Conf." *SCA*, 9-17-1863, bp.
"Dalton Cir., N. GA Conf." *SCA*, 10-16-1872, p. 162.

Leatherwood, Acquilla
b. Burke Co., NC; d. Jefferson Co., AL; LE 8-1-1813; LP 12-4-1813.

Ledbetter, Benjamin E.
"Canton Cir., N. GA Conf." *SCA*, 9-24-1873, p. 151.

Ledbetter, Charles M.
mv/ Oct. 1886, Lula Maddox of Flowery Branch, GA.

"Christian Literature." *WCA*, v100, n20, 5-15-1936, p. 12.

Ledbetter, Henry
Travis, Joseph. *Autobiography*, p. 207.

Ledbetter, Henry W. (d. 1877)
*not the same as Henry Ledbetter, d. NC, 1852.
Tribute by Glennville Sta., AL Conf.

Ledbetter, Joel (7-27-1811 - 10-25-1873)
b. Anderson Dist., SC; d. Franklin Co., GA; lp Providence Church, Pendleton Cir. (SC); le 1839; lp 1842; Tribute by Hartwell Cir.

11-27-1847, recom. for deacon's orders, Pendleton Cir. (Wof.).

Ledbetter, Lewis L. (1816 - 6-4-1867)
bv. 1818; lp 1842; bur. at Habersham UMC, 8 m. from Millen, GA, n. off Hwy. 24 in unmarked grave.

"Wilkes Cir., GA Conf." *SCA*, 9-7-1866, p. 5.

Ledbetter, Samuel B.
bur. Citizens Cem., Cobb Co., GA. m/ Susie A. Ellis (10-23-1861 - 5-3-1903). She b. Greenville, GA.

Ledford, Charles M. (d. 1905).
m/ Lillian Price, d. 1905. both died of pneu. leaving 5 daus. who were orphaned. One, Leona, was placed in Orphan's Home, Decatur, GA.

Lee, James W.
expose of his playing cards on a train. *SCA*, 2-4-1870, p. 18.

"Van Wert Cir., N. GA Conf." *SCA*, 9-19-1876, p. 150; 10-31-1876, p. 174. "Infedility, Its Tendencies." (series). *SCA*, 2-19-1878, fp.

Lee, Jesse
founded the Meth. church at the forks of the Oconee & Apalachee rivers in 1799, now called Fork Chapel near Greshamville & Swords MC in Swords, GA.

in 1780 he was drafted into the militia but refused to accept the rifle that was presented to him. He was placed under guard, and his singing, prayers and preaching had an impressive effect upon the officers, soldiers and a tavern keeper. He was made a wagon driver and traveled with the army through sections of W. NC. He was discharged on 10-29-1780. See: Clark, Elmer T. *Methodism in Western North Carolina.* Nashville, Historical Soc. of W. NC Conf., 1966, p. 47.

May, James W. "Glimpses of Jesse Lee, 1758 - 1816." *HH*, v3, n1,
      June, 1973, pp. 6-9.

Jenkins, James. *Experiences,* etc., pp. 84-85.

Leet, Arthur J.
"Warrenton Cir., GA." *SCA*, 6-16-1843, p. 3.

Legg, Russell Reno (4-1-1847 - 9-26-1909)
b. Fannin Co., GA; d. Winston Co., AL. son of Laten Legg & Eliza Thomas. GA Militia CSA; bur. Mt. Vernon, Cullman Co., AL w. wife.m/ 1-30-1863, Fannin Co., GA, Sarah Elizabeth Carson (1-17-1846 - 8-26-1917). chrn. James Wardlaw (1-9-1865 - 12-25-1935); Addison Laten (12-26-1868 - 11-2-1947); Margaret M. (2-20-1869 - 9-7-1952); Irva Ella Ista Lana (1-28-1872 - 12-17-1952); Norah O. (12-4-1876 - 4-25-1947); Dotery Franklin (8-8-1877 - 6-25-1945); John Feldon (2-2-1884 - 3-30-1961). lst 6 chrn. b. GA, d. AL; 7th child b&d AL.

Leggett, Ebenezer
story of his father, Rev. Jesse Leggett, of Marion, SC, in Travis, Joseph, *Autobiography,* pp. 91-92.

Leigh, Richard
emigrated from NC to Chattooga Co., GA in 1837; moved to Ridge's Valley, Floyd Co., GA; bro. was Rev. Hezekiah G. Leigh of NC Conf.

Leonard, Thomas K.
"Decatur Cir., S. GA Conf." *SCA*, 10-14-1874, p. 163; 8-11-1875, p. 126. "Camilla & Newton, S. GA Conf." *SCA*, 9-26-1876, p. 154.

Leslie, Hamilton W.
wife Evaline W. (1843 - 1-12-1875), d. Wytheville, VA.

Lester, Artemas
"A Voice From Lincoln." *WCA*, v50, n19, 5-12-1886, p. 2.

Lester, Bernard H.
m/ 4-3-1873, Alzoah Standley, dau. of Charles Standley of Randolph Co., GA.

Lester, Robert B.
Chap., 3rd GA Reg., CSA.

"Atlanta, GA Conf." *SCA,* 9-23-1858, p. 67; 10-14-1858, p. 78.
"Talbotton, GA Conf." *SCA,* 8-21-1856, p. 47.
"SS Convention, Hamilton Cir." *SCA,* 10-4-1867, p. 158.
"Fort Valley, S. GA Conf." *SCA,* 9-8-1875, p. 142.
"Fort Valley & Marshallville, S. GA Conf." *SCA,* 9-29-1875, p. 154.

Letson, Samuel H.
*not a minister
"Milner Cir., Pike Co., N. GA Conf." *SCA,* 9-30-1874, p. 154.

Lewis, J.B.E.
"Rome Cir." *SCA,* 10-21-1874, p. 166.

Lewis, Josiah
"Sparta Cir., GA." *SCA,* 10-23-1840, p. 74; 8-20-1841, p. 38.
"Rock Fish Church, GA." *SCA,* 11-19-1841, p. 90.

Lewis, Josiah, Jr.
wife Mary Rose Hubert (6-7-1845 - 4-14-1873), b. Taliaferro Co., GA;
d. Athens, GA.

"Masonic FC, Covington, GA." *SCA,* 7-17-1868, p. 114.
"That Eccentric Church." *SCA,* 10-1-1869, p. 158.
"When the Cause is Lost, There is Enough of Words." *SCA,* 11-15-1871, fp.
"Athens Dist. Conf." *SCA,* 9-18-1872, p. 146.
"Some Thoughts on Regeneration." *SCA,* 9-22-1875, fp.
"Regeneration, Christian Obedience & Christian Education." *SCA,* 9-29-
    1875, fp.

Lewis, Miles W.
m/ 10-20-1873, Amie C. Champion of Greene Co., GA.

Lewis, Walker
m/ 10-18-1871, Lula Trammell of Cartersville, GA.

"Quitman, S. GA Conf." *SCA,* 7-28-1875, p. 118.
"Smithville, S. GA Conf." *SCA,* 9-19-1876, p. 150.

Lewis, William F.
son of Rev. Josiah. m/ 11-22-1871, Mary Hulit Speer.

Ley, John C.
"Ocean Pond Mis.." *SCA*, 5-9-1845, p. 190.
"Benton Mis., FL Conf." *SCA*, 7-31-1846, p. 30; 12-4-1846, p. 102.
"St. Augustine & Pilatka Mis., FL." *SCA*, 5-16-1851, p. 198; 8-1-1851,
        p. 34; 10-31-1851, p. 86.
"The Work — E. FL Seminary." *SCA*, 6-26-1856, p. 15.
"Micanopy, E. FL." *SCA*, 3-18-1870, p. 42.
"Key West." *SCA*, 4-3-1877, p. 54.
"The Tampa Dist. Conf." *SCA*, 5-15-1877, p. 78.

Lindsay, John C. W. (11-26-1795 - 5-22-1870)
b. Wilkes Co., GA; d. Upson Co., GA; m/ 11-26-1817, Nancy Horton
of Greene Co., GA. lp age 50.

Linson, William T.
"Randolph Mis., GA." *SCA*, 4-5-1839, p. 166; 6-14-1839, p. 206;
        9-27-1839, p. 59; 12-6-1839, p. 98.

Little, John H.
m/ Janie Penelope Waller (3-11-1853 - 4-4-1916). She bur. Smyrna,
Hancock Co., GA.

Little, John J.
"Hamilton Cir., GA Conf." *SCA*, 11-3-1848, p. 86.
"Chalybeate Spring Cir., N. GA Conf." *SCA*, 9-16-1870, p. 146
        10-21-1870, p. 166; 9-27-1871, p. 155.
"Franklin Cir., N. GA Conf." *SCA*, 9-18-1872, p. 146.

Littlejohn, Jesse R.
"Murphy Mis., GA." *SCA*, 7-30-1852, p. 34.
"Americus, GA." *SCA*, 9-20-1855, p. 68.
"Butler Cir., S. GA Conf." *SCA*, 11-20-1872, p. 182.

Lively, William
"State Line Mis.." *SCA*, 11-25-1853, p. 102.

Lloyd, William F.

"Kadesh Barnea." (Wesleyan Doctrine of Holiness pamphlet). J.W. Burke, Macon, 1886. uv.

"Pay Your Preacher." *SCA,* 11-13-1872, fp.

Lockwood, Robert M.

"Letter from Hawkinsville, GA." *SCA,* 6-12-1872, p. 90.

"Hawkinsville Dist. Conf." *SCA,* 7-10-1872, p. 109.

"Hawkinsville Dist." *SCA,* 11-6-1872, p. 175.

"A Word for Organs & Choirs." *SCA,* 4-15-1874, p. 58.

"Bainbridge, S. GA Conf." *SCA,* 4-26-1876, p. 66; 1-23-1877, p. 14.

"Thomasville Dist. Conf." *SCA,* 6-20-1876, p. 98.

"Notes of a Traveler." *SCA,* 6-26-1877, p. 102.

Longstreet, Augustus B.

oldest Chap. in CSA.

"Baccalaureate Address." (Emory College). *SCA,* 8-6-1841, fr. p.

"The Life & Character of ..." (by Hon. Jas. Jackson). *SCA,* 8-16-1871, fp.

"There's Room Enough in Paradise." (poem). *SCA,* 7-6-1866, p. 2.

Lovejoy, Anderson Ray (8-12-1819 - 6-24-1903)

b. Jasper Co., GA; d. Decatur, GA; m/1-10-1843, Mary Ann Hatton (d. 12-11-1890) of Meriwether Co., GA, d. Clarkston, GA. chrn. Sarah Cornelia, 1843; William Pressley (1845 - 1914); James Emory, 1847; Medora Elizabeth, 1848; Mary Ophelia, 1850; John, 1852; Andrew Simmons, 1854; Almede Ann, 1855; Laura Imogene (1857 - 1895); Anderson Bascom, 1859; Pauline Elada, 1861; Charles Henry (1866 - 1886). All chrn. b. in Meriwether Co., GA.

Lovejoy, William Capers (4-27-1825 - 1901)

b. Jasper Co., GA; d. Denton, TX, bur. Oak Grove Cem. m/1-10-1843, Laura Dunlap Hatton *(see above)* (d. 3-18-1910) of Meriwether Co., GA, d. Tillman, OK. chrn. Emma (1848 - 1944); John Fletcher (1850 - 1904); William, 1853; Franklin Early (1854 - 1927); Pleasant, 1853; Robert E., 1856; Allen W., 1859. All chrn. b. in Meriwether Co., GA. John Fletcher m/ Mary Louise Cotter, dau. of Rev. Wm. Jasper Cotter.

Lovejoy, William Pressley

left presiding of Saul College, TN, to join the N. GA Conf. CSA. chrn. Annie Lowe (1874 - 1876); Ruth Trippe, 1875; Katharine Ray, 1882;Paul, 1884; Hatton, 1887.

"What Shall Be Done With the Woman's Parsonage & Home Mission Society?"
WCA, v58, n5, 2-7-1894, p. 2
"Eatonton, N. GA Conf." *SCA*, 8-5-1874, p. 123.
"Summerville Cir., N. GA Conf." *SCA*, 9-29-1875, p. 154; 10-31-1876,
p. 174.
"White Plains, N. GA Conf." *SCA*, 10-9-1877, p. 162.

Lovett, William C.
m/ 12-20-1877, Mamie Smith, dau. of Rev. J. Blakeley Smith.

Lowe, James M.N.   (1813 - 5-24-1870)
d. Clay Co., GA; was in FL Conf. until 1860 when he suffered a heart attack.

"Warrior Mis., FL Conf." *SCA*, 5-21-1847, p. 198;1 10-22-1847, p. 78;
7-6-1849, p. 18.
"Marion Mis., FL." *SCA*, 7-23-1852, p. 30.
"Holmesville Cir., FL Conf." *SCA*, 7-24-1856, p. 31.

Lowe, James T.
"Palmetto & Grantville Sta." *SCA*, 9-27-1867, p. 154.
"Quitman Cir." *SCA*, 8-28-1877, p. 138.

Lowrey, Basil   (1-12-1812 - 4-13-1894)
b. Franklin Co., GA; bur. Citizens Cem., Cobb Co., GA. m/ Emily Yarbrough
(3-14-1815 - 12-3-1905). Two minister sons: Geo. Pierce Lowery, d. Johnson
City, TN; John M. Lowrey.

Lowrey, John M.   (1-23-1842 - 12-18-1898)
bur. Citizens Cem., Cobb Co., GA. m/ 1866, Sophia A.G. Davis, d. 3-17-
1876, b. Barnwell, SC; d. Norcross, GA; m2/ 12-12-1877, Ella O. Latimer.

"Dublin Cir., GA Conf." *SCA*, 9-15-1864, np.
"Irwinton Cir., GA Conf." *SCA*, 11-16-1866, fp.
"Lawrenceville, N. GA Conf." *SCA*, 10-11-1867, p. 162; 8-14-1868, p. 130.
"White Plains Cir., N. GA Conf." *SCA*, 10-21-1870, p. 166;
10-18-1871, p. 166.
"Thomson Cir., N. GA Conf." *SCA*, 11-6-1872, p. 174.
"Canton Cir., N. GA Conf." *SCA*, 11-6-1877, p. 178.

Luckey, Reuben H.

"Wesley Manual Labor School." *SCA*, 12-18-1840, pp. 106-107.
"A College in the Florida Conference." *SCA*, 9-24-1857, fp.
"Bible Work in GA." *SCA*. 8-21-1868, p. 134.

Lumsden, Richard P.   (MPC) (CMC)

bur. Mt. Zion UMC, Carroll Co., GA.

Lyne, Denis B.

"South Western Georgia." *SCA*, 8-14-1856, p. 43.
"Albany, GA, FL Conf." *SCA*, 12-11-1856, p. 110.
"Revival in Brunswick, GA." *SCA*, 3-25-1858, p. 171.

McAfee, John W.   (1799 - 6-19-1870)

d. Forsyth Co., GA; joined church 1819.

McAfee, William Hamilton

Chap., 22nd GA Reg., CSA.
wife Mary E. (3-3-1843 - 10-11-1867) b. Dahlonega, GA.

McAlpin, Alexander

was missionary on the Morgan Col. Mission for many years after he
located. He served Morgan Circuit at one time.

McArver, James H.

"Jacksonville Mis., E. FL." *SCA*, 8-2-1839, p. 26-27.

McCaine, Alexander   (d. 6-5-1856)

b. Ireland; d. Augusta, GA; lived in Talledega, AL.
a GA preacher in 1797-98, located in 1821, probably joining the MPC
at its formation. Wrote in 1826, *History and Mystery of Methodist
Episcopacy,* a foundation document of the MPC.

McCall, H. S.   (9-18-1846 - 5-8-1870)

b. Liberty Co., GA; d. Taylor's Ck., Liberty Co., GA; lp 1868;
1869 Bryan Cir. d. pneumonia.

McCann, B.H.   (d. 3-9-1904)

bur. Citizens Cem., Cobb Co., GA.

McCarty, Thomas F. (d. 7-25-1868)
Tribute by Zebulon Cir., N. GA Conf.

McCleskey, Greene L.
"Monroe Cir., GA." *SCA,* 11-10-1848, p. 91.

McClure, Charles M.
*listed as McCluse in error in Lawrence, MPG, p. 335.

"Canton Cir., N. GA Conf." *SCA,* 10-28-1870, p. 170.

McCook, McKendree F. (d. 1893)
ed. of the *Brunswick Times.*
obit. notice in *WCA,* 3-1-1893, p.4.

McCorkle, Archibald (6-16-1796 - 8-29-1872)
b. Lincoln Co., GA; joined church at Campmeeting, Oglethorpe Co.,
GA. vet. War of 1812.

McCullers, John G.
wife Henrietta Shivers (1825 - 5-3-1874) b. Pulaski Co., GA; d. Calhoun
Co., GA; dau. of Daniel & Eliza Shivers.

McCurry, Benjamin C.
Lt. Col., 22nd GA Reg., CSA, fought at Gettysburg.

McDaniel, Charles B.
b. Carroll Co., GA; d. Atlanta, GA; bur. Montgomery, AL.

S. GA. CONFERENCE: 1915 t/f MPC and served 11 yrs. as Dist. &
Conf. Evangelist and for 6 months on Graymont Summit Charge.
N. GA. CONFERENCE: 1928-31 Mary Branan; 1932 St. James,
Atlanta; 1933 Milton Mem.; 1934 St. Luke, Atlanta; 1934 Sup.
Served Avondale before retirement.

McDaniel, Daniel G.
Sketch of ... see: *SCA,* 7-24-1868, fp.

McDaniel, Simeon C.
Chap. 19th GA Reg. CSA.

McDonald, George M.
"Clinch Mis., FL Conf." *SCA*, 7-5-1855, p. 19.

McEwen, Alexander M.
nv McEwin.
1815, proceedings in his case in Conference. (Wof.).
McFarland, John B.
m/ 11-21-1871, Louisa A. Hamilton of Chattooga Co., GA.

"Subligna Cir., N. GA Conf." *SCA*, 8-23-1871, p. 134; 5-17-1871, p. 78;
11-22-1871, p. 186.

McFerrin, John B. (6-15-1807 - 5-10-1887) (MEC)
(MECS)
b. Rutherford Co., TN; bur. Nashville, TN; son of Rev. James McFerrin;
cvt. 1820; 8-8-1825 lp Cambridge, AR; OT in TN Conf. and served
Franklin Cir. McFerrin came to GA in 1828 as a missionary to the
Cherokees. He served Limestone Cir. (AL) & Huntsville Sta. He served
Nashville, TN; 1836 PE Florence Dist.; 1837 PE Cumberland Dist.;
1840-58 Edt. *CA;* 1858 Bk. agt., MECS; 1861-65 Missionary to Army
of TN, CSA; 1866-78 Mission Bd., MECS; 1879 Bk. agt. See: Minutes
of TN Conf.

"Incidents In Missionary Life." *SCA*, 3-13-1856, p. 160.
(from *The Home Circle*).
"Infant Baptism." *SCA*, 8-16-1871, fp.
Letter from ... (series). *SCA*, 2-11-1864, np.
"Revival at Kingston, GA." *SCA*, 2-25-1864, np.
"Three Charges, Yea Four." *SCA*, 3-3-1864, np.
"Letter." *SCA*, 11-9-1863, fp.
"Religion in the Army of TN." *SCA*, 1-14-1864, np; 3-24-1864, np.
"Report to the Bishops and Missionary Board." *SCA*, 6-2-1864, np.
"From Gen. Hood's Army." *SCA*, 12-1-1864, np.
"Letter from Nashville." (series). *SCA*, 9-21-1865, np.
"The Old Missionary Debt." *SCA*, 8-3-1866, fp.
"Meeting of the Board of Domestic Missions." *SCA*, 9-28-1866, fp.
"Methodist Itinerancy." *SCA*, 11-12-1869, fp.
"Evidences of Pardon." *SCA*, 2-4-1874, fp.

McGarity, Joseph A.
d. Jersey, GA; son of Solomon Seaborn McGarity & Carolyn Biggers of
Pleasant Grove Church (MPC), Carroll Co., GA.

McGarity, Robert S.
d. Jefferson, GA; son of Solomon Seaborn McGarity & Carolyn Biggers of Pleasant Grove Church (MPC), Carroll Co., GA.

McGee, James P.
"Lineville Cir., AL Conf." *SCA*, 8-20-1863, bp.

McGehee, Edward A. H.
"Revival in Thomasville, GA." *SCA*, 6-4-1873, p. 86; 9-2-1874, p. 138.

McGehee, Edward T.   (1807 - 4-16-1870)
b. Jasper Co., GA; d. Henderson, GA; lived in Baldwin, Jones & Putnam; orphaned at age 15; MD; m/ Miss Owen & settled in Perry, GA; cvt. 1834; lp 1839; (L); 2 sons members of S. GA Conf.

McGehee, John B.
"Revival in Hancock Co., GA Conf." *SCA*, 10-27-1859, p. 295.
"Mt. Zion, Hancock Circuit, GA Conf." *SCA*, 11-24-1859, p. 310.
"Hancock Cir., GA Conf." *SCA*, 10-13-1859, p. 286.
"Ft. Gaines Cir., GA Conf." *SCA*, 11-6-1856, p. 91.
"Clinton Cir., GA Conf." *SCA*, 9-18-1862, p. 143.
"Revival in Greenville, GA." *SCA*, 7-2-1863, fp.
"Greenville, GA." *SCA*, 7-30-1863, bp; 8-20-1863, bp; 9-10-1863, bp.
"To the Delegates of the Gen. Conf. of the MECS." *SCA*, 3-23-1866, bp.
"About the Crusade." *SCA*, 6-14-1867, p. 94.
"The Church - The LaGrange Dist." *SCA*, 9-13-1867, p. 138.
"Americus Dist., S. GA Conf." *SCA*, 7-24-1868, p. 118; 9-18-1868, p. 151; 11-13-1868, p. 182.
"Americus, GA." *SCA*, 6-11-1869, p. 94.
"The Americus Dist. & Other Church Interests." *SCA*, 8-6-1869, p. 126.
"Letter From Americus." *SCA*, 9-10-1869, p. 146.
"To the Americus Dist., S. GA Conf." *SCA*, 3-4-1870, p. 34.
"Class Meetings, Revivals, South." *SCA*, 9-9-1870, p. 142.
"Another Innovation." *SCA*, 9-23-1870, p. 150.
"Columbus Dist." *SCA*, 4-22-1874, p. 62; 8-12-1874, p. 126; 8-11-1875, p. 126; 9-8-1875, p. 142; 10-27-1875, p. 170.
"To the Columbus Dist." *SCA*, 8-28-1877, p. 138.
"Make Haste Slowly." *SCA*, 12-11-1877, fp.

McGehee, John William (7-31-1833 - 10-7-1874)
b. Meriwether Co., GA; d. White Sulphur Springs, GA of apoplexy;
son of Thos. F. & Sarah K. McGehee; lp 1855; Missionary, Stovall's
Brigade, CSA. Tribute by Greenville-Trinity Cir., LaGrange Dist. (L).

"West Point, GA Conf." *SCA*, 10-28-1858, p. 87.
"Dalton Station, GA Conf." *SCA*, 10-20-1859, p. 291.
"Warrenton Cir., GA Conf." *SCA*, 11-13-1862, p. 175.
"Elberton Cir., GA Conf. *SCA*, 9-24-1857, p. 67.
"Experiences of an Army Missionary." *SCA*, 5-12-1864, fp.
"The Revival in the Army of TN." *SCA*, 6-16-1864, np.

McGiboney, William
d. Greene Co., GA; dv. 1848. lived on Shoulderbone Ck.; bro. John was JP in
Greene Co., GA. m/ ca 1795 to wife, Nancy (1776 - Apr. 1849), b. GA.
She was a charter member of the White Plains MC. Known chrn. James C.
(2-3-1796 - 5-22-1847); Lucretia, 1798; Matilda, 1800 (d. by 1841); William
Jr. 1802-4; Maria, 1805 (d. by 1850); Erasmus, 1806-7. See: *FP*, 4-13-1991,
p. 14.

McHan, Harvey H.
Chap., 36th GA Reg., CSA.

"Dade Mis.." *SCA*, 7-5-1855, p. 19.
"Dublin Cir., GA Conf." *SCA*, 10-9-1856, p. 75.
"With What Measure Ye Meet it Shall be Measured to you Again." *SCA*,
        7-2-1873, fp.

McHan, William B.
"Chatham & Bryan Mis., GA." *SCA*, 8-19-1853, p. 46.
"Bullock & Bryan Mis., GA." *SCA*, 4-28-1854, p. 190.
"Fairhaven Mis., GA Conf." *SCA*, 5-11-1855, p. 16; 11-22-1855, p. 99.
"Bethel Cir., GA Conf." *SCA*, 11-18-1858, p. 98.
"Sylvania Cir., GA Conf." *SCA*, 9-15-1859, p. 271; 11-24-1859, p. 311.
"A Useful Invention." *SCA*, 3-31-1864, fp.
"Cuthbert, S. GA Conf." *SCA*, 11-29-1871, p. 190.
"Letter From Cuthbert, GA." *SCA*, 3-20-1872, p. 42.

McKibben, Marcus A.
12-12-1835, rec. for traveling connection; 1843, letters & reports of his case.
(Wof.).

"Bethel Cir., S. GA Conf." *SCA*, 10-15-1869, p. 166.
"Valdosta, GA." *SCA*, 11-18-1870, p. 182.
"Second Voice From SC." *SCA*, 12-9-1874, fp.

McKinnie, William (d.1873)
an exhorter in Long Cane Cir., N. GA Conf.

McKinzie, James (d. 6-10-1867)
member New River Lodge #94, Corinth, Heard Co., GA.

McKissick, M. E.
"Ocmulgee Cir., N. GA Conf." *SCA*, 10-9-1877, p. 162; 11-13-1877, p. 182.

McMichael, William T.
"Sylvania Cir., S. GA Conf." *SCA*, 8-23-1871, p. 134.
"Mt. Vernon Mis., GA Conf." *SCA*, 11-12-1863, bp; 10-6-1864, np.
"Bulloch Co., GA." *SCA*, 10-5-1866, p. 5.
"Statesboro Cir., GA Conf." *SCA*, 11-30-1866, fp.
"Isabella Cir., S. GA Conf." *SCA*, 5-31-1867, p. 86.
"Waresboro Cir., S. GA Conf." *SCA*, 6-5-1868, p. 90; 11-6-1868, p. 178.
"The Waresboro, GA, Sunday School." *SCA*, 7-31-1868, p. 122.
"Blackshear Cir., S. GA Conf." *SCA*, 8-27-1869, p. 138; 10-8-1869, p. 163.
"Pine Grove Church, Blackshear Cir." *SCA*, 10-1-1869, p. 158.
"Sylvania Cir., S. GA Conf." *SCA*, 8-5-1870, p. 122; 10-7-1870, p. 153;
        10-21-1870, p. 166; 11-4-1870, p. 174; 10-25-1871, p. 170;
        12-6-1871, p. 195; 9-18-1872, p. 146; 11-5-1873, p. 171.
"Jackson Cir. & Ocmulgee Mis." *SCA;* 8-26-1874, p. 130; 9-16-1874, p. 147.
"Jackson Cir., N. GA Conf." *SCA*, 8-18-1875, p. 130.
"Clinton Cir., N. GA Conf." *SCA*, 10-3-1876, p. 158-59.

McPherson, Angus
1837, memoir. (Wof.).

McPherson, James M.
"Leon Cir., FL." *SCA*, 8-2-1839, p. 26; 10-25-1839, p. 75.
"Brunswick Cir., GA." *SCA*, 9-30-1842, p. 81.
"Dahlonega Mis., GA." *SCA*, 6-18-1841, p. 2.

McRae, J. H. D.
m/ 6-18-1877, Susan J. Newton of Scriven Co., GA.

"Columbia Cir., FL." *SCA*, 7-31-1872, p. 118.

"Ocapilco Mis., S. GA Conf." *SCA*, 9-15-1875, p. 146; 10-17-1876, p. 166.
"Oak Grove, Ocapilco Cir." *SCA*, 1-16-1877, p. 10.
"A Child's Question." *SCA*, 3-6-1877, fp.

McVean, John
1810, letter to Asbury & McKendree; 7-24-1818, report on charges of
drunkenness against him. (Wof.).
He ws formerly expelled from the Church for intemperance and then received
later back on trial. Being a preacher of acknowledged abilities, he was stationed
in Georgetown. He was popular, with crowded congregations. Prior to the 2nd
Quarterly meeting for the station, he became dead drunk and left the place.
Brandy had sealed his doom and gave the church a grievous wound. He later
professed to be reclaimed, joined the Church again, and became a local preacher
a few years before his death. I think he found his way to heaven. -Travis,
Autobiography, p. 110.

McWhorter, Samuel W.
"Cove Cir., N. GA Conf." *SCA*, 8-28-1872, p. 134.

McWilliams, David R.
m/ 12-17-1848, Civility ? (10-19-1824 - 7-10-1870), b. NC; d. Lumpkin, GA.

"Springfield Cir., GA Conf." *SCA*, 9-25-1862, p. 147; 10-25-1867, p. 170.
"Lumpkin, S. GA Conf." *SCA*, 11-19-1869, p. 185.

MacDonell, George G.N.
"City Mis., Savannah, GA Conf." *SCA*, 12-6-1855, p. 107.
"Macon Colored Mis.." *SCA*, 5-15-1856, p. 199.
"Green Hill, GA Conf." *SCA*, 9-23-1858, p. 66.
"Stewart Campmeeting." *SCA*, 10-7-1858, p. 74.
"Church Dedication, Lumpkin, GA." *SCA*, 10-6-1859, p. 286.
"Macon, GA Conf." *SCA*, 7-24-1856, p. 31.
"Bibb County Campmeeting, Macon, GA Conf." *SCA*, 10-2-1856, p. 70.
"Atlanta, GA." *SCA*, 10-30-1862, p. 166.
"Columbus, GA." *SCA*, 5-28-1857, p. 207.
"From Augusta Dist., GA Conf." *SCA*, 8-24-1866, p. 4; 11-16-1866, fp.
"Andrew FC." *SCA*, 7-5-1867, p. 107.
"Americus, S. GA Conf." *SCA*, 10-4-1867, p. 158.
"From Savannah, GA." *SCA*, 3-27-1868, p. 50.
"Trinity Church, Savannah." *SCA*, 2-19-1869, p. 30.
"Savannah, GA." *SCA*, 6-11-1869, p. 94; 9-3-1869, p. 142.
"Sunday School Missionary Society." *SCA*, 2-1-1871, fp.

"Savannah Dist. Conf." *SCA*, 6-14-1871, p. 94; 5-29-1872, p. 82;
6-4-1873, p. 86.
"To the Churches in LaGrange Dist." *SCA*, 6-10-1874, p. 90.
"Fort Valley, S. GA Conf." *SCA*, 9-9-1874, p. 139.
"Laying of the Cornerstone of Wesley Monumental Church, Savannah, GA."
SCA, 8-18-1875, p. 130.
"Savannah Dist., S. GA Conf." *SCA*, 9-19-1876, p. 150.

Mabrey, Thomas
Dec. 1827, letter to Conf. asking for sup. relation. (Wof.).

Maddux, Patrick N. (1-25-1801 - 7-4-1870)
b. Warren Co., GA; cvt. 1820 Sparta CG; lp 12-25-1822.
m/ Martha Neville (8-25-1807 - 7-28-1873), b. Charleston, SC;
d. Barnesville, GA.

"Warrenton, GA." *CA*, 9-16-1831, p. 10.
"Zebulon Cir., GA Conf." *SCA*, 9-23-1858, p. 66.

Mahaffy, E. Varnel W.
"Lawrenceville Cir., N. GA Conf." *SCA*, 9-20-1871, p. 150.

Mallette, Gideon A.
"To the Planters on Satilla River." *SCA*, 12-27-1855, p. 107.
"Bethel Mission, FL Conf." *SCA*, 6-14-1850, p. 6.

Maloy, William C.
"Dalton, GA Conf." *SCA*, 9-28-1866, p. 5.

Malsby, Marshall F.
"Carrollton & Bowdon Cir., N. GA Conf." *SCA*, 4-1-1870, p. 50;
11-18-1870, p. 182.

Mann, Alfred T.
wife, Julia Pierce, d. 6-18-1863; m2/ must have been 1864 not 1854.

"Meeting of MEC, Sparta, GA." *SCA*, 8-16-1844, p. 39.

Manning, Henry Allen (3-2-1831 - 11-14-1891) (MECS)
d. Cobb Co., GA.
(L) N. GEORGIA CONFERENCE: No record.

Manning, Walter T.
father of Pitchford Parks Manning (L); was in Cobb Co., GA, by 1840. The property on which he lived once held a church which he organized, Antioch, which was on the Marietta Circuit. Manning is bur. in the Antioch cem., Cobb Co., GA. which is there beside the church.

"Roswell, N. GA Conf." *SCA*, 8-25-1875, p. 134.

Manson, Frances E. (3-19-1800 - 8-9-1874)
b. Dinwiddie Co., VA; d. Henry Co., GA; 1822 grad. Univ. of MD; moved to GA 1825; to Jasper Co.; to McDonough 1828; served a term in State Senate; lp 4-23-1831 at Ebenezer, Yellow River Cir.; Deacon 1-17-1836; Elder 1-9-1842; Mason.

Mapp, Jeremiah J.M.
"Jefferson Mis., GA." *SCA*, 4-28-1843, p. 180; 9-15-1843, p. 54.
"Black River Mis., GA." *SCA*, 7-2-1841, p. 10.

Marsh, William (8-30-1800 - 5-4-1874)
(L); b. VA; d. Putnam Co., GA; lp 1862; Tribute by Putnam Cir.

Marshall, John M.
wife Margaret Amanda Wade (1-16-1830 - 8-28-1869) b. Orangeburg Dist., SC' dau. of Rev. Daniel F. & Catherine E. Wade; 1849 grad. Wesleyan FC. m2/ 5-24-1870, Mrs. Amanda M. Sims of Coweta Co., GA.

"Perry Cir., GA Conf." *SCA*, 10-9-1856, p. 75.
"The Converted Consumptive." *SCA*, 11-5-1857, fp.
"Painful But Pleasant Memories." *SCA*, 4-26-1867, fp.
"A Fine Prospect." *SCA*, 5-10-1867, p. 74.
"Balm for a Troubled Soul." *SCA*, 2-14-1872, p. 22.
"Evil Speaking." *SCA*, 5-1-1872, fp.
"Obituaries, Funeral Sermons." *SCA*, 3-5-1873, fp.

Martin, Hicks
founded Mt. Zion MEC(N) Seminary, Carroll Co., GA, in 1865; M.D.

Martin, James W.
son of Hicks Martin.

Martin, M.
"Greenville Cir., GA Conf." *SCA*, 8-30-1855, p. 51.

Martin, McCagn C. (b. 1811)
b. SC; 1860 in Dalton, GA.

Martin, William
"Congaree Mis., SC Conf." *SCA*, 7-24-1846, p. 26; 10-16-1846, p. 74;
    5-14-1847, p. 194; 11-19-1847, p. 94; 9-1-1848, p. 50; 8-31-1849,
    p. 50; 10-25-1850, p. 84.
"Relief in SC." *SCA*, 9-27-1867, p. 154.
"Dr. Jesse Boring." (sketch). *SCA*, 8-7-1868, p. 126.
"Washington St. Church, Columbia, SC." *SCA*, 4-8-1870, p. 54.
"Wofford College." *SCA*, 7-8-1870, p. 106.
"My Trip Southwest." *SCA*, 3-8-1871, p. 38.
"On the Wing Notes." *SCA*, 2-7-1872, p. 18.
"Columbia Dist., SC Conf." *SCA*, 7-9-1873, p. 106.
"The Angel Friend." *SCA*, 3-3-1875, fp.
"A Semi-Centennial Sermon." *SCA*, 1-22-1878, fp.

Martin, William A.
son of Hicks Martin

Martin, William D.
"Mission in Meriwether & Troup, GA." *SCA*, 6-24-1842, p. 6.

Martyn, Robert P.
"Lawrenceville Cir., N. GA Conf." *SCA*, 7-31-1872, p. 118; 8-13-1873,
    p. 126; 9-10-1873, p. 142.
"Cleveland Cir., N. GA Conf." *SCA*, 6-17-1874, p. 94.

Mashburn, John H.
gave 4 a. for Ebenezer Church & cem., Forsyth Co., GA, 1865;
wife Catherine (2-15-1799 - 4-20-1869) b. Rutherford Co., NC; d. Forsyth
Co., GA. prob. bur. Ebenezer. mv m2/ 8-27-1869, Nancy M. Butler.
Chap., 38th GA Reg., CSA.

"Calhoun Cir., GA Conf." *SCA*, 10-21-1858, p. 82.
"Carnesville Cir., N. GA Conf." *SCA*, 10-7-1870, p. 153.
"Mulberry Cir., N. GA Conf." *SCA*, 11-13-1872, p. 179.

Mashburn, John H., Jr.
m/ 11-1-1874 not 1875.

"Toogalo Cir. & Currihee Mis." *SCA*, 9-10-1873, p. 142.

Mathews, Bro. (?) (1797 - 11-19-1872)

(L). d. Danburg, Wilkes Co., GA.

Mathews, Moses, Jr.

nv Matthews

son of Moses Mathews, Sr.; bro. of Phillip Mathews; d. Stewart Co., GA
ca 1840 after having moved there in 1830. Most of his chrn. moved to TX
prior to Civil War.

Mathews, Phillip

nv Matthews

bur. 1st Episcopal Church cem., Georgetown, SC; brother of Moses, Jr.
and son of Moses, Sr.; g.son of Isaac Matthews. 4 chrn. in cluding Mary,
1818; and Rev. Theodore. Moved from Winnsboro, SC, to Georgetown with
his father in 1783; grew displeased with the MEC and connected himself with
the Episcopal Church and moved to Beaufort, SC. A cousin of Gov. George
Mathews of GA. One child lost by drowning in Georgetown; another lost
at sea.

Episcopal clergyman in 1809 in Georgetown; identified by Travis (p. 58) as a
former Methodist preacher. He left the connection to join Hammet, who was
a seceder from the ME Church ca 1792. See: Jenkins, *Experiences,* etc., p. 49.

Matthews, Willis D.

12-18-1829, recom. by Coweta & Carol Mis. to SC Conf. (Wof.).

"Greenville Cir., GA." *SCA,* 10-14-1837, p. 66.
"Hamilton & Talbot Cir., GA." *SCA,* 10-18-1839, p. 71.
"Troup Cir., GA." *SCA,* 8-21-1840, p. 38.
"Columbus Dist., GA." *SCA,* 8-6-1841, p. 30; 10-15-1841, p. 70.
"LaGrange, GA." *SCA,* 9-10-1841, p. 50.
"Troup Cir., GA." *SCA,* 9-27-1855, p. 67.
"Cassville Cir. QC." *SCA,* 8-8-1844, p. 33.
"Cherokee Dist., GA Conf." *SCA,* 11-1-1844.
"Newnan Cir., GA." *SCA,* 10-25-1850, p. 79.
"Talladega Dist., AL Conf." *SCA,* 7-28-1859, p. 242.
"Troup Cir., GA Conf." *SCA,* 9-18-1856, p. 63.

Maulden, Americus

bur. Waco Bapt. Cem., Waco, GA.

Mauldin, James D.

"Waresboro Cir., FL Conf." *SCA*, 9-4-1862, p. 132.

"Letter from Southeastern GA." *SCA*, 9-20-1871, p. 150.

"Sylvania Cir., S. Ga Conf." *SCA*, 9-30-1874, p. 154; 9-15-1875, p. 146;
 9-1-1875, p. 138.

"Is There Any Legislation Necessary." *SCA*, 4-17-1877, fp.

Mayson, James R.

"Acworth, N. GA Conf." *SCA*, 8-23-1871, p. 134; 10-25-1871, p. 170;
 10-16-1872, p. 162.

"Fulton Cir., N. GA Conf." *SCA*, 12-9-1870, p. 193.

"McDonough Cir., N. GA Conf." *SCA*, 9-3-1873, p. 138; 8-19-1874, p. 131;
 9-16-1874, p. 146; 10-28-1874, p. 170.

Meacham, Robert B.

b. NC; See: 1860 Census, Heard Co., GA.

Means, Alexander

preached the funerals of Wilbur Fisk and Pres. Taylor (1850). See: *WCA*,
5-3-1935, p. 6. See: *WCA*, v50, n.1, 1-6-1886 for an obit. of a dau.

"Dr. Alex Means." *WCA*, v47, n29, 7-18-1883, p. 2.

"Superintendent's Report, GA Conf. Manual Labor School." *SCA*, 9-21-1837,
 p. 42; 9-30-1837, p. 59.

"Letter on Revivals In Georgla." *SCA*, 9-7-1838, p. 46.

"Letter on the Manual Labor School." *SCA*, 9-14-1838, p. 50.

"The Golden Girdle." (poem). *SCA*, 9-21-1838, p. 56.

"Aurora Borealis." (poem). *SCA*, 9-13-1839, p. 51.

"Letter." *SCA*, 10-11-1839, p. 66.

"Lines Written in the Album of a Female Friend." *SCA*, 10-18-1839, p. 68.

"Lines." (poem). *SCA*, 11-22-1839, p. 88.

"Anniversary of the Missionary Society, GA Conf." *SCA*, 2-12-1841, p. 137.

"Commencement Address." Macon FC. *SCA*, 9-1-1843, p. 47.

Letter, 7-5-1851. *SCA*, 8-8-1851, p. 38.

"Campmeeting Hymn." (poem). *SCA*, 5-9-1851, p. 192.

"The Sound of the Gospel is Passing Away." (poem). *SCA*, 11-11-1858, fp.

"A Trip to E. FL." *SCA*, 12-22-1859, pp. 326-327.

"To An Itinerant Minister's Wife." (poem). *SCA*, 1-15-1863, fp.

"Oxford, GA." *SCA*, 5-6-1858, p. 195.

"The Twilight of the Millennium." *SCA*, 9-11-1862, fp.

"Poetic Paraphase." (poem). *SCA*, 11-26-1863, fp.

"Emory College Alumni Appeal." *SCA*, 1-4-1867, fp.
"Denominational Colleges, Valuable Statistics." *SCA*, 5-14-1873, fp.
"From My Diary." *SCA*, 6-18-1873, p. 94.
"Lines Commemorative of Our Sainted Little Charlie Capers." *SCA*,
    6-25-1873, fp
"A Tribute to the Memory of Mrs. Cornelia H. Hopkins." (poem). *SCA*,
    9-23-1874, fp.

Means, Olin S.
"Putnam Cir., GA Conf." *SCA*, 8-18-1859, p. 254.

Mebane, W. K.   (1835 - 1-21-1878)
b. Richmond, VA; d. Thomasville, GA. (denom. not given in obit.).
(L). Tribute, Decatur Cir., Whigham, GA.

Menefee, Richard Alexander
d. & bur. in Chirino, Nacogdoches Co., TX; son of Geo. Menefee, RS.
Held Meth. services in his home in Talbot Co., GA.

Merk, Andrew B.   (4-4-1859 - 9-7-1903)
bur. Dry Pond UMC, Jackson Co., GA. m/ Mollie Pinson (3-22-1860 -
1-7-1950).

Merk, Henry   (12-8-1799 - 1868)
b. Edgefield Dist., SC; cvt. 1821; le 1825; moved to Athens, GA 1827;
Jackson, GA 1828; lp 1837; deacon 1842; (L); moved to Carroll Co., GA
1857 where he died.

*Merritt, Mickleberry   (1802 - 11-24-1866)
+not a minister. A layman in whose house the MPC was formed in GA.
b. Greene Co., GA; reared in Morgan Co., GA; moved to Monroe Co., GA
in 1826. m/1826, Jane Broom (10-19-1808 - 4-6-1870); joined MECS 1828;
formed MPC, 1852, Monroe Co., GA.

Merritt, William B.   (d. 2-24-1894)
d. near Buena Vista, GA. m/ 3-19-1871, Schley Co., GA, Fannie Williamson.

"Weston Cir., GA Conf." *SCA*, 9-10-1863, bp.
"The Lumpkin Dist. Meeting." *SCA*, 10-5-1866, fp.

Middleton, James R. (b. 7-10-1803 - 8-18-1874)
b. McIntosh Co., GA; moved to FL 1854; le 1834; lp 1835; Deacon 1839; Elder 1848; (L) in FL CONF. after his move there.

m/ Rachel Carter, b. 3-29-1812. chrn. Mary Ann, 1829; Charlton Hines; William Cooper; David Alexander; James Wesley; George Carter; Charles Bascom; Andrew West, 1852; Delilah, 1832.

"Altamaha Mis., GA." *SCA*, 9-9-1837, p. 46.

Miller, John M.
"Harpersville Cir., AL." *SCA*, 10-30-1846, p. 83.

Mills, John W.
d. Shelby Co., TX; Delegate to Gen. Conf. 1858, 1866.

"Albany Cir., FL Conf." *SCA*, 5-18-1855, p. 199; 8-23-1855, p. 47; 4-27-1855, p. 67.
"Satilla Mis., GA Conf." *SCA*, 8-16-1844, p. 38.
"Satilla Mis., FL Conf." *SCA*, 5-30-1845, p. 203.
"Sumter Mis., FL Conf." *SCA*, 7-3-1856, p. 19.
"Madison Dist., FL Conf." *SCA*, 11-27-1856, pp. 102-103.
"Bainbridge Dist., S. GA Conf." *SCA*, 4-12-1867, p. 58.
"Relief for the Poor." *SCA*, 6-14-1867, p. 94.
"Randolph Cir., S. GA conf." *SCA*, 9-11-1868, p. 146.
"Unfruitfulness of Preaching - Woman's Influence." *SCA*, 9-25-1868, fp.
"Weston Cir., S. GA Conf." *SCA*, 8-20-1869, p. 134; 10-15-1869, p. 166.
"Ellaville & Oglethorpe Cir., S. GA Conf." *SCA*, 9-16-1870, p. 146.

Mills, William
"Chattahooche Mis., GA." *SCA*, 6-25-1841, p. 6.

Mitchell, Archelaus H.
1846, 5 letters to H. Bass. (Wof.).

"Cokesbury Manual Labor School." *SCA*, 10-28-1837, p. 75; 12-15-1837, p. 103; 10-26-1838, p. 74; 11-23-1838, p. 90.
"The Sabbath." (poem). *SCA*, 7-5-1839, p. 8.
"Address, Centenary Institute, AL." *SCA*, 8-23-1850, p. 45.
"Religious Needs in the Army." *SCA*, 4-23-1863, p. 62.
"Reminiscences of Bishop Andrew." (series). *SCA*, 6-21-1871, fp.

Mitchell, Cicero A.
"Clinton Cir., N. GA Conf." *SCA*, 10-28-1870, p. 170.
"County Line Cir., S. GA Conf." *SCA*, 9-4-1872, p. 139; 9-9-1874, p. 139.

Mitchell, James
wrote a book in 1885 on Bishop Scott. No ref.

Mixon, J. Fletcher
wife Georgia E. Smith (12-4-1840 - 8-19-1874), dau. of Henry & Carrie Smith; b&d. Jasper Co., GA.

"Atlanta Dist. Conf." *SCA*, 8-19-1870, p. 130.
"The Bainbridge Dist. Conf." *SCA*, 4-26-1871, p. 66; 5-1-1872, p. 66.
"Monroe Cir., N. GA Conf." *SCA*, 10-27-1875, p. 170.
"Broad River Cir., N. GA Conf." *SCA*, 9-18-1877, p. 150.

Mizelle, Luke T.   (8-29-1803 - 9-8-1877)
b. Bulloch Co., GA; d. Powder Springs, GA; m/ ? McCall & settled in Russell Co., AL; father was (L); Deacon 1850 AL. 2Lt., 7th GA Reg., CSA.

Montgomery, Silas
40th GA Reg., CSA.

Montgomery, T. F.
wife Mary Achsah Turner (10-3-1829 - 4-24-1869).

Moore, Charles A.
"County Line Cir., S. GA Conf." *SCA*, 9-27-1871, p. 155; 9-10-1873, p. 142.

Moore, George W.
bur. Spartanburg, SC, remains temporarily interred.

12-16-1836, letter to Conf. re his ill health. 1799-1863, memorial and acct. of his life. (Wof.).

"Letter on SC Campmeetings." *SCA*, 9-7-1838, p. 46.
"Newberry Cir., SC." *SCA*, 1-28-1842, p. 130; 10-23-1840, p. 74.
"Laurens Cir., SC." *SCA*, 11-4-1842, p. 81.
"Beaufort Mis., SC." *SCA*, 9-12-1851, p. 58; 4-30-1852, p. 190; 12-19-1851, p. 114; 8-13-1852, p. 42; 12-31-1852, p. 26; 11-11-1853, p. 94.

"Cooper River Mis., SC." *SCA*, 7-5-1855, p. 19; 11-22-1855, p. 98;
    4-7-1859, p. 178; 11-24-1859, p. 310; 11-27-1856, p. 103; 4-9-1857,
    p. 179; 7-16-1857, p. 27.
"Flatwoods Mis., SC." *SCA*, 1-15-1847, p. 126.

Moore, Henry D.
Chap. 12 Reg. AL Vols., CSA.
m/ 9-26-1859, Caroline F. Thomason.

"From the AL Regiment." *SCA*, 12-3-1863, bp.
"Albany, GA." *SCA*, 6-19-1868, p. 99; 7-16-1869, p. 114.
"AL Correspondence." (series). *SCA*, 10-5-1878, fp.

Moore, Joseph
"A Biographical Sketch of the Rev. Joseph Moore." *SCA*, 3-7-1851, p. 153.
"Darlington, SC." *CA*, 12-31-1830, p. 78.

Moore, S. S.
"On the St. John's River." *SCA*, 2-22-1871, p. 30.
"A Visit to St. Augustine, FL." *SCA*, 9-20-1871, p. 150.
"On the Oclawaha River." *SCA*, 2-7-1872, p. 18.
"Religious Life in S. FL." *SCA*, 7-3-1872, p. 102.

Moore, Thomas M.
wife Sarah Margaret Huckabee (11-22-1843 - 8-5-1873) b. Coweta Co., GA;
d. Camilla, GA; dau. of W.G. Huckabee.

Moore, William A.
"About Chaplains." *SCA*, 3-19-1863, p. 44-45.

Morehouse, Norman D.
"Springfield Cir., GA Conf." *SCA*, 10-5-1866, p. 5.
"Swainsboro Cir., S. GA Conf." *SCA*, 11-26-1869, p. 190.
"Spring Vale, S. GA Conf." *SCA*, 10-25-1871, p. 170.
"Springfield Cir., S. GA Conf." *SCA*, 8-13-1873, p. 126.
"Alexander Cir., S. GA Conf." *SCA*, 8-25-1875, p. 134; 10-6-1875, p. 158;
    9-12-1876, p. 146.

Moreland, B. T.
"Hogansville Cir., N. GA Conf." *SCA*, 10-2-1872, p. 154; 9-3-1873, p. 139.

Morgan, Hobson
(L); Class Leader, Exhorter, Steward & Deacon
m/ 4 chrn.

Morgan, John J.
"Decatur Cir., GA Conf." *SCA*, 11-16-1865, np; 8-17-1866, p. 4;
    9-7-1866, fp; 11-2-1866, fp.
"From Hawkinsville Cir., GA." *SCA*, 5-8-1867, p. 70.

Morris, J. V. M.
"Altamaha Dist., S. GA Conf." *SCA*, 10-20-1875, p. 166.

Morton, Henry   (d. 1863)
m/ 1854 Sarah A. Phillips, d. 12-21-1877, dau. of Geo. & Sarah Phillips
of VA; she m1/ 1829, Rev. Jas. C. Talbot (d. 1840) of Wilkes Co., GA.
6 chrn.

Morton, William A.
Rivers, W.P., "Elegiac Lines." (poem on the death of Wm. H? Morton).
    SCA, 10-16-1856, fp.

Moss, William H.
55th GA Reg., CSA.

"Elbert Cir., GA Conf." *SCA*, 9-23-1858, p. 67.

Mote, John P.   (3-6-1793 - 9-4-1867)
nv Moate. b. SC; d. Dooly Co., GA; cvt. age 13; lp 1813.

Murchison, Colin
"The Cokesbury School." *SCA*, 7-29-1858, p. 35.
"Marion Cir., SC." *SCA*, 10-30-1846, p. 83.

Murchison, Kenneth
letter to Conf. asking for sup. relations; papers charging him with intoxication.
(Wof.).

"MacKannan Cir., SC." *CA*, 2-3-1832, p. 90.

Murdock, C. H.
*do not have other than this data.
m/ 6-20-1858, Narcissa E. Roberts (2-20-1841 - 7-11-1871), b. Twiggs Co.,
GA; d. Welborn, FL; dau. of Rev. D. & N.H. Roberts.

Murdock, Charles P.
"Alapaha Mis., FL Conf." *SCA*, 4-24-1856, p. 187.

Murdock, David   (9-26-1790 - 3-2-1875)
b. SC; d. DeKalb Co., GA; joined MEC at Bush River, Anderson Dist., SC,
May 1816; le 1832; lp 1847; Deacon Dec. 1856, Americus; 1829 moved to
Newton Co., GA; united w/ Ebenezer Church; 1872 moved to DeKalb Co.,
GA; united w/ Ousley Church; d. cancer of face.

Murff, Samuel   (12-26-1776 - 1860)
b. SC, d. Winston Co., MS. Served as circuit rider in Clarke Co., GA.

Murphy, Henry D.
"Louisville Cir., Savannah Dist., S. GA Conf." *SCA*, 9-17-1873, p. 146.

Murphy, John   (1812 - 1897)
MD; 3 p. typescript by S.B. Dorsey.

Murphy, William L.
"The Lives of a Whole Family Saved by Prayer." *SCA*, 12-2-1858, fp.
"It is Even So." *SCA*, 12-23-1858, fp.
"Tampa Dist., FL Conf." *SCA*, 8-14-1862, p. 122.

Murrah, Ebenezer G.
"Watkinsville, GA." *SCA*, 11-18-1870, p. 182.
"Hancock Cir., N. GA Conf." *SCA*, 10-25-1871, p. 170.
"Monticello, N. GA Conf." *SCA*, 10-2-1872, p. 154.
"Mulberry Cir., N. GA Conf." *SCA*, 9-30-1874, p. 154.

Murrah, William
"Mobile, AL." *SCA*, 7-27-1838, p. 22.

Murray, John P.   (d. 1873)

Myers, Aaron
Sgt. 15th GA Reg., CSA.

Myers, Edward H.
"Methodism in Darien, GA." *SCA*, 6-17-1842, pp. 2-3.
"Address at Wesleyan FC." *SCA*, 8-6-1852, p. 37.
"Review of Rogers on Election." *SCA*, 12-20-1850, p. 113; 12-27-1850,
     p. 117; 1-31-1850, p. 121; 1-10-1850, p. 125; 1-17-1850, p. 129;
     1-24-1850, p. 132.
"Prevalent Social Sins." (sermon). J.W. Burke & Co., 1866. nv.
"Baccalaureate Address, Wesleyan, 7-16-1873." *SCA*, 7-23-1873, p. 114.
"Episcopal Ministry & Slavery in 1844." (series). *SCA*, 9-9-1874, fp.
"Legislation on Temperance in the MECS." (series). *SCA*, 10-14-1874, fp.
Disruption of the MEC. ca 1875, uv.

Rivers, W. P. "An Ode, Savannah's Death-Roll." (poem in tribute to Myers).
     SCA, 10-10-1876, fp.

Myers, Herbert P.
"Keeping Labors out of the Harvest Fields." *WCA*, v50, n43, 11-3-1886,
     p. 5.
"Letter From Blackshear, GA." *SCA*, 5-7-1873, p. 70.
"Dawson Dist. Conf." *SCA*, 4-29-1874, p. 66.
"Brunswick Dist. Conf." *SCA*, 4-30-1878, p. 66.

Myers, James N.
"Atlanta Cir., GA Conf." *SCA*, 10-19-1866, p. 5.
"Villa Rica Cir., N. GA Conf." *SCA*, 10-28-1870, p. 170; 10-18-1871, p. 166.
"Cherokee Cir., N. GA Conf." *SCA*, 10-31-1876, p. 174.
"Dawsonville Cir., N. GA Conf." *SCA*, 11-20-1877, p. 186.

Myers, Lewis
m/ 6-30-1816, Rebecca Russell

1820, statement of accounts, Book Concern; 1821, accounts along w/ Jas.
Travis & Jesse Richardson; 1-18-1827, receipts to bk. committee. (Wof.).

"Old Wesley College." (Succoth Academy). *SCA*, 12-24-1841, p. 110.
"Springfield Cir., GA." *SCA*, 9-27-1839, pp. 58-59.
Dougharty, George. "Letter to Lewis Myers." 1806. *SCA*, 10-28-1837, p. 75.
"Effingham Campmeetings." *SCA*, 11-20-1846, p. 95.
"Autobiography." (series). *SCA*, 8-20-1869, fp.

Myers, Oscar A.
"From the TN Army." *SCA*, 7-23-1863, bp.

Myrick, Daniel J.
"Sandersville Cir.." *SCA*, 9-2-1858, p. 55; 10-28-1858, p. 86.
"Hinesville Cir., GA Conf." *SCA*, 11-13-1856, p. 95.
"Bartow Cir., GA Conf." *SCA*, 9-11-1862, 138; 9-18-1862, p. 143.
"Manassas, Bartow Co., GA." *SCA*, 10-30-1862, p. 166.
"Sandersville, GA Conf." *SCA*, 9-10-1857, p. 59.
"Watkinsville Cir., GA Conf." *SCA*, 10-29-1863, bp.
"Lexington Cir., N. GA Conf." *SCA*, 9-18-1868, p. 151; 10-9-1868, p. 162.
"Baptismal Demonstrations." ca 1868 uv.
"Intemperance as a Moral Evil." *SCA*, 3-25-1870, fp.
"Rum Selling & Its Consequence." *SCA*, 4-1-1870, fp.
"Covington, GA." *SCA*, 9-23-1870, p. 150; 10-21-1870, p. 166.
"Forsyth, GA." *SCA*, 10-30-1872, p. 170.
"Dalton, GA." *SCA*, 5-5-1875, p. 70; 8-25-1875, p. 134.
"Dalton Cir., N. GA Conf." *SCA*, 10-6-1875, p. 158.

Nash, Reuben
19th GA Reg., CSA.

Neeley, Thomas
grave is in the Hutchison-Johnson cem. off Winterville/Arnoldsville Rd. in Oglethorpe Co., GA.

Neese, Levi P.
"Jonesboro Cir., N. GA Conf." *SCA*, 8-30-1871, p. 138.
"Swainsboro Cir., S. GA Conf." *SCA*, 11-8-1867, p. 178.
"Hartwell Cir., N. GA Conf." *SCA*, 8-28-1868, p. 138.
"Cave Spring, GA, SS." *SCA*, 5-28-1869, p. 87.
"Cave Spring, N. GA Conf." *SCA*, 9-24-1869, p. 155; 11-26-1869, p. 190.
"Bethel, Zoar & Concord." *SCA*, 9-23-1870, p. 150.
"Fulton Cir., N. GA Conf." *SCA*, 10-21-1874, p. 166.
"Fairburn Cir., N. GA Conf." *SCA*, 9-18-1877, p. 150.

Nelson, Art
black preacher mentioned in *History of Pine Log MC*. p. 30.

Newell, John
a problem with English grammar discouraged him in itinerant ministry.
See: Burke, John B. *Autobiography*, p. 41.

Nolan, David Atticus (3-28-1819 - 6-29-1905)
b. NC; d. Senoia, Coweta Co., GA. m/ 3-27-1838, Henry Co., GA, Louisa
R. Peebles, dau. of Lewis J. Peebles. chrn. Joseph Thomas, 1839; James R.,
1841; John Y., 9-4-1843; William T., 1846; David T., 1851; Jesse H., b.
7-29-1852.

Nolan, J. David
"Jackson Cir., N. GA Conf." *SCA*, 10-1-1869, p. 158; 10-14-1870, p. 162.
"Fayetteville Cir., N. GA Conf." *SCA*, 9-27-1871, p. 154.

Norman, Gideon G. (1808 - 1867)
native of Wilkes Co., GA; d. Washington, GA; Capt., 3rd GA Reg., CSA.

Norman, William T.
"Ocmulgee Mis., GA." *SCA*, 10-3-1851, p. 70; 12-5-1851, p. 106.
"Carnesville Cir., GA Conf." *SCA*, 9-9-1858, p. 59.

Norris, John T.
wife Ella R. DeJarnette, d. 4-28-1878, Cartersville, GA.

"Washington, GA Conf." *SCA*, 9-25-1862, p. 147.
"Rome Dist. Conf." *SCA*, 9-10-1873, p. 142.

Norris, William B.
Chap., 8th GA, CSA.

Norsworthy, Frederick P.
10-15-1825, recom. to SC Conf. from Athens Dist. Conf. (Wof.).

Norton, Archibald H.
wife Huldah (9-8-1821 - 10-4-1873)

"Haralson Mis., N. GA Conf." *SCA*, 10-7-1870, p. 153.

Odom, Alexander
deserter, 4th GA Reg., CSA.

"Rome Cir., N. GA Conf." *SCA*, 9-16-1870, p. 146; 10-21-1870, p. 166.
"Spring Place Cir., N. GA Conf." *SCA*, 6-10-1874, p. 90.

O'Driscoll, Dennis
"Dooly Mis., GA." *SCA*, 8-26-1853, p. 50.
"Upson Cir., GA Conf." *SCA*, 10-21-1858, p. 82.
"Missionary Collection, Sylvania Circuit, GA Conf." *SCA*,
    9-18-1856, p. 63.
"Weston Cir., GA Conf." *SCA*, 10-12-1866, p. 5.
"Cusseta Cir., S. GA Conf." *SCA*, 10-8-1869, p. 163.

Ogletree, Absalom H.   (5-13-1847 - 1-1-1892)
dv. 51st GA Reg., CSA.

"Smithville Cir., S. GA Conf." *SCA*, 9-9-1874, p. 139.

Olin, Stephen
1-26-1828, Request to Conf. for location. (Wof.).

Travis, Joseph. *Autobiography.* pp. 129-133.
Letter. *SCA*, 10-11-1839, p. 66.
"Social and Economical Reforms of Christian Missions." *SCA*,
    6-30-1854, p. 14.
"Christian Education." *SCA*, 7-21-1864, fp.
"Be Not Anxious For Your Life." (poem). *SCA*, 11-21-1876, fp.

Oliver, Charles J.
wife Nannie Ameila, d. 9-16-1868, Atlanta, GA. m2/ 1-26-1871, Fannie T.
Shropshire of Floyd Co., GA.

Oliver, Dionysius C.
bur. New Salem, Banks Co., GA.

Oliver, Jackson   (d. 1873)
bur. New Salem, Banks Co., GA. Tribute by Homer Cir.

Oliver, John L.   (1796 - 9-24-1872)
b. Granville Co., NC; d. Dade Co., AL; m/ 1820 Lucy Glenn; moved to
Clarke Co., GA where wife & child died; 1824 cvt.; m2/ 1825, Mary K.
Watson; located due to financial embarrassment; lived between Madison &
Athens, GA; 1847 moved to Barbour Co., AL.

AL CONF. 1867-68 Clopton Cir.; 1869 Choctawhachie Cir.; 1870-71
Chanahatchie Cir.; 1872 Choctawachie Cir.

Oliver, R. C.
"My People are Destroyed for Lack of Knowledge." *SCA*, 6-2-1864, np.

Orr, Adolphus J.
"Carnesville Cir., GA Conf." *SCA*, 7-31-1846, p. 31.
"Madison Mis., GA Conf." *SCA*, 8-4-1848, p. 34; 12-29-1848, p. 118.

Orr, Gustavus J.
"Emory College." *SCA*, 5-25-1866, fp.

Osborn, Nelson   (11-28-1798 - 9-3-1873)
b. Lincoln Co., GA; d. Carnesville Cir.; cvt. 1818; m/ 1819, Liney Watson; 10 chrn.; bur. Carroll's Church, Franklin Co., GA.

Oslin, John   (11-5-1809 - 5-2-1885)
bv. 1810; dv. 1865; bur. Jonesville City Cem.; m1/ Millie Arnold Hines; m2/ Sarah Traylor McDonald.

Oslin, Nelson   (b. 1798)
1850 Census Franklin Co., GA identifies him as Meth. minister. m/ Sinney ?

Oslin, Reuben E.   (5-12-1812 - 1-24-1876)
d. Fredonia, AL. m2/ Martha J. Johnson of Chambers Co., AL.

"Dahlonega Mis., GA." *SCA*, 11-27-1840, p. 94.

Oslin, Simeon S.
m/ Susan Worthy

Oslin, William W.
Chap., 43rd GA Reg., CSA.

"Old Methodist Usages," *SCA*, 7-15-1858, p. 25.
"Liberty Church, Greene Co., GA." *SCA*, 3-27-1868, fp.
"Reminiscences of Liberty and Salem Churches." *SCA*, 4-24-1868, fp.
"A Good Camp Meeting (AL)." *SCA*, 10-28-1870, p. 170.
"Putnam Cir., N. GA Conf." *SCA*, 9-13-1871, p. 146; 9-4-1872, p. 138; 10-23-1872, p. 166.
"Watkinsville Cir., N. GA Conf." *SCA*, 11-3-1875, p. 174; 9-4-1877, p. 142.

Ousley, Newdaygate B. (1824 - 1894)

attempting to break the ice on a frozen unbridged stream for his horses, he fell and was injured. He died a few days later and is bur. in Poulan, Worth Co., GA. father of 8 girls and 1 set tw. boys.

"Decatur Cir., GA Conf." *SCA*, 9-23-1858, p. 67.
"Valdosta Cir., FL Conf." *SCA*, 9-25-1862, p. 147.
"Morven Dist. Meeting, FL Conf." *SCA*, 11-9-1866, fp.
"Quitman Dist., FL Conf." *SCA*, 11-16-1866, fp.
"Matters About Thomasville, GA." *SCA*, 5-8-1868, p. 74.
"Thomasville, GA - Conf. For Colored People." *SCA*, 9-18-1868, p. 151.
"A Sabbath School in the Pine Woods." *SCA*, 7-16-1869, p. 114.
"Burke Co., GA." *SCA*, 8-6-1869, p. 126.
"Waynesboro Cir., S. GA Conf." *SCA*, 9-17-1869, p. 150; 10-1-1869. p. 158;
　　　　11-18-1870, p. 182; 10-25-1871, p. 170; 4-3-1872, p. 50.
"Camp Meetings." *SCA*, 6-10-1874, p. 90.
"Americus Dist." *SCA*, 9-30-1874, p. 154.
"Revival at Brunswick." *SCA*, 4-28-1875, p. 66.
"Lowndes & Echols Mis., S. GA Conf." *SCA*, 9-12-1876, p. 146.

Overby, Enoch M.
"The Fine Art of Living." *WCA*, v101, n25, 12-17-1937, p. 10.

Owen, Jacob R.
"Cuthbert, GA." *SCA*, 10-5-1866, p. 5.
"Randolph Cir., S. GA Conf." *SCA*, 9-20-1867, p. 150; 8-14-1868, p. 130.

Ozier, Jacob
1-3-1836, letter to Conf. asking for leave of absence. (Wof.).

"Cuthbert Cir., GA." *SCA*, 10-2-1840, p. 62.

Pace, C. D.
"Meeting at Covington, GA." *SCA*, 8-2-1844, p. 29.

Paden, Robert St. Clair (12-22-1836 - 2-21-1876)
b. Roswell, GA; cvt. age 14; le 10-19-1867 Alpharetta; lp 9-12-1868; bur. Roswell Meth. Cem. m/ Elizabeth Samantha Tippens (1834 - 1921). 5 chrn.

Palmer, Augustus H.
10-26-1829, rec. to Conf. from Walton Cir. QC for itinerancy. (Wof.).

Palmer, Noah H.
bur. Quillian Cem., Dawnville, GA. wife Julia (6-21-1823 - 5-26-1896).

"Cleveland Cir., N. GA Conf." *SCA*, 9-20-1867, p. 150.

Park, George R.
"A Wonderful Spring." *SCA*, 5-29-1872, p. 82.

Parker, Benjamin B.
m3/ Jane Taylor (1820 - 8-15-1870) d. Hart Co., GA.

Parker, John R.
b. Franklin Co., GA. Co. F, 39th GA Reg., CSA.

"Canton Cir., GA Conf." *SCA*, 9-7-1866, fp.
"Jefferson Cir., GA." *SCA*, 8-21-1872, p. 130; 10-2-1872, p. 154.
"Gainesville Dist., N. GA Conf." *SCA*, 10-27-1875, p. 170; 11-17-1875,
    p. 182.

Parker, Joshua M.
m/ 11-14-1872, Laura V. Neal of Warrenton, GA.

"Cumming Cir., N. GA Conf." *SCA*, 11-15-1871, p. 182.
"Roswell Cir., N. GA Conf." *SCA*, 10-21-1874, p. 167.

Parks, Harwell H.
"A Day of Anguish." *SCA*, 6-15-1866, fp.
"Athens, GA." *SCA*, 9-7-1866, p. 5.
"Revival at Athens, GA." *SCA*, 11-2-1866, fp.
"Rome, N. GA Conf." *SCA*, 9-24-1869, p. 154.
"Letter From Augusta." *SCA*, 9-6-1871, p. 142.
"Letter From Savannah." *SCA*, 1-15-1873, p. 6.
"Augusta, GA." *SCA*, 5-30-1876, p. 86.

Parks, Isaac G.
bv. 8-28-1841.

"Two Revivals." *SCA*, 9-12-1876, p. 146.
"Ocmulgee Cir., N. GA Conf." *SCA*, 10-31-1876, p. 174.

Parks, James W.
dv 8-11-1886. m/ 10-15-1833, Sarah Frances Newton (9-10-1816 - 3-6-1885); son, Rev. Isaac G. Parks, bv. 8-28-1841. All bur. Ebenezer UMC, Forsyth Co., GA.

"Cumming Cir., GA Conf." *SCA*, 12-8-1864, np.

Parks, Wesley F.
Capt., 24th GA Reg., CSA.

Parks, Wiley G.
*Wiley G. Parks (1817 - 6-15-1877), b. Yadkin Co., NC; d. Dawson, Terrell Co., GA is listed in the obits. of the *SCA* with the title, Hon. He is not referred to in the obit. as a preacher, though it is probably the same man.

The charges against Parks during the Conference from which he was expelled were these: 1) Drunkenness; 2) Gambling and playing cards while in the Army; 3) Using profane language; 4) Adultry on visiting houses of ill fame. (Handwritten conf. minutes, Pitts Lib., Emory Univ.). CSA.

"Lumpkin, GA Conf." *SCA*, 6-18-1857, p. 11.

Parks, William A.
cvt. by Lucius H. Holsey, later CME Bishop.

"Athens Colored Mis., GA Conf." *SCA*, 7-15-1858, p. 27.
"A Waste Place Reclaimed." *SCA*, 11-4-1858, p. 90.
"Letter from Texas." *SCA*, 9-11-1862, p. 138.
"Letter from Hood's Army." *SCA*, 11-24-1864, np.
"Bainbridge, GA." *SCA*, 6-28-1867, p. 102.
"Hamilton Cir., S. GA Conf." *SCA*, 9-11-1868, p. 146.
"Whitesburg Cir., N. GA Conf." *SCA*, 9-18-1877, p. 150.
"The Baptists and the Immersion." (series). *SCA*, 10-23-1877, fp.
"Pills In Prose & Poetry." (series). *SCA*, 1-29-1878, fp.

Parks, William J.
"Athens Dist., GA." *SCA*, 9-30-1837, p. 58; 8-24-1838, p. 38; 9-14-1838, p. 50; 10-5-1838, p. 62.
"Letter." *SCA*, 5-1-1840, p. 182.
"Bold Springs Camp Meeting." *SCA*, 8-7-1840, p. 30.

"Cherokee Dist., GA." *SCA*, 8-5-1842, p. 31.
"A Review of 'A Sermon on Election.'" *SCA*, 8-16-1850, p. 41; 8-25-1850,
    p. 45; 8-30-1850, p. 49; 9-13-1850, p. 57; 9-27-1850, p. 65; 10-4-
    1850, p. 69; 10-11-1850, p. 73.
"Newton Co., GA." *CA*, 11-5-1830, p. 38.
"Franklin & Jackson Cos., GA." *CA*, 11-11-1831, p. 42.
"Athens Dist.." *CA*, 11-18-1831, p. 46.
"Revival Influence In Georgia." *SCA*, 10-20-1848, p. 78.
"A Trip to AL." *SCA*, 10-7-1858, p. 74.
"Thoughts on Christian Union & Union Meetings." *SCA*, 11-4-1858, fp.
"A Georgian in FL." (series). *SCA*, 1-8-1857, p. 126.
"Notes From Charleston." *SCA*, 4-2-1857, pp. 174-175.
"Thou Carriest Them Away as With a Flood." *SCA*, 11-6-1862, fp.
"A Short Essay on Apostacy." uv, ca 1858.
"Out of Soap." *SCA*, 3-11-1858, fp.
"Poor Logic." *SCA*, 6-25-1857, fp.
"Emory College." (series). see: 7-23-1857, p. 31.
"The Elberton Dist. Meeting." *SCA*, 9-20-1867, p. 150.
"About Parsonages." (series). *SCA*, 10-25-1867, fp.
"A New Religious Sect in GA." *SCA*, 1-17-1868, fp.
"From Oxford, GA - Odds & Ends." *SCA*, 4-24-1868, p. 66.
"Not Caught as Yet." *SCA*, 10-25-1871, p. 170.
"Emory College." *SCA*, 3-13-1872, p. 38.

Rivers, William P. "A Tribute to Rev. W.J. Parks." (poem). *SCA*,
    12-3-1873, fp.

Parrish, David L.
"Belton Mis., N. GA Conf." *SCA*, 9-8-1875, p. 142.

Parsons, James
3-26-1819, report on his case. (Wof.).

Pate, John R.
"Jonesboro Cir., N. GA Conf." *SCA*, 9-8-1875, p. 142.
"Upson Cir., N. GA Conf." *SCA*, 10-31-1876, p. 174.

Patillo, Charles L.
"Dawsonville Cir., N. GA Conf." *SCA*, 10-6-1875, p. 158.
"Hall Cir., N. GA Conf." *SCA*, 10-31-1876, p. 174.

Patillo, George H.
m/ 11-15-1859

"Jonesboro, GA Conf." *SCA*, 10-21-1858, p. 82.
"Talbotton, GA." *SCA*, 10-30-1862, p. 166.
"St. James Church, Augusta, GA." *SCA*, 10-18-1867, p. 166.
"Romanism Exposed." *SCA*, 4-16-1869, p. 62.
"Romanism Again." *SCA*, 6-18-1869, fp.
"A Letter From Atlanta." *SCA*, 10-22-1873, p. 163.
"Hancock Cir., N. GA Conf." *SCA*, 10-23-1877, p. 170.

Patillo, Samuel
10-25-1828, letter to Conf. (Wof.).

Patterson, James
1816, personal Bible; letters to his son; 1821, letters & papers of his case;
1820, Journal, notes and sermons; 11-9-1821, letter to Josiah Askew
expressing his belief. (Wof.).

Pattillo, William P.
"Atlanta Dist. Conf." *SCA*, 8-30-1871, p. 138.

Payne, James B.
Mary Martin nv Morton (1803 - 1893).

"Perry Cir., GA." *SCA*, 9-2-1837, p. 42; 9-30-1837, p. 58.
"LaGrange, GA." *SCA*, 7-6-1838, p. 10; 7-27-1838, p. 22; 9-14-1838, p. 50.
"LaGrange & West Point, GA." *SCA*, 10-25-1839, p. 75.
"Ft. Gaines Dist., GA." *SCA*, 11-13-1840, p. 86; 7-16-1841, p. 19.
"Our Local Preachers." *SCA*, 6-3-1853, p. 213; 6-10-1853, p. 5; 6-17-1853,
        p. 9; 6-24-1853, p. 13; 7-1-1853, p. 17.
"Augusta Dist. Preacher's Meeting." *SCA*, 5-15-1856, p. 198.
"Covington & Oxford Cir., GA Conf." *SCA*, 10-16-1846, p. 75.
"Sacraments Not Regular Among Us." *SCA*, 3-25-1858, fp.
"Our Financial Management in the Support of the Ministry." *SCA*,
        6-25-1857, fp.
"Atlanta Dist., GA Conf." *SCA*, 9-7-1866, p. 5.

Payne, James T.
wife Elizabeth (1810 - 7-21-1870).

Payne, Lewis B.

"Irwinton Cir., GA." *SCA*, 8-30-1855, p. 51.

"Fighting and Praying." *SCA*, 6-9-1864, np.

"Brunswick Dist., S. GA Conf." *SCA*, 10-9-1872, p. 158.

Payne, Warren D.

"Sandtown Cir., N. GA Conf." *SCA*, 11-19-1873, p. 179; 8-27-1873, p. 134.

Peacock, Jesse   (1792 - 1870)

d. Selma, AL. m/ 10-21-1869, Marietta R. Anderson of Forsyth Co., NC.

Pearce, Gadwell J.

"Revival at Athens, GA." *SCA*, 10-2-1846, p. 67.

"Revival on Cassville Cir., GA." *SCA*, 9-16-1842, p. 55.

"LaGrange, GA." *SCA*, 10-5-1865, np.

"Rome Dist., N. GA Conf." *SCA*, 4-5-1871, p. 54.

Peek, Leonard C.

"Irwin Cir., GA Conf." *SCA*, 11-1-1844, p. 81.

Peeler, Anderson

"Lowndes Cir., GA." *SCA*, 9-6-1839, p. 47; 6-28-1839, p. 6.

"Monticello Cir., FL." *SCA*, 7-24-1840, p. 22.

Peeler, Benjamin   (2-5-1793 - 7-5-1877)

reared in Elbert Co., GA; d. Jewells; cvt. 1830; 1845 moved to Princeton; remained member (Clarke Co., GA); lp; no record of ordination.

Pegg, William H.   (11-14-1814 - 8-10-1873)

d. 1st MECS, Atlanta, GA.

Pendergrass, John   (1778 - 1-20-1868)

d. Jackson Co., GA.

Pendergrass, John J.

bur. Salem, Banks Co., GA.

Pendleton, Edmund M.

"Rev. Richmond Nolley." (poem). *SCA*, 7-1-1837, p. 8.

"Summerfield." (poem). *SCA*, 7-8-1837, p. 12.

"Sanctification." *SCA*, 7-15-1837, pp. 14-15.

"A Contrast." *SCA*, 7-29-1837, p. 22.

"Charity Never Faileth." (poem). *SCA*, 7-29-1837, p. 24.

"To Consumption." (poem). *SCA*, 8-5-1837, p. 28.

"My Friends Away." (poem). *SCA*, 8-12-1837, p. 32.

"Thoughts In A Dissecting Room." *SCA*, 8-19-1837, p. 40.

"Christian Aristocracy." *SCA*, 8-26-1837, p. 39.

"The Destroying Angel." (poem). *SCA*, 8-26-1837, p. 40.

"The Dead." (poem). *SCA*, 9-2-1837, p. 44.

"Jerusalem." (poem). *SCA*, 10-7-1837, p. 64.

"The Transfiguraiton." (poem). *SCA*, 10-21-1837, p. 72.

"A Sister's Love." (poem). *SCA*, 10-28-1837, p. 76.

"The Ocean." (poem). *SCA*, 11-24-1837, p. 92.

"Christ At Prayer - Walking On the Water." (poem) *SCA*, 12-29-1837, p. 112.

"Soliloquy of Judas." (poem). *SCA*, 2-16-1838, p. 140.

"The Fall of Jerico." (poem). *SCA*, 4-13-1838, p. 172.

"To J. On The Death Of Her Mother." (poem). *SCA*, 6-4-1838, p. 184.

"On Reading Novels." *SCA*, 9-7-1838, p. 47.

"Emmaus." (poem). *SCA*, 1-4-1839, p. 112.

"The Rose of Sharon." (poem). *SCA*, 2-8-1839, p. 122.

"The Post Horn." (poem). *SCA*, 3-1-1839, p. 132.

"Mount Sinai." (poem). *SCA*, 3-15-1839, p. 152.

"Thirsting For Immortality." (poem). *SCA*, 5-3-1839, p. 180.

"Destruction of Jerusalem." (poem). *SCA*, 8-2-1839, p. 24.

"Congregational Singing." *SCA*,AA "Sparta GA Conf." *SCA*, 10-13-1859, p. 286.

"Responses in Worship." *SCA*, 10-2-1856, fp.

"How and What We Should Sing." *SCA*, 10-20-1864, fp.

"The Davidic Exercises." *SCA*, 11-24-1864, fp.

"The Polity of Methodism." (series). *SCA*, 3-2-1866, bp.

"History of the Methodist Church in Sparta, GA." *SCA*, 2-14-1868, fp.

"Infant Membership." *SCA*, 4-8-1870, fp.

"Local Preachers." *SCA*, 4-22-1870, fp.

"Our Local Preacher System." *SCA*, 4-29-1870, fp.

"Local Preachers Once More." *SCA*, 6-3-1870, fp.

"Financial Plan for Circuits & Smaller Stations." *SCA*, 2-15-1871, p. 20.

"Letter from Sparta." *SCA*, 9-27-1871, p. 154.

"Baltimore & the Protestant Episcopal Connection." *SCA*, 11-1-1871, p. 174.

"Liquor Dealers." *SCA*, 10-16-1872, fp.

"Dram Drinking." *SCA*, 7-30-1873, fp.

"The Temperance Controversy." *SCA*, 12-2-1874, fp.

"The Rule of Giving." (series). *SCA*, 11-27-1877, fp.

Pennington, Abraham

"Cumming Cir., GA." *SCA,* 11-10-1837, p. 82.
"Fayetteville & Zebulon Cir., GA." *SCA,* 8-19-1842, p. 39.

{There are two Ephraim Penningtons as follows, correcting
the personal data on the listing on p. 418 of text}.

Pennington, Ephraim   (7-30-1792 - 12-23-1862)

b. NC; d. from small pox vaccination; bur. New Hope M.E. Church. 1st Sgt.
GA Militia; 2nd Sgt. 8-13-1813. m/ 6-10-1820, Jasper Co., GA, Lucy Brown,
d. 6-14- 1872. She spent the last 6 years of her life in TX. bur. in what was
in 1976 a pasture near Station Creek, TX, a few miles outside of Oglesby,
Coryell Co., TX. chrn. Sara M., 8-30-1822; William B., 7-21-1824; Mary B.,
3-10-1827; Jane M., 1-16-1830; Eliza A., 1-1-1832; Abraham Parks, 1-6-1835;
J.O.A., 11-22-1839.

Pennington, Ephraim   (b. 3-31-1809)

b. GA, son of Thos. Pennington, bro. of Frederick Pennington. m1/3-6-1828,
Jasper Co., GA, Mary Ann Phillips (1834 - 1847). chrn. Thadeus H., 1-5-1834;
Mary Ann, 5-27-1836; Dawson J., 7-18-1839; Ephraim Wade, 8-2-1841;
Martha Ann, 7-20-1845. m2/ 1-25-1848, Troup Co., GA, Eliza B. Hicks;
one child, Susan. m3/ 4-13-1852, Martha Jane Corry. chrn. James Ephraim,
2-24-1853; Della Ector, 10-12-1856; Amie Ector, 10-25-1862.

** data on Ephraim M. Pennington from *SCA,* 9-24-1869, gives the following
dates of birth and death and data which differ from both the above:

(7-29-1829 - 8-30-1869) b. Newton Co., GA; d. Social Circle, GA; lp 1867;
5 chrn.

Pennington, Samuel S.   (b. 1830)

b. Morgan Co., GA; son of Samuel Pennington (3-16-1800 - 2-22-1873) &
Eliza Shy (1805 - 5-9-1852), dau. of Samuel Shy & Jane Patterson. g.son of
Thos. Pennington (ca 1760 - 1850) & Lietha Bell.

Pennington, Thaddeus

lp 10-7-1837.

Penny, J. E.

"SS Celebration, Barnesville Cir." *SCA,* 10-7-1870, p. 153.

Penny, John
"Satilla Mis., FL." *SCA,* 10-10-1851, p. 74; 1-6-1852, p. 130; 6-27-1851,
    p. 14.
"Warrior Mis." *SCA,* 5-2-1845, p. 186.
"Orange Mis., FL." *SCA,* 1-15-1847, p. 126.
"Marion Mis., FL." *SCA,* 6-18-1847, p. 6; 10-22-1847, p. 78.

Perry, Dow
m/ 10-15-1828, McDonough, GA, Tabitha T. T. Hunt (7-8-1811 - 3-29-1876)
b. Jasper Co., GA; d. Tallassee, AL; dau. of Turner & Martha Hunt.

Perry, T. J.
"Morgan Co., Camp Meeting, S. GA Conf." *SCA,* 11-4-1870, p. 174.

Perry, William C.D.   (d. 3-27-1863)
d. smallpox.

Perryman, James L.
"Bowdon Cir., N. GA Conf." *SCA,* 10-16-1877, p. 166.

Persons, George W.
"Letter from Perry Cir., GA." *SCA,* 10-5-1838, p. 62.
"Long Beards." *SCA,* 5-10-1867, p. 76.

Peurifoy, Archibald M.
1857-59, 3 diaries. *SCHS* 920-71 p46+ (Wof.).

11-2-1833, recom. to trav. connection by Black River Cir. QC. (Wof.).

"The Buena Vista Christian Association." *SCA,* 10-4-1867, p. 158.

Peurifoy, McCarroll   (d. 11-7-1859)
"Greensborough Cir., GA." *SCA,* 11-8-1839, p. 83.

Peurifoy, Tilman D.   (1-21-1809 - 6-3-1872)
b. Putnam Co., GA; d. Edgefield Co., SC; cvt. age 14; lp age 17.

"Letter of the Alachua Mission." (letter tells of the murder of his family by
    Indians during the time he was a missionary to them). *SCA,* 4-27-
    1838, p. 178.
"Ft. Gaines Cir., GA." *SCA,* 7-7-1843, p. 15.

Pharr, Joseph Wilson
"Ellijay Mis., GA Conf." *SCA*, 7-7-1848, p. 18; 11-12-1847, p. 90.

Pharr, Joseph William Burke (1859 - 8-10-1931)
nv. John W.B. (see p. 420, text).
b. Cherokee Co., GA; son of Artessiman Emory Pharr (1836 - 1915) and
Mary ? (b. 1837); lived in Woodstock, GA; his father served as a Pvt. in Co.
B., 38th Reg., GA Vol. Inf. (Milton Co., GA). The family moved to Mt.
Zion, Carroll Co., GA, in 1890. J.W.B. Pharr was postmaster of Mt. Zion
from 1901 - 1931. m1/ Missouri ?; m2/ ? Frizzell. No issue. Named for
g.father, Joseph Wilson Pharr (9-14-1796 - 11-16-1858), also a Meth.
preacher in GA. bur. Mt. Zion.

Pharr, Theodore A.
son of Joseph Wilson Pharr.

Pierce, Alfred M.
"Love Will Triumph." *WCA*, v100, n31, 2-5-1937, p. 8.
"Worship." *WCA*, v100, n40, 10-9-1936, p. 12.

Pierce, George F.
"An Address before the Few and Phi Gamma Societies of Emory College,
    7-19-1842." *SCA*, 9-9-1841, fp.
"Incidents of Western Travel." (serial). *SCA*, 2-14-1856, p. 146; 2-21-1856,
    pp. 150-151; 2-28-1856, pp. 154-155; 3-27-1856, p. 170; 4-17-
    1856, pp. 182-183; 4-24-1856, p. 186; 5-1-1856, p. 191; 5-8-
    1856, p. 195; 5-15-1856, p. 198; 6-12-1856, fp; contd.
"Address Before Methodist Educational Convention of GA." *SCA*, 8-13-
    1847, p. 37.
"Address to Sons of Temperance." *SCA*, 5-25-1849, p. 201.
"Notes By The Way." (series). *SCA*, 3-24-1859, p. 170.
"Across the Continent." (series). *SCA*, see: 6-9-1859, p. 215.
"Notes Of A Western Tour." (series). *SCA*, see: 2-26-1857, p. 154.
"To the Preachers of the MECS." *SCA*, 9-15-1864, np.
"Report of the Army Mission Committee to the Annual Conferences of
    the MECS." *SCA*, 10-27-1864, np.
"To the Methodists of GA." *SCA*, 8-3-1866, p. 4.
"Letter." *SCA*, 9-21-1866, p. 4.
"The Rev. Allen Turner." *SCA*, 5-10-1867, fp.
"A Visit to NC." (series). *SCA*, 7-12-1867, p. 110.
"The Dist. Meeting - The Dahlonega Meeting." *SCA*, 9-20-1867, p. 150.
"Over The River." (series). *SCA*, 7-30-1869, fp.

Pierce, James L.

Valedictory Address, Madison, FL." *SCA*, 7-28-1859, fp.

"White Plains Cir., N. GA Conf." *SCA*, 10-14-1874, p. 163.

Pierce, Lovick

12-15-1818, Feb., 1825, 2-7-1829, letters to Conf.; 1-12-1829, letter from Daniel Grant containing part of his father's will. (Wof.).

"Biographical Sketch of..." by Wm. H. Milburn, pub. in *National Magazine,* Oct. 1853.

"awakened at Weatherby's, Edisto Circuit, 1801," Jenkins, *Experiences,* etc., pp. 103-104.

Cannon, William R. "The Pierces: Father & Son." *HH*, v11, n1, Jun. 1981, pp. 5-15.

"Apalachicola." *SCA*, 5-14-1841, p. 190.

"Sermon on the Occasion of the Death of Mrs. Anna V. Calhoun, Consort of the Hon. Jas. S. Calhoun, late of Columbus, GA." *SCA*, 12-24-1841, p. 10; 12-31-1841, fp.

"Decrease of Members." *SCA*, 2-14-1856, p. 144; 2-7-1856, p. 140; 1-31-1856, p. 136.

"Final Address to the GA Conf." *SCA*, 3-13-1856, p. 161.

"Columbia Dist., GA." *SCA*, 11-10-1848, p. 91.

"Women: Their Faults & True Ornaments." *SCA*, 3-17-1859, fp.

"Hurried Sacraments." *SCA*, 11-3-1859, fp.

"Overtasked Gen. Confs. and Annual Confs." *SCA*, 12-1-1859, fp.

"Proposed Changes Vindicated." (series). *SCA*, 7-3-1856, fp.

"No Revolution Advocated." *SCA*, 9-4-1856, fp.

"Proposed Alterations." (series). see: *SCA*, 2-26-1863, fp.

"Class Meeting." *SCA*, 4-16-1863, fp.

"Long Prayers." *SCA*, 6-25-1857, fp.

"Columbus, GA." *SCA*, 6-25-1857, p. 15.

"Cassville, GA." *SCA*, 8-13-1857, p. 43.

"Relations of Itinerant Ministers." *SCA*, 9-24-1857, fp.

"Class Meeting Continued." *SCA*, 4-7-1864, np.

"Further Suggestions." *SCA*, 4-14-1864, np.

"The Class Meeting Question." *SCA*, 4-21-1864, np; 6-9-1864, np.

"A Visit to the SC Conf." *SCA*, 1-7-1864, fp.

"Class Meetings." *SCA*, 1-14-1864, fp.

"The Causes of the Decline in Class Meeting Interest." *SCA*, 1-21-1864, fp.

"Family Prayer." (series). *SCA*, 2-11-1864, fp.

"The Infidelity of Prejudice." *SCA*, 7-28-1864, fp.

"The Final Address." *SCA*, 8-11-1864, np.

"The Law of Moral and Religious Obligation." *SCA*, 3-2-1865, fp.
"My Second Appeal to Men of Conscience Who Believe In A Whole Bible"
        SCA, 4-6-1865, fp.
"A Lecture Before the Historical Soc. of SC." *SCA*, 6-8-1866, p. 2.
"Church Membership - Its Obligations & Duties." (series). *SCA*,
        7-12-1867, fp.
"Comparative View of Methodism for Sixty Years." *SCA*, 8-16-1867, fp.
"The General Rules." (series). *SCA*, 9-6-1867, fp.
"To the Lay Delegates of the N. & S. GA Confs." *SCA*, 11-15-1867, p. 182.
"Emotional Sensuality." (series). *SCA*, 3-27-1868, fp.
"To the Bainbridge Dist. Meeting." *SCA*, 4-24-1868, fp.
"Baptism Not an Ordinance But a Rite." (sermon). J.W. Burke & Co., 1869 uv.
"How Should a Regular Minister Dress." *SCA*, 3-25-1870, fp.
"Moderation a Moral Obligation." *SCA*, 4-15-1870, fp.
"The Mystery of Evil and God." (sermon). 1870 uv.
"Brunswick and Methodism." *SCA*, 4-29-1870, p. 66.
"Moderation - Total Abstinence - Intemperance." *SCA*, 6-24-1870, fp.
"On Revivals." (series). *SCA*, 11-4-1870, fp.
"The Efficacy of Moral Sentiment." (series). *SCA*, 11-25-1870, p. 185.
"Ornamental Dress: Is it a Soul-Destroying Evil." (series). *SCA*, 9-6-1871, fp.
"Indifferentism Rebuked." (series). *SCA*, 2-7-1872, fp.
"A Dissertation for Thoughtful Church Members." (series). *SCA*,
        10-9-1872, fp.
"An Address to Young Preachers." (series). *SCA*, 1-15-1873, fp.
"The Eldership." (series). *SCA*, 4-16-1873, fp.
"To the Itinerant Preachers of the MECS." *SCA*, 12-2-1874, fp.
"Theology in Miniature." (series). *SCA*, 2-24-1875, fp.
"My Ninety-First Birthday." *SCA*, 3-31-1875, p. 50.
"Christian Fraternity." (series). *SCA*, 8-18-1875, fp.
"Wesley Monumental Church." *SCA*, 8-25-1875, p. 134.
"Valedictory Address To Ladies." (series). *SCA*, 9-29-1875, fp.
"Thoughts on Sanctification." (series). *SCA*, 2-16-1876, fp.
"Exegetical Inquisition." *SCA*, 6-27-1876, fp.
"Wesleyan FC." (series). *SCA*, 9-19-1876, fp.
"Important Inquiry." *SCA*, 3-6-1877, fp.
"Our Protracted Meeting Policy." *SCA*, 3-20-1877, fp.
"Salutations on my 93rd Birthday." *SCA*, 4-10-1877, fp.
"Ministerial Apostolic Succession" (series). *SCA*, 9-4-1877, fp.
"Giving No Offense to Anything." *SCA*, 9-18-1877, fp.
"My 94th Birthday." *SCA*, 3-26-1878, p. 46.

"The Rev. Lovick Pierce, DD, On Reading Sermons & Preparing For The Pulpit." (by John E. Edwards). *SCA*, 11-23-1866, p. 2.
"Rev. Lovick Pierce." (poem). by one who sat at his feet. *SCA*, 9-15-1875, fp.

Pierce, Reddick
11-27-1836, communication to the Conf.; report of com. examining him. (Wof.).

Smith, Whitefoord. "Some Recollections of the Rev. Reddick Pierce." *SCA*, 12-6-1871, fp.

Pierce, Thomas F.
wife Ann Dickey Malone, d. 2-4-1860, Washington, GA; State service, CSA;

Pierce, Thomas R.
"Pueblo Church." *SCA*, 1-13-1875, p. 6.

Pierce, Wilds L.
"Sermon." found by preachers in the Cent. Anniv. of the Mt. Pleasant MC, Oglethorpe Co., GA, 1920. Atlanta, GA. by C.C. Cary. pp. 52-53.

Pinson, William W.
d. & bur. Nashville, TN. honorary degrees from UGA & Southern Meth. Univ.; Pinson College in Camaguey, Cuba, named for him; wrote: *In Black & White; Missions In A Changing World.* uv.

Pitchford, Henry P.
had dau. by lst wife named Lydia Marley Ami who d. 6-11-1848.

"Brunswick Cir., GA." *SCA*, 6-28-1839, p. 6.
"Jefferson Mis., GA." *SCA*, 11-5-1841, p. 82; 7-1-1842, p. 10.
"Spring Place, GA Conf." *SCA*, 10-28-1858, p. 87.
"Summerville Cir., GA Conf." *SCA*, 8-28-1856, p. 51.
"Dalton Cir., GA Conf." *SCA*, 9-10-1857, p. 59.
"Protracted Meeting at Bethel, MS." *SCA*, 9-9-1870, p. 143.
"Old and New." *SCA*, 10-11-1871, fp.

Pledger, Thomas M.
"Tunnel Hill Cir., N. GA Conf." *SCA*, 8-28-1868, p. 138; 10-9-1868, p. 162; 10-1-1869, p. 158.
"Calhoun Cir., N. GA Conf." *SCA*, 9-2-1870, p. 138; 9-30-1870, p. 154.

Pledger, Wesley P.
suicide. See: Burke, *Autobiography*, p. 130; Co. H., 12th GA Reg., CSA.

"Dublin Cir., GA." *SCA*, 10-4-1855, p. 70.
"Reidsville Cir., GA Conf." *SCA*, 12-17-1857, p. 115; 9-24-1857, p. 67.
"Dahlonega Dist., GA Conf." *SCA*, 10-5-1866, p. 4.
"The SS Convention Question." *SCA*, 6-26-1872, fp.
"Rome Dist., N. GA Conf." *SCA*, 10-3-1876, p. 158.

Pope, Benjamin B.
m/ Eliza S. Roundtree; 2 daus. died. Mary Susan 8-13-1844; Clara Henry 5-21-1840.

Pope, Cadesman
"Lehi Cir., Wachita Conference." *SCA*, 8-18-1859, p. 254.
"Letter From AR." *SCA*, 4-9-1869, p. 58; 10-1-1869, p. 158.

Porter, Hezekiah H.
"Spring Place, N. GA Conf." *SCA*, 10-21-1870, p. 167.

Porter, John   (1780 - 1-19-1847)
bur. Tabernacle Cem., Greenwood Co., SC; m/ E.D. (1788 - 5-30-1855); chrn. bur. same: Martha M. (1819 - 1-26-1841); Henry nd.

Potter, Ira L.
raised on a farm in Laurens Co., SC, on Lick Ck., 4 m. from county seat; attended Rock Spring Academy at Laurens; siblings were Adam (one of the first graduates of Emory College) and Prudence who m/ Joshua Franks. m/ in the home of wife's father by Lewis Rector, a Baptist preacher. child not mentioned in book entry, p. 432, Rosa.

cvt. lp 1815; 1835 OT SC CONF; 1846 tf FL CONF.
served circuits in NC and SC - Pickens, Greenville, Darlington. tf. GA CONF. in 1845.

8-22-1831, recom. to Conf. for deacon's orders from Laurens Cir., Saluda Dist.; 11-29-1834, recom. to itinerancy from Greenville Circuit. (Wof.).

"Lancaster Cir., SC." *SCA*, 9-9-1837, p. 46.
"Rockingham Cir., NC." *SCA*, 11-4-1842, p. 81.

Potter, John M.

"Plattville, GA." *SCA*, 7-24-1872, p. 114.
"Colquit Cir." *SCA*, 8-21-1872, p. 130.
"Stewart Cir., S. GA Conf." *SCA*, 7-22-1874, p. 114; 9-30-1874, p. 155.
"Oglethorpe Cir., S. GA Conf." *SCA*, 9-22-1875, p. 152; 9-29-1875, p. 154;
    8-1-1876, p. 122.

Potter, Stephen

m/ 3-2-1817, Anna (11-16-1797 - 6-19-1871), b. Spartanburg Dist., SC;
d. Oxford, GA.

12-25-1835, recom. for deacon's orders by Laurens QC. (Wof.).

Potter, Weyman H.

"Life in the Camp." *SCA*, 2-19-1863, p. 30.
"A Sabbath with the Army." *SCA*, 1-29-1863, p. 18.
"Augusta Dist., N. GA Conf." *SCA*, 11-4-1870, p. 174.
"Progress in the Church in Atlanta." *SCA*, 5-3-1871, p. 70.
"Athens, GA." *SCA*, 5-5-1875, p. 70; 10-24-1876, p. 170.

Pournelle, George Washington

"Chattahoochee Mis., GA" *SCA*, 3-13-1840, p. 155; 1-29-1841, p. 130.
"Irwinton Mis., AL." *SCA*, 7-24-1840, p. 22.

Powell, John B.

Co. E, 5th GA Reg., CSA.

Powell, William F.   (12-31-1818 - 9-20-1870)

d. Dade Co., GA; member Trion Lodge; m/ 1843, Martha A. Simmons,
sister ot Rev. Jno. C. Simmons; 4 chrn.

(L); le 2-2-1850; lp 3-7-1857; 1867 Deacon;
1862 Supply on Lafayette Cir.; 1864 Summerville Cir.; 1867 same;
1868 Oostanaula Cir.; 1869 Rome Cir.

*b&d dates vary but appts. suggest same as below whose death date in
MPG by Lawrence is confused with L.T.G. Powell.

Powell, William Francis Spaight

organized Powell's Chapel, Carroll Co., GA, 1850.

Pratt, George W.
"Leon Cir., FL Conf." *SCA*, 7-29-1858, p. 35; 7-30-1857, p. 37.
"Linwood Church Dedication by Bishop Pierce." *SCA*, 8-12-1858, p. 43.
"Benton Mis., FL Conf." *SCA*, 12-31-1847, p. 118.
"Marion Mis., FL Conf." *SCA*, 5-12-1848, p. 194; 6-16-1848, p. 6.
"Morven Mis., FL Conf." *SCA*, 11-24-1848, p. 98.
"Tampa Dist., FL Conf." *SCA*, 5-22-1856, p. 203.
"Gadsden Cir., FL Conf." *SCA*, 12-8-1859, pp. 318-319.

Prickett, James P.
"Sandtown Mis., N. GA Conf." *SCA*, 9-18-1868, p. 151.

Puckett, Hastings
"Flint River Mis., S. GA Conf." *SCA*, 8-20-1869, p. 134; 9-3-1869, p. 142;
10-1-1869, p. 158; 10-7-1870, p. 153; 11-25-1870, p. 185.

Purvis, John B.
"Ogeechee River Mis., S. GA Conf." *SCA*, 8-28-1872, p. 134.
"Wrightsville Cir., S. GA Conf." *SCA*, 9-11-1877, p. 146; 12-4-1877, p. 194.

Quantock, John   (2-9-1795 - 6-15-1870)
b. E. Lambrook, Somersetshire, England; d. Polk Co., GA; cvt. 1823 in
Savannah; le & lp in England; resided in Savannah, GA.

Quantock, William
"Cherokee Hill Mis., GA." *SCA*, 7-22-1837, p. 18; 12-22-1837, p. 106.

Quillian, Asbury H.
"Letter from Colorado Territory." *SCA*, 9-20-1871, p. 150.

Quillian, Bethel B.
m3/ 11-10-1870, Lizzie Gaines.

Quillian, Clayton
son of Lewis Wagener Quillian & g.son of Clemmon & Anna K. Quillian.

Quillian, Frank
"The Great Physician's Cure For Troubles." *WCA*, v100, n39, 4-2-1937, p. 9.

Quillian, James   (d. 1-27-1869)

"Ellijay Mis., GA Conf." *SCA,* 7-5-1850, p. 18.
"Murphy Mis., GA Conf." (principally in NC). *SCA,* 4-28-1848, p. 186; 7-7-1848, p. 18.

Quillian, John B.C.

"Blairsville Mis., GA." *SCA,* 7-20-1849, p. 26.
"Autumn Leaves." (serial begins). *WCA,* v50, n30, 7-28-1886.
"The Star of Bethlehem." *SCA,* 7-2-1869, fp.
Star of Redemption. uv.
"A Few Incidents of a Trip to Mossy Ck. Campmeeting in White Co., GA." *SCA,* 9-18-1872, fp.
"Camp Meeting at Salt Springs." *SCA,* 10-24-1876, p. 170.

Quillian, Smith C.

correction: son of Clement/Clemmon Quillian & Anna King; g.son of James Monroe Quillian and Sarah Ann Wagner; g.g.son of James Quillian & ? Herring. His son, Marcus N. did not serve in war, though died in that time period.

"Dade Mis., GA Conf." *SCA,* 12-13-1858, p. 110; 7-12-1850, p. 22.
"Barnesville, GA Conf." *SCA,* 6-18-1857, p. 11.
"Zebulon Cir., GA Conf." *SCA,* 10-29-1857, p. 87.

Quillian, William F.

mother, Jane Williams (4-20-1820 - 10-30-1916), d. Gainesville, GA.

"Divine Purpose of the Family." (sermon) uv.
"Homer Cir., N. GA Conf." *SCA,* 9-11-1872, p. 142; 10-30-1872, p. 170.
"Broad River Cir., N. GA Conf." *SCA,* 9-29-1875, p. 154; 11-17-1875, p. 182.
"Carrollton Sta., N. GA Conf." *SCA,* 2-20-1877, p. 30.

Raiford, Capel

"Carnesville Cir., GA." *SCA,* 8-17-1838, p. 34.
"Jackson County, GA." *SCA,* 11-30-1838, p. 94.
"Quincy, FL." *SCA,* 11-29-1839, p. 95.

Randle, Josias

3-20-1812, letter to Francis Asbury. (Wof).

Rankin, George C.
*pos. same as Geo. R.

"Calhoun Cir., N. GA Conf." *SCA*, 8-6-1873, p. 122.

Ray, Joseph
dv 1-1-1864, Telfair Co., GA.

Raybun, I. C.
m/ 4-3-1873, Susan A. Louge of Gibson, GA.

Rea, William T.
m1/ Rhoda Maria Brown, (1818 - 4-15-1867) b. SC, d. Subligna, Chattooga Co., GA. bv on her 1823; m2/ Mary Brantley.

"Wrightsville Cir., S. GA Conf." *SCA*, 8-14-1872, p. 126; 8-28-1872, p. 134; 8-13-1873, p. 126.

Overstreet, Hazel & Cain, Martha T., "Odum UMC, 1888-1898, Witnessing For Christ For One Hundred Years." *HH*, v18, n2, Fall, 1988, p. 44-51.

Read, William T.
"Revival in McDonough, N. GA Conf." *SCA*, 8-19-1870, p. 130.

Reagan, Daniel   (b. 2-12-1834)
held 3 appts. in Holston Conf., left his last circuit on acct. of the Federal Invasion and took refuge w/ friends in Meriwether Co., GA where he died. Educated Hiawassee College.

Redding, Arthur
wife Mary (2-12-1780 - 3-26-1867) b. NC; d. Chattahoochee Co., GA; m1/ Peyton R. Clemmons.

Redding, Leonidas R.   (3-20-1830 - 3-22-1872)
d. consumption, Harris Co., GA. Capt. 31st GA Reg., CSA.

"Army Missionary Experience." *SCA*, 3-17-1864, np.
From Gen. Gist's Brigade." *SCA*, 5-19-1864, fp.
"The Army Work." *SCA*, 7-28-1864, np.
"A Good Work." *SCA*, 7-6-1866, fp.
"A Great Work of Grace." (Centerville Cir.). *SCA*, 9-7-1866, fp.

Redding, R. J.
"Americus Dist. Conf." *SCA,* 7-3-1872, fp.

Rees, Elias B.
M.D.; m/ 11-23-1876, Oglethorpe Co., GA, Katie E. Dozier, dau. of Augustus Dozier.

"Subligna Cir., N. GA Conf." *SCA,* 4-3-1877, p. 54; 3-21-1877, p. 134.

Reese, James H.
"A Good Meeting at Antioch, Marietta Cir." *SCA,* 8-16-1855, p. 43.
"Hawkinsville Cir., GA Conf." *SCA,* 7-24-1856, p. 31; 11-19-1857, p. 99.

Reese, Jere
wife Esperann ? (1820 - 9-13-1867) d. Eufaula, AL.

Reese, Jeremiah (d. 1921)
Co. B, 38th GA Reg., CSA.

Remshart, John W.
dau. Georgia Few, d. 7-31-1837.

Rentz, Edward J.
"Ellaville Cir., S. GA Conf." *SCA,* 10-15-1869, p. 166.
"Weston, S. GA Conf." *SCA,* 10-4-1871, p. 159.
"Butler, S. GA Conf." *SCA,* 8-19-1874, p. 131; 8-11-1875, p. 126;
        9-8-1875, p. 142; 10-6-1875, p. 158.
"Buena Vista Cir., S. GA Conf." *SCA,* 9-19-1876, p. 150.
"Camilla & Newton Cir., S. GA Conf." *SCA,* 9-18-1877, p. 150;
        9-25-1877, p. 154.

Reynolds, Andrew J.
"Scriven Mis., GA." *SCA,* 11-7-1851, p. 90; 7-11-1851, p. 22.
"Murphy Mis., GA Conf." *SCA,* 11-13-1846, p. 90.
"Burke Mis., GA Conf." *SCA,* 5-12-1848, p. 194; 7-28-1848, p. 30;
        10-20-1848, p. 78; 1-15-1849, p. 122; 1-11-1850, p. 116; 7-19-
        1850, p. 26; 1-3-1851, p. 122; 7-6-1849, p. 18.

Reynolds, Edmund W.

"Eatonton Cir., GA." *SCA*, 10-21-1837, p. 70.

"McDonough Cir., GA." *SCA*, 10-11-1839, p. 67; 1-3-1840, p. 115.

"Greenville Cir., GA." *SCA*, 11-12-1841, p. 87.

"Talbot Cir., GA." *SCA*, 11-1-1850, p. 87.

Reynolds, Freeman Franklin

son of Charles Reynolds; d. Battle Hill Sanitorium in Atlanta; bur. Westview cem., Atlanta; m1/ 10-15-1840, Elbert Co., GA, Elizabeth E. Andrew (1-10-1820 - 5-16-1870), dau. of Benjamin Andrew & Lucy Tate of Elbert Co., GA. She d. Bethany Community & is bur. at Bethany CG. m2/ New Hope Church, Lawrenceville, 4-21-1872, Emily Zinnila Griffin Coffee, b. 1843. chrn. Benjamin Andrew, 1848; Joseph Melville, 8-3-1855; Mollie, 1858; Lou, 1860; Franklin Parks, 1865; John, 1878; Flora, 1875.

charges against him. See: *SCA*, 1-26-1866, np.

invented the Reynolds Plow (ad). *SCA*, 5-7-1869, p. 75.

"Burke Cir., GA." *SCA*, 8-9-1855, p. 39.

"Dade Mis., GA Conf." *SCA*, 7-3-1846, p. 14.

"Lawrenceville, N. GA Conf." *SCA*, 10-4-1871, p. 159; 11-15-1871, p. 182; 8-21-1872, p. 130.

Reynolds, John A.

"Length of Sermons - Consecration & Sanctification."
    WCA, v50, n23, 6-9-1886, p. 2.

"Wilkes Cir., GA Conf." *SCA*, 9-24-1863, bp.

"News From Afar - Summerville, N. GA Conf." *SCA*, 3-19-1869, p. 46.

"Summerville Cir., N. GA Conf." *SCA*, 9-10-1869, p. 146.

"Cedartown Cir., N. GA Conf." *SCA*, 10-28-1870, p. 170.

"Not Dead." *SCA*, 11-25-1870, p. 185.

"Kingston Cir., N. GA Conf." *SCA*, 11-1-1871, p. 174.

"Letter from N. GA." *SCA*, 5-29-1872, p. 82.

"Our Educational Interest." *SCA*, 7-2-1873, fp.

"Letter from Kingston, GA." *SCA*, 10-22-1873, p. 163.

"Forsyth Cir., N. GA Conf." *SCA*, 3-11-1874, p. 38; 11-25-1874, p. 186; 1-27-1875, p. 14; 10-27-1875, p. 170.

"Letter from Decatur, GA." *SCA*, 5-9-1876, p. 74.

"Decatur Cir., N. GA Conf." *SCA*, 12-12-1876, p. 198.

"Letter from Payne's Chapel, Atlanta." *SCA*, 3-27-1877, p. 50.

"Letter from Atlanta." *SCA*, 7-3-1877, p. 106.

"Taking Up The Cross." *SCA*, 4-26-1876, p. 66.

"Our Welcome in LaFayette." (Mollie B. Reynolds). *SCA*, 1-13-1875, p. 6.

"Things I Do Not Like." (Mollie B. Reynolds). *SCA*, 3-10-1875, fp.

Reynolds, John Wesley (2-10-1828 - 12-27-1869)

b. DeKalb Co., GA; d. Culloden, GA; only son of Rev. Edmund W. Reynolds. cvt. 1844.

"Stewart Cir., GA Conf." *SCA*, 9-16-1858, p. 63.

"Cave Spring Cir., GA Conf." *SCA*, 9-11-1862, p. 138; 9-10-1863, bp.

"Upson Cir., GA Conf." *SCA*, 10-12-1866, p. 5.

"Thomaston Cir., N. GA Conf." *SCA*, 11-1-1867, p. 174.

Reynolds, Joseph Melville (8-3-1855 - 1-17-1941) (MPC)

b. Waynesboro, GA; son of Rev. Freeman F. Reynolds & Elizabeth E. Andrews. The 2nd of 7 chrn., he attended Emory College. m1/ 1-1-1886, (mv 1-3-1886), Mary A. Elrod (10-2-1870 - 4-2-1887), bur. Hopewell MC cem. m2/ 10-4-1887, Lou Elrod (6-4-1868 - 3-23-1950), dau. of John Elrod & Laura King. (Laura King was dau. of Robt. A. King and g.dau. of Rev. Robt. King, Jr.). 11 chrn. as follows: John DeWitt, 9-7-1888; Lucille, 2-7-1890; Joseph Franklin, 7-4-1893; Herschel Bates (Tom), 11-13-1894; Mollie Ellen, 6-6-1896; Paul Leonard, 2-9-1898; Allen, 4-23-1899; Horace Lee, 10-26-1901; Andy Watkins, 2-21-1903; Louise, 3-27-1904; Melville, 4-15-1907.

In the 1890s the family moved to Buckhead section of Atlanta. Then to Avondale (Ingleside) abt. 1900. In 1903 to Cedar Grove in DeKalb Co. Reynolds was pastor there from 1905-1928. Other churches on the circuit were Ellenwood, Kellys Chapel & Anvil Block, all MPC. After leaving Cedar Grove, he was chaplain at the Decatur jail. He & Lou Elrod are bur. at Cedar Grove w/ 4 chrn.

Reynolds, Perry G.

"Rome Cir., N. GA Conf." *SCA*, 10-25-1871, p. 170.

"Coosa Cir., N. GA Conf." *SCA*, 10-9-1872, p. 188.

"Dalton Cir., N. GA Conf." *SCA*, 9-24-1873, p. 151.

"Calhoun Cir., N. GA Conf." *SCA*, 8-5-1874, p. 123; 11-8-1874, p. 182.

"Gordon Cir., N. GA Conf." *SCA*, 11-17-1876, p. 178.

Richards, John J.
"St. Illa Mis. to Blacks, FL." *SCA*, 7-21-1854, p. 26.
"Satilla Mis., FL Conf." *SCA*, 7-23-1852, p. 30; 9-15-1848,
     p. 58; 10-25-1850, p. 84.
"Newnansville Ci.t, FL Conf." *SCA*, 10-30-1856, p. 87.
"Marion Cir., FL Conf." *SCA*, 9-3-1857, p. 55.

Richardson, Jesse
2nd Lt., 52nd GA Reg., CSA. Prisoner of war. d. Pt. Lookout, MD.

Richardson, Jesse L.
b. Bedford Co., VA.
m/ 1-27-1794, Surry Co., NC, Ruth A. Jones (Sept. 1770 -
12-16-1855), b. Surry Co., NC; d. Habersham Co., GA, dau.
of James Jones, Sr. and Elizabeth Ferree. (add child): Susannah
(1798 - 2-23-1872/3), d. Wichita, KS, m/ Rev. Wm. M. Grantham.

1-18-1825, Letter to Conf. re work in Grove Circuit, GA; 1825,
Letter to Rev. Samuel K. Hodges, Fayetteville, re charges brought
against Warwick; 1-1-1830, letter to Conf.; 1-1-1825, letter to Conf.
re work on Grove Circuit. (Wof.).

Jenkins, James. *Experiences*, etc. pp. 50-55.

Richardson, John M. (8-30- - 9-21-1872)
b. Rutherford Co., NC; d. Dalton, GA; lp 1840.

Richardson, John T.
"Tunnel Hill Cir., 7-29-1872." *SCA*, 8-7-1872, p. 122.

Richardson, Russell J.
1-7-1830, recom. to Conf. for traveling connection by Conquest-Cedar Ck.
Circuit, Milledgeville Dist. (Wof.).

Richardson, Simon P.
"Additional Appointment of an Evangelist." *WCA*, v50, n19, 5-12-1886, p. 2.
"Key West, FL." *SCA*, 11-13-1846, p. 91; 7-9-1847, p. 19.
"Tallahassee Dist., FL Conf." *SCA*, 7-28-1859, p. 242.
"Bible Cause in FL Conf." *SCA*, 1-29-1857, p. 136.
"Overhaul the Old Ship." *SCA*, 3-21-1866, bp.
"One Bible Society Enough For Us." *SCA*, 3-16-1866, bp.
"St. Augustine - In the Past." *SCA*, 3-4-1874, p. 34.

"The Power to Conquer." *SCA*, 1-30-1877, fp.
"Central CG." *SCA*, 7-3-1877, p. 106.
"Conditions of Church Membership." *SCA*, 2-19-1878, fp.

Richardson, William C.
"The Vicar of Christ." *SCA*, 4-15-1874, fp.

Rivers, William P.
"A Sacramental Hymn." (poem). *SCA*, 11-15-1855, p. 93.
"Elegiac Lines" (poem on the death of Wm. H. Morton). *SCA*, 10-16-1856, fp.
"A Funeral Sonnet." (to the memory of Rev. H.S. Bradley). *WCA*, 10-25-1893,
    p. 5.
"The Story and the Song." *WCA*, 12-20-1893, p. 5.
"A Vision of the Night." (poem). *SCA*, 2-25-1864, fp.
"Our Country's Prayer." (poem). *SCA*, 8-27-1863, fp.
"Whitfield Cir., GA Conf." *SCA*, 8-24-1866, p. 4; 9-7-1866, p. 5.
"What I Would Live For." (poem). *SCA*, 2-1-1867, fp.
"Stand For The Right." (poem). *SCA*, 3-29-1867, fp.
"Lines Suggested by the Motto: Fortiter, Fideliter, Feliciter." *SCA*,
    1-3-1868, fp.
"What Shall I Do To Inherit Eternal Life." (poem). *SCA*, 6-12-1868, fp.
"Birth of our Savior." (poem). *SCA*, 1-1-1869, fp.
"Consolation." (poem). *SCA*, 1-15-1869, fp.
"Jonesboro Cir., N. GA Conf." *SCA*, 9-3-1869, p. 142.
"Mother's Love & Prayers." (poem). *SCA*, 10-15-1869, fp.
"The Soldier's Widow." (poem). *SCA*, 11-19-1869, fp.
"My Mother." (poem). *SCA*, 4-8-1870, fp.
"Christ's Victory Over Death." (poem). *SCA*, 5-6-1870, fp.
"Cave Spring Cir." *SCA*, 8-26-1870, p. 134; 9-9-1870, p. 143;
    9-20-1871, p. 150.
"The Rest of Prayer or The Thorns Shall Disappear." (poem). *SCA*,
    9-16-1870, fp.
"Triumph in Death." *SCA*, 10-21-1870, fp.
"The New Year." (poem). *SCA*, 1-11-1871, fp.
"A Narrow Escape." *SCA*, 4-5-1871, p. 54.
"The Roses of Spring." *SCA*, 5-3-1871, fp.
"Ora et Labors." (poem). *SCA*, 10-4-1871, fp.
"Memorabilia." *SCA*, 10-4-1871, p. 158.
"Hymn." (poem). *SCA*, 12-13-1871, fp.
"Night Thoughts in December or Communion with Death." (poem). *SCA*,
    1-17-1872, fp.
"Consolation." (poem). *SCA*, 2-28-1872, fp.

"Be Holy - Be Happy." (poem). *SCA*, 3-20-1872, fp.
"Intemperance or the Court of Alcohol." *SCA*, 4-24-1872, fp.
"The Song in the Heart." (poem). *SCA*, 6-12-1872, fp.
"Dreamings of the Sainted Dead." (poem). *SCA*, 6-26-1872, fp.
"The Rome Dist. Conf." *SCA*, 8-14-1872, p. 126.
"The Pilgrim's Song." *SCA*, 9-4-1872, fp.
"The Reapers." (poem). *SCA*, 9-18-1872, fp.
"Letter from N. GA." *SCA*, 10-9-1872, p. 158.
"Forrestville Cir., N. GA Conf." *SCA*, 10-30-1872, p. 170; 8-27-1873, p. 134.
"A Poetical & Scriptural Collation of the Names, Titles & Offices of Christ."
    SCA, 11-6-1872, fp.
"The Old and the New." (poem). *SCA*, 1-8-1873, fp.
"Another Life." (poem). *SCA*, 2-5-1873, fp.
"A Voice O'er The Sea." (poem). *SCA*, 2-19-1873, fp.
"The Church of God." (poem). *SCA*, 4-2-1873, fp.
"The Song of the Miser." (poem). *SCA*, 4-16-1873, fp.
"God Pity the Man." (poem). *SCA*, 3-19-1873, fp.
"The Death - Frost in Springtime." *SCA*, 5-28-1873, fp.
"Cardiphonia - Hope's Soliloquy." (poem). *SCA*, 6-4-1873, fp.
"Maury's Last Voyage." (poem). *SCA*, 6-25-1873, fp.
"Faithful." (poem). *SCA*, 7-30-1873, fp.
"Education." *SCA*, 9-10-1873, fp.
"Little Birdie Sing for Me." (poem). *SCA*, 10-22-1873, p. 168.
"To the Evangelical Alliance." (poem). *SCA*, 11-5-1873, fp.
"A Prayer for Submission to the Will of God in Bereavement." (poem). *SCA*,
    11-26-1873, fp.
"A Tribute to Rev. W.J. Parks." (poem). *SCA*, 12-3-1873, fp.
"Christian Love." (poem). *SCA*, 1-28-1874, fp.
"Oxford Visited." (poem). *SCA*, 8-26-1874, fp.
"Jesus, A Hymn." (poem). *SCA*, 9-16-1874, fp.
"The Love of Jesus." (poem). *SCA*, 10-21-1874, fp.
"Break it Gently to Mother." (poem). *SCA*, 10-28-1874, fp.
"A Sabbath Hour." (poem). *SCA*, 1-27-1875, fp.
"A Poetical Illustration of The Lord's Prayer." (poem). *SCA*, 2-17-1875, fp.
"My Jesus, My Savior." (poem). *SCA*, 5-12-1875, fp.
"Emory." (poem). *SCA*, 7-14-1875, p. 112.
"Sympathy." (poem). *SCA*, 8-25-1875, fp.
"Elberton Cir., N. GA Conf." *SCA*, 10-20-1875, p. 167.
"Faithful Stewards." (poem). *SCA*, 10-27-1875, fp.
"The Church Victorious." (poem). *SCA*, 12-1-1875, fp.
"Another Year." (poem). *SCA*, 1-12-1876, fp.
"Death Among the Reapers." (poem). *SCA*, 3-8-1876, fp.

"An Allegory." (poem). *SCA*, 4-26-1876, fp.
"Sub Cruce." (poem). *SCA*, 6-13-1876, fp.
"God." (poem). *SCA*, 7-4-1876, fp.
"An Ode, Savannah's Death-Roll." (poem). *SCA*, 10-10-1876, fp.
    (tribute to Rev. E.H. Myers).
"Bright Days Will Come." (poem). *SCA*, 11-7-1876, fp.
"A Plea For Foreign Missions." (poem). *SCA*, 11-28-1876, fp.
"Another Ship - The New Year." *SCA*, 1-30-1877, fp.
"Christianity The Hope of the Country." *SCA*, 2-13-1877, fp.
"Sabbath Bells." (poem). *SCA*, 3-13-1877, fp.
"The Soul Without God." (poem). *SCA*, 4-3-1877, fp.
"Life's Mystery." (poem). *SCA*, 7-24-1877, fp.
"Fallen." (poem). *SCA*, 9-11-1877, fp.
"Barnesville, N. GA Conf." *SCA*, 9-18-1877, p. 150; 10-2-1877, p. 158.
"Affliction." (poem). *SCA*, 10-2-1877, fp.
"Patience." (poem). *SCA*, 11-20-1877, fp.
"There's No Fate Enthroned & Frowning." *SCA*, 11-27-1877, fp.
"Christmas Hymn." (poem). *SCA*, 12-25-1877, fp.
"There's No Hell." (poem). *SCA*, 1-29-1878, fp.
"Veni Creator Spiritus." (poem). *SCA*, 5-14-1878, fp.
"Life's Sweetest Thoughts." (poem). *SCA*, 5-21-1878, fp.

*the following attributed to him:
"Desirableness of Truth as an Element of Moral Character." *SCA*,
    7-31-1868, fp.
"Truth Desirable For its Practical Benefit." *SCA*, 8-7-1868, fp.
"Tattlers and Whispers." *SCA*, 8-14-1868, fp.

*the following attributed to wife Mary Frances:
"A Wife's Prayer." (poem). *SCA*, 8-21-1868, fp.
"My Boy." (poem). *SCA*, 8-28-1868, fp.
"Music." (poem). *SCA*, 9-25-1868, fp.
"The Death of Eli." (poem). *SCA*, 10-9-1868, fp.

Roark, Jones W.
"Gainesville Cir., GA Conf." *SCA*, 11-13-1856, p. 95.

Robb, Robert H.
Character Sketches - Some Early Official Members of the GA Conf.,
MEC. nd., pvt. copy. (Lawrence).

Roberts, Bryan   (1-23-1804 - 11-6-1871)
b. Iredell Co., NC; d. Gilmer Co., GA.

Roberts, Joseph W.
"Camden Mis., S. GA Conf." *SCA,* 11-3-1875, p. 174.

Roberts, Thomas F.P.   (d. 2-3-1883)
bur. Charleston, SC.

Roberts, William F.
"Colquitt Cir., S. GA Conf." *SCA,* 9-9-1870, p. 142; 9-23-1870, p. 150.
"Ocmulgee Cir., S. GA Conf." *SCA,* 11-13-1872, p. 179.

Robertson, Andrew
"Clayton Mis.." *SCA,* 8-19-1853, p. 46; 12-23-1853, p. 118.

Robins, John B.
wrote, *Life of Francis Asbury.*

Robinson, Adam A.
Chap., 11th GA Bttn. Artillery, CSA.

"Theological Compend." *SCA,* 10-4-1871, fp.
"Letter from Key West." *SCA,* 7-24-1872, p. 114.
"Letter from FL." *SCA,* 6-11-1873, p. 90.
"In the Newly Born Infant, a Child of God or Satan." *SCA,* 7-8-1874, fp.
"The Temperance Rule." *SCA,* 11-11-1874, fp.
"Home Training." *SCA,* 10-27-1875, fp.
"About Key West." *SCA,* 3-15-1876, p. 42.
"The Lord's Table, Who Are Invited." *SCA,* 10-9-1877, fp.
"The Lord's Supper Again." *SCA,* 1-22-1878, fp.

Robinson, George M.
"Roswell Cir., N. GA Conf." *SCA,* 10-15-1873, p. 163.

Robinson, John H. (11-9-1801 - 1872)

b. Fairfield Dist. SC; d. Oglethorpe, GA; son of Adam & Elizabeth Robinson; moved to Jones Co., GA as a child; cvt. campmeeting age 17; le age 18; SC CONF. OT 1821; 1826 Elder; m/ 1827, Pheriby Godwin, of Horry Dist. SC, d. May, 1856; m2/ Dec. 1857, Isabella Grayson of Williamsburg Dist. SC.

1859 GA CONF., Cusseta Cir.; 1860 Butler Cir.; 1860 Sup. member Oglethorpe Cir.;

Robinson, William C.

"Uchee Mis., AL." *SCA*, 10-3-1851, p. 70.

Robison, William F.

Chap. 15th GA Reg.
dv. on wife Savannah Stillwell, 10-5-1888 (see: *WCA*, 10-10-1888).

"Methodism in Hawkinsville, GA." *SCA*, 6-25-1869, p. 102.

Savannah Stillwell wrote the following poems:
"These Earthly Ties." *WCA*, v47, n8, 2-21-1883, p. 1.
"Beneath The Mold." *WCA*, v49, n26, 7-1-1885, p. 2.
"I Wonder." *WCA*, v48, n27, 7-2-1884, p. 2.
"Near Thee." *WCA*, v48. n25, 6-18-1884, p. 2.
"Farewell." *WCA*, v49, n46, 11-18-1885, p. 3.
"Higher." *WCA*, v45, n26, 7-2-1881, p. 2.
"Homesick." *WCA*, v45, n14, 4-9-1881, p. 1.
"Sequestered Places." *WCA*, v49, n17, 4-29-1885, p. 2.
"The Promises of God." *WCA*, v48, n16, 4-16-1884, p. 2.
"There Is But One." *WCA*, v49, n40, 10-7-1885, p. 2.

Robison, Wingfield W.

"Thomaston Cir., GA." *SCA*, 9-27-1839, p. 59.
"Talbotton Cir., GA." *SCA*, 7-17-1840, p. 18; 10-16-1840, p. 70;
        9-18-1840, p. 54.
"Revival in Perry Cir., GA." *SCA*, 8-5-1842, p. 31; 8-19-1842, p. 39.
"Lumpkin Cir., GA." *SCA*, 9-10-1841, p. 50.

Rogers, J.W.

d. Macon, GA; Co. D, 25th GA Reg., CSA.

Rogers, James A.
dv. 4-26-1863; Co. C, 18th GA Reg., CSA.

Rogers, James T.
bur. Trinity UMC, Clairmont, GA. (Hall Co.).

Rogers, Richard W.
"Millen Mis., S. GA Conf." *SCA*, 7-22-1874, p. 114; 8-19-1874, p. 131; 11-4-1874, p. 174.

Rogers, Robert H.   (d.4-1-1887)
d. Hayneville, AL; bro. to Rev. W.A. Rogers.

*m/ data says Robt. A. formerly of GA Conf., but is prob. the above: m/ 5-4-1870, Mrs. M. Jennie Hill, Spalding Co., Ga.

"Flowery Branch Cir., N. GA Conf." *SCA*, 9-4-1877, p. 142; 10-16-1877, p. 166.

Rogers, William   (1805 - 4-2-1870)
attended Lawrenceville Academy; preached around Chattahoochee, GA; d. in what was Milton and is now Fulton Co., GA, within a mile of his birthplace; part Cherokee Indian.

Rogers, William A.
"Address to the Graduating Class of Griffin FC." *SCA*, 7-24-1868, fp.

Rogers, William H.
Co. F., 5th Reg., GA State Troops; 1862, Co. G, 58th GA Reg., CSA.

Rolander, William Joseph
arrived in the U..S. from Germany in 1828; parents died at sea, leaving him responsible for a yr. old sister, Mary Magdalena. Traveled from foster home to foster home throughout GA. cvt. 1834; LE 1835; 1840, lived in Fulton Co., GA; 1861, lived in Sand Mtn., AL. Returned to Fulton Co. after the War. bur. Sardis Meth., Fulton Co.
m/ Anna Gunter (8-1-1820 - 1-9-1905) b. GA; bur. Sardis. chrn. Eliza Ann (5-11-1845 - 3-23-1849); Mary Louisa (1-11-1849 - 12-20-1886); Thomas Andrew (Feb. 1848 - 5-13-1923); Lorenzo Dow (11-28-1854 - 5-8-1937); William Washington (8-7-1856 - 3-19-1922); David Haliburton (5-28-1859 - 10-14-1914); John Wesley (7-28-1861 - 3-6-1917).

1860s, member & pastor of Mt. Vernon MECS, Fulton Co., GA; 1877-78, preached at Pleasant Hill MC, now Paces' Ferry; 1879, joined Sardis MC. He wd. walk 20-25 m. to his appts.; fasted every Friday for 40 yrs.

Rorie, James E.
"Gibson Cir., S. GA Conf." *SCA,* 11-11-1874, p. 178.

Rosser, James A.
"Alexander Cir., N. GA Conf." *SCA,* 10-2-1872, p. 154; 10-28-1874, p. 170.

Round, George H.
"GA Conference Manual Labor School." *SCA,* 12-18-1840, p. 107.
"Northern Notes." (series). see: *SCA,* 7-23-1857, p. 30-31.
"The Northwest." (series). see: *SCA,* 10-8-1857, p. 74-75.
"NC Letters." (series). *SCA,* 9-14-1878, fp.

Rowan, John F.   (12-10-1832 - 12-30-1901)
preached at Union MC which is now on Hwy. 138 near line of Henry & Rockdale cos. Enlisted CSA, Calhoun, GA; came to GA from AL; bur. near Union Church. m/ Frances A. Parker (8-17-1833 - 5-9-1908). Co. E, 30th GA Reg., CSA.

Rowland, Albert W.
"LaFayette Cir., GA Conf." *SCA,* 10-28-1858, p. 87.
"Monroe Cir., N. GA Conf." *SCA,* 11-5-1873, p. 171.

Rowland, William C.
m/ 12-10-1873, Charlotte I. Lockhart of Tallapoosa Co., AL.

"Dublin Cir., GA Conf." *SCA,* 10-15-1857, p. 79.

Rush, Jackson
"Franklin Cir., GA Conf." *SCA,* 10-2-1856, p. 71.

Rush, Leonard
Chap., Montgomery's Artillery; later 2rd GA Cavalry Chap., CSA.

"Black River & Pee Dee Mis." *SCA,* 1-18-1839, p. 122; 5-24-1839, p. 194.

Rushing, Richard R.

m/ 12-9-1829, Martha A. (4-11-1813 - 2-28-1867) b. Colleton Dist., SC. She was killed by a Negro as she slept. The assailant having stolen her husband's gun, raised her bedroom window and discharged it against her head. He was a hired worker who had married a woman reared by Mrs. Rushing and was jealous and enraged when his wife elected to remain with Mrs. Rushing rather than go with him.

"Sandersville Cir., GA." *SCA*, 1-20-1843, p. 125.
"Scriven Mis., GA Conf." *SCA*, 8-16-1844, p. 38.
"Columbus Mis., GA." *SCA*, 5-28-1847.

Russell, Augustus D.

"Black River Mis., GA Conf." *SCA*, 5-27-1842, p. 198; 9-9-1842, p. 50.

Russell, James

"Sketch of the late James Russell." *SCA*, 6-24-1837, p. 1.

Russell, John

"applied to the conference to come back, but was not received. He afterward prevailed on the society at Rembert's to receive him on the condition that he would be peaceable; but he soon slabbed off again, and has done us no good since." (1827). Jenkins, James. *Experiences*, etc., p. 192.

Russell, Thomas B.

"Fort Valley, GA Conf." *SCA*, 10-15-1863, bp.

Russell, Willis M.

"Decatur Co., FL Conf." *SCA*, 10-2-1862, p. 151.
"Miracles." *SCA*, 8-18-1864, fp.
"Spring Ck. Mis., S. GA Conf." *SCA*, 11-26-1869, p. 190.

Ryburn, Peter M.

"Jeffersonville Cir., GA Conf." *SCA*, 10-9-1856, p. 75.
"West Point, GA." *SCA*, 9-20-1867, p. 150.
"Interesting Revival Incidents." *SCA*, 9-27-1867, fp.
"Bad Taste." *SCA*, 7-23-1869, fp.
"The Villa Rica Church." *SCA*, 3-8-1871, p. 38.
"Marietta Dist." *SCA*, 4-5-1871, p. 54; 10-4-1871, p. 159.
"West Point, GA." *SCA*, 1-21-1874, p. 10.
"Dalton Station, N. GA Conf." *SCA*, 1-16-1877, p. 10.

Rylander, John E.
attended Emory College; le there; shot in head at Gaines' Mill, VA.
b. Sumter Co., GA. indicted posthumously in 1865 as a war criminal
or forbidding Union chaplains access to prisoners. CSA.

Saffold, A.G.
"Meeting of the ME Church at Madison, GA." *SCA*, 8-2-1844, p. 29.

Samford, Thomas
"Harris & Talbot Cir., GA Conf." *SCA*, 10-18-1844, p. 73.

Sanders, Britton
wife Sarah E. ? bur. Danielsville, GA.

"Hartwell Cir., N. GA Conf." *SCA*, 9-20-1867, p. 150.
"Canton Cir., N. GA Conf." *SCA*, 10-25-1871, p. 170.
"Fayetteville Cir., N. GA Conf." *SCA*, 1-22-1878, p. 10.

Sanders, Ernest A.
bur. Stapleton, GA.

Sasnett, Bolling H.
"Gordon Cir., S. GA Conf." *SCA*, 9-10-1873, p. 142.

Sasnett, William J.
"Endowment of Emory College." *SCA*, 1-24-1856, p. 133; 2-7-1856, p. 141;
    1-31-1856, p. 137.
"The Secular On Art: Denominational Educational Movement in GA."
    (series). *SCA*, see: 10-28-1858, fp.
"A Vindication on the Common School Question." (series). *SCA*,
    see: 6-16-1859, fp.
"Pewed Methodist Churches." (series). *SCA*, 6-12-1856, fp.
"The Relations of the Divine Providence to our Present National Struggle."
    (series). see: *SCA*, 2-26-1863, fp.
"Lay Representation." (series). see: *SCA*, 4-1-1858, fp.
"The LaGrange Female College." *SCA*, 6-11-1857, fp.
"Our Academy System." (series). see: *SCA*, 9-24-1857, fp.
"A Short Essay on Apostasy." *SCA*, 10-29-1857, fp.
"The Present Crisis." (series). *SCA*, 3-10-1864, fp.
"Instrumental Music in Church Service." *SCA*, 6-30-1864, fp.

"The Wants of Methodism." (series). *SCA*, 10-20-1864, np.
"Another Picture - A Defence." *SCA*, 11-24-1864, np.
"Recollections of the Late Wm. Arnold of the GA Conf." *SCA*, 4-13-1865, fp.

Saunders, Robert M.
"European Correspondence." (series). *SCA*, 9-6-1867, p. 142.
"A Sabbath in Florence, Italy." *SCA*, 9-18-1868, p. 151.

Scarborough, James B.
m/ 6-13-1869, Mrs. P.W. Cheak, both of Madison Co., GA.

Scott, William J.
"Americus, GA Conf." *SCA*, 11-4-1858, p. 90.
"Atlanta, GA Conf." *SCA*, 10-16-1862, fp.
"Revival in Americus, GA." *SCA*, 3-11-1858, p. 163.
"Dalton Dist., N. GA Conf." *SCA*, 6-7-1871, p. 90; 11-6-1872, p. 174.
"The Dalton Dist. Conf." *SCA*, 5-22-1872, p. 78.
"Trinity Church, Atlanta, GA." *SCA*, 8-25-1875, p. 134.

Scruggs, Richard H.   (1816 - 1870)
le 1841; lp 1862; joined church at Old Church CG.

Seale, Robert A.
"Zebulon Cir., N. GA Conf." *SCA*, 10-18-1867, fp.
"Richmond Cir., N. GA Conf." *SCA*, 1-9-1877, p. 6.
"What of Fiction." *SCA*, 11-27-1877, fp.

Seals, Thomas A.
"Cave Spring Cir." *SCA*, 6-26-1868, p. 102; 9-18-1868, p. 151.
"Warrenton Cir., N. GA Conf." *SCA*, 9-24-1869, p. 154; 9-9-1870, p. 142;
    11-4-1870, p. 174; 11-29-1871, p. 190.
"An Old Campground to be Reoccupied." *SCA*, 9-2-1870, p. 138.
"Mt. Gilead Campmeeting." *SCA*, 11-18-1870, p. 182.
"Greenville, Trinity & Fletcher's Chapel, N. GA Conf." *SCA*, 10-16-1872,
    p. 162.
"Asbury Church, N. GA Conf." *SCA*, 11-18-1874, p. 182.

Searcy, Benjamin R.   (1-16-1797 - 2-6-1873)
b. Cumberland Co., NC; 1818-1828 lived in Jones Co., GA; then in Talbot
Co., GA; lp 1820.

Sears, William N.
"Andrew Mis. to Blacks, AL." *SCA*, 12-10-1852, p. 114; 5-13-1853,
    p. 202; 8-26-1853, p. 50.
"Chambers Mis. to Blacks, AL." *SCA*, 6-23-1854, p. 10; 7-28-1854, p. 30.

Seay, William
Co. E, 23rd GA Reg., CSA.

Sego, William
Co. H, 62nd GA Reg., CSA.

Seldom, Johnny
*prob. not a preacher

"Crawford Cir., S. GA Conf." *SCA*, 9-17-1873, p. 146.

Sessions, John J.
m3/ 6-25-1877, Karen Elizabeth Wimberly of Calhoun Co., GA.

Sewell, Christopher A.
Co. E, 36th GA Reg., CSA.

Sewell, Isaac
b. Franklin Co., GA; bur. Citizens Cem., Cobb Co., GA; m/ Louisa
Lane (1803 - 10-11-1881), b. Franklin Co., GA; bur. same.

Shanks, Asbury H.
"Florida Dist., AL." *SCA*, 11-2-1838, p. 78.
"Selma, AL." *SCA*, 11-15-1839, p. 86.
"Pikeville Mis., AL." *SCA*, 8-7-1840, p. 30.

Sharp, John D.
"Marietta Cir., GA Conf." *SCA*, 8-30-1855, p. 51.

Sharpe, Hamilton W.
"Hahira, GA." *SCA*, 9-20-1867, p. 150.
"Mt. Zion Camp-Meeting, S. GA Conf." *SCA*, 10-29-1869, p. 175.
"Brunswick Dist. Meeting." *SCA*, 4-22-1870, p. 62; 6-3-1870, fp.
"Morven Cir., S. GA Conf." *SCA*, 9-2-1870, p. 138.
"Old Mt. Zion CG, Brooks Co., GA." *SCA*, 10-28-1870, p. 170.
"The Brunswick Dist. Conf." *SCA*, 4-26-1871, p. 66; 5-10-1871, p. 74.
"Mt. Zion Campmeeting." *SCA*, 11-1-1871, p. 174.

Sharpe, William
wife Judan Smith was the dau. of Gen. Daniel Smith (10-28-1748 - 6-16-1818), b. Stafford Co., VA., d. Rochcastle, TN. He was son of Capt. Henry Smith, b. Somerset Co., MD.

chrn. include: Eliza E.; Elizabeth H., d. 1841; Harriet S., d. 1847.

Shaw, Simeon
"Oothcalooga Valley." *WCA*, v53, n6, 2-9-1889, p. 8.

Shea, William D.
"Revival in Oglethorpe, GA." *SCA*, 3-27-1856, p. 171.
"A Voice From Georgia." *SCA*, 4-3-1856, p. 175.
"Putnam Circuit: Weekday Preaching." *SCA*, 10-28-1858, p. 86.
"From Beyond the Mississippi." *SCA*, 10-30-1862, p. 165.

Sheldon, Vardy H.
m/ 10-26-1870, Frances M. Sexton of Alachua Co., FL.

Shell, Stephen
"Hiwassee Mis., GA Conf." *SCA*, 4-9-1847, p. 174; 6-25-1847, p. 10.
"Greensboro Mis., GA." *SCA*, 5-25-1849, p. 202; 8-10-1849, p. 38; 10-19-1849, p. 78.

Shellman, Thomas P.C.
8-29-1829, recom. to itinerancy by Warrenton Cir. (Wof.).

"Pensacola Mission." *CA*, 5-27-1831, p. 154; 10-28-1831, p. 34.

Shockley, Gideon   (1779 - 1856)
b. SC; d. Randolph Co., AR; son of Thomas Shockley, Sr. & Prudence ?; m1/ Manoah ? (d. 4-30-1847); m2/ Catherine ? chrn. Mary, 1790; Thomas (1801 - 1852); Cornelius (5-2-1803 - 7-5-1884); Martha, 4-1-1807; Margaret; Abdi C. (1809 - 1877); Gideon, b. ca 1849; Wiley G., 1851.

Short, William J.
m/ 12-25-1860, Nancy Wallis (11-12-1840 - 7-15-1875) of Marion Co., GA.

Sikes, Daniel   (12-18-1804 - 5-10-1869)
M.D. b&d Tatnall Co., GA; m/ 1824, Elizabeth J. Eason, dau. of Rev. Wm. Eason.

Simmons, J. Crockett (d. 7-26-1880)

Simmons, John
"Revivals in Covington & Monroe Cir." *SCA*, 11-25-1842, p. 93.

Simmons, John C., Sr. (d. 4-3-1868)
d. Thomaston, GA at residence of Thos. Bethel.

"St. Augustine & Nassau Mis., FL." *CA*, 8-24-1832, p. 206.
"Ringgold, GA Conf." *SCA*, 7-15-1858, p. 27.
"Cassville, GA." *SCA*, 12-10-1841, pp. 102-103.
"Rome Dist., GA Conf." *SCA*, 9-16-1858, p. 63; 9-18-1856, p. 63.
"Watkinsville Cir., GA Conf." *SCA*, 9-15-1859, p. 271.
"Revival in Dalton" *SCA*, 3-18-1858, p. 167.
"Lookout Mountain Mis., GA Conf." *SCA*, 9-10-1857, p. 59.
"Stewart Cir., GA Conf." *SCA*, 8-20-1863, bp.
"A Terrible Explosion." *SCA*, 6-15-1866, p. 6.
"Light Wanted." *SCA*, 7-6-1866, fp.
"Revival in Forsyth, GA." *SCA*, 9-20-1867, p.150.

Simmons, John C., Jr.
"Elberton Cir., GA Conf." *SCA*, 10-5-1849, p. 71.
"A Call from Oregon." *SCA*, 3-11-1858, p. 162.
"California Correspondence." (series). *SCA*, 5-7-1873, p. 70.

Simmons, John W.
"Brunswick Dist., S. GA Conf." *SCA*, 8-14-1868, p. 130; 9-11-1868, p. 146;
        10-30-1868, p. 174.
"Letter from CA." *SCA*, 6-25-1869, p. 102.
"Affairs in the Brunswick Dist., S. GA Conf." *SCA*, 7-8-1870, p. 106.
"Brooks Campmeeting." *SCA*, 10-21-1870, p. 166.
"Affairs in Hinesville Dist." *SCA*, 12-11-1872, p. 194.
"Jones Chapel, S. GA Conf." *SCA*, 10-6-1875, p. 158.
"Brunswick Dist. Conf." *SCA*, 5-16-1876, p. 78.

Simmons, Oliver C.
m/ Carrie E. Moore, dau. of J.C. Moore of Floyd Co., GA.

Simmons, Thomas J.
"Whitfield Cir., N. GA Conf." *SCA*, 11-22-1867, p. 186.

Simmons, William A.
1st wife was a Maddox (ux); 5 chrn. Marry, Will, Addie, Sally, Ethel.
At least 3 chrn. by m2/, namely, Ralph Allen, Ellene, Carlton Hill.

"From the Army Near Suffolk." *SCA*, 5-14-1863, p. 66.
"Revival in Gen. Anderson's Brigade." *SCA*, 10-15-1863, bp.
"Calhoun Cir., GA Conf." *SCA*, 11-23-1866, p. 5.
"Dahlonega Dist., N. GA Conf." *SCA*, 10-18-1867, p. 166; 8-6-1869, p. 126.
"The Dahlonega Dist. Meeting." *SCA*, 10-2-1868, p. 158.
"Whitesburg Cir., N. GA Conf." *SCA*, 11-3-1875, p. 175.

Simpson, William J.
of Houston Co., GA.

Simpson, William W. (b. 1835)
b. Hall Co., GA; Co. D, 55th GA Reg, CSA; 1865 5th Reg. US Vols.

Sinclair, Elijah
1823, Committee report of charges against him - 1) married without
consulting brethren; 2) gallanted ladies through the streets; 3) married
a woman not in communion with any church. 2-3-1825, letter to SC
Conf. w/ resignation. (Wof.).

Sinclair, Jesse
12-23-1824, letter to Conf. and resignation. (Wof.).

Singleton, Joseph J.
"Covington & Oxford, *SCA*, 10-18-1867, fp.
"Oxford Cir., N. GA Conf." *SCA*, 10-29-1869, p. 175.

Singleton, William A.
m/ 1855, C.A.E. Bryan (1828 - 1-31-1876); b. Scriven Co., GA; d. Buena
Vista, GA; dau. of Jesse & Mary A. Bryan.

Sistrunk, Samuel H. J. (9-9-1818 - 3-6-1878)
(L) b. Orangeburg, SC; d. Fort Valley, GA; served Lane's Chapel,
Perry Cir., 1854.

"Good Meetings." *SCA*, 11-5-1869, p. 178.
"Oglethorpe Cir., S. GA Conf." *SCA*, 9-5-1876, p. 142.

Slade, John
Temple, Robert M. Jr. *Florida Flame.* pp. 35-37.

Smith, Alfred B.
"Hancock Mis., GA Conf." *SCA,* 6-22-1849, p. 10.

Smith, Alfred H.   (d. 2-5-1865)
d. Camp Chase, OH; Co. E, 41st GA Reg.; 1862 Co. F, 22nd AL Reg., CSA.

Smith, Anderson   (MPC)
bur. Mt. Pleasant (Smith's Chapel) MPC, Carroll Co., GA;
son of Seaborn Smith.

Smith, Anthony Garnett, Sr. (8-30-1776 - 1-18-1852)
b. Cumberland Co., VA. In 1787 he and his parents had a religious experience
and joined the Methodist Church. That same year his family and others moved
to GA (that part of Wilkes Co. that became Oglethorpe Co.). m/ 1797, Mary
(Polly) Allen. He and parents were charter members of Mt. Pleasant Church,
Oglethorpe Co., GA, founded in 1820. In 1827 he moved his family to
Crawford Co., GA where he lived the rest of his life. His home still stand, and
he and wife are buried near it. A son, Wesley Fletcher, was also a Meth.
preacher.

began ministry in 1807; LP 1801; ordained in 1811 and 1812 by Asbury &
McKendree.

12-8-1824, 12-9-1827, recom. to elder's orders; 2-21-1825, 12-15-1825, letters
to SC Conf. (Wof.).

Smith, Barnett
7-5-1823, letter to Bro. Major. (Wof.).

Smith, Burgess   (9-27-1808 - 6-26-1857)
bur. Concord UMC, Elbert Co., GA. m/ Harriet W. (11-29-1808 - 8-20-1899).

Smith, Cosby W.
son of Rev. Noah Smith.

m/ 12-23-1851, Matilda C. Flowers (11-3-1831 - 1-25-1877), dau. of Rev.
Drury & Catherine Flowers, b. Jasper Co., GA; d. DeKalb Co., AL.

Smith, Edwin I.
"Prospect Cir., N. GA Conf." *SCA*, 10-16-1877, p. 166.

Smith, Eli
"Cleveland Cir., N. GA Conf." *SCA*, 10-20-1875, p. 167.
"Roswell Cir., N. GA Conf." *SCA*, 11-6-1877, p. 178.

Smith, Fletcher
12-1-1849, recom. for traveling by Greenville SC QC. (Wof.).

"Pickens Cir., SC Conf." *SCA*, 10-15-1857, p. 79.

Smith, George E.
(L). bur. Cokes Chapel, Coweta Co., GA.

Smith, George G.
LP at St. John's, Augusta; was SS Agt. for the Church for many years.
Asst. Pastor at Macon & Vineville, 1859; moved to MD and became a
member of that Conf. on acct. of wife's illness. Co. A, 7th GA Reg.,
Co.H, 4th GA Cavalry, CSA.

wife Sarah Joanna Ousley (2-14-1840 - 3-25-1869) b. Culloden, Monroe Co.,
GA; d. Lewisburg, W. VA; dau. of R.F. Ousley; grad. Wesleyan 1858; bur.
Rose Hill, Macon, GA. m2/ mv 12-25-1870.

Just Saved. Southern Methodist Publishing House, 1885. uv.
"Chaplains in the Army." *SCA*, 5-14-1863, fp.
"Old & New." *SCA*, 7-5-1871, p. 106.
"Preacher's Mutual Aid Society." *SCA*, 7-19-1871, p. 114.
"Old Times & New." *SCA*, 8-23-1871, fp.
"Say Brothers, Will Ye Yield?" (poem). *SCA*, 4-7-1864, fp.
"Sprague's Annals of the American Pulpit." *SCA*, 8-10-1866, p. 2.
"Letter from Lowndes, GA." *SCA*, 11-16-1866, p. 5.
"Letter from Baltimore." *SCA*, 8-16-1867, p. 130; 8-30-1867, p. 138;
        9-20-1867, p. 150.
"Letter from Western VA." *SCA*, 5-6-1870, p. 70.
"A Day at the Baltimore Conf." *SCA*, 4-12-1871, p. 58.
"Our Sunday School Mission Work." *SCA*, 5-29-1872, p. 82.
"A Monday's Letter." *SCA*, 10-16-1872, p. 162.
"Memories." *SCA*, 4-30-1873, fp.
"Marietta Cir., N. GA Conf." *SCA*, 11-19-1873, p. 179.
"Letters to a Young Preacher." *SCA*, 6-17-1874, p. 94.

"A Village Campmeeting." *SCA*, 9-16-1874, p. 146.
"Methodism in Savannah." *SCA*, 10-13-1875, fp.
"The First Missionary to the Negroes in GA." *SCA*, 11-3-1875, fp.
"LaGrange Dist. Conf." *SCA*, 8-15-1876, p. 130.
"With the Dead." *SCA*, 2-26-1878, fp.
"Revival in Milledgeville." *SCA*, 4-9-1878, p. 54; 4-23-1878, p. 62.

Smith, Hubert M. (10-28-1862 - 6-29-1935)
d. Crystal City, TX. m/ Anne Meddlers (Meaders) of the Reinhardt College faculty.

Smith, Isaac
1826, letters and papers of charges against him in Indian disturbances; 2-3-1824, letter to Conf. at Charleston concerning the Asbury School; (Wof.).

Reason For Becoming A Methodist. Boston: Chas. H. Pierce, 1851. (Wof.).

Teasley, Luke. "Isaac Smith: He Persevered." *HH*, v14, n1, June, 1984, pp.
        21-31; v14, n2, Dec. 1984, pp. 35-44.
"Biographical Sketch." (series, his autobiog.). *SCA*, 3-24-1859, fp.

Smith, J. Blakey
"Carrollton Cir., GA." *SCA*, 10-20-1848, p. 78.
"The Journeyings of a Tract Agent." *SCA*, 4-2-1857, p. 174.
"A Good Campmeeting." (Warm Springs, Meriwether Co., GA). *SCA*,
        9-24-1863, fp.
"An Orphan's Home, GA Conf." *SCA*, 7-21-1864, np.
"Greenville Cir., GA Conf." *SCA*, 11-2-1865, np.
"Macon Dist. Conf." *SCA*, 8-19-1870, p. 130.
"Americus Dist. - Turnpike Campmeeting." *SCA*, 9-13-1871, p. 146.
"Cuthbert, S. GA Conf." *SCA*, 10-4-1871, p. 158.
"Americus Dist., S. GA Conf." *SCA*, 9-4-1872, p. 138; 9-18-1872, p. 146.

Smith, James Bradford
"Jefferson Mis., GA Conf." *SCA*, 5-28-1847, p. 206; 12-31-1847, p. 118.
"Scriven Mis., GA Conf." *SCA*, 9-1-1848, p. 50.
"Augusta Colored Charge, GA." *SCA*, 12-14-1849, p. 110.

Smith, James M.
"Sunday-School Celebration at Pleasant Hill, Oglethorpe Co., GA." *SCA*,
        9-18-1868, p. 151.

Smith, James Rembert

"Sandersville Cir., GA." *SCA*, 10-21-1837, p. 70; 12-8-1837, p. 98.

(Note: A James Rembert Smith, M.D., of this vintage m/ 1-10-1838, Elizabeth Tankersly Crawford (nv Crafton) (2-16-1817 - 1-3-1877), b. Richmond Co., GA; d. Sandersville, GA; dau. of Bennett Crawford. 9 chrn. It is not known if these are separate persons or the same).

Smith, James Rembert

*not the same as above.
m/12-8-1875, Carrie Palmer, dau. of Jas. E. Palmer.

"Toccoa, N. GA Conf." *SCA*, 3-20-1877, p. 46.
"From Toccoa." *SCA*, 11-13-1877, p. 182.

Smith, John M. (b. 11-27-1789)

b. Elbert Co., GA; LP, Monroe Cir., 10-17-1825; preached 1878 sermons, 716 of which were funeral sermons. He baptized 1291 persons and was the father of 4 Meth. preachers: Milton, Peyton P., Sidney M. & Joseph T. Smith. Lived in DeKalb Co., GA. See: *WCA*, 5-4-1887.

Smith, Joseph Tarply (5-27-1816 - 10-28-1874)

b. Franklin Co., GA; d. Jonesboro, GA; son of Rev. John M. Smith (L); cvt. 1835 Mt. Gilead CG; bro. to Sidney, Peyton & Milton Smith, Revs.; lp 10-23-1842.

Smith, Luther M.

a president of Emory College.
m/ 5-16-1865, Callie Lane (8-13-1843 - 7-13-1877), grad. 1860, Madison FC; dau. of Prof. Geo. Lane of Oxford, GA.

"Report on Emory College." *SCA*, 1-4-1871, fp.

Smith, Milton C.

son of Rev. John M. Smith.

"Sandersville Cir., GA." *SCA*, 11-1-1850, p. 87.

Smith, Noah

"Fayetteville Cir., GA Conf." *SCA*, 9-2-1858, p. 55.
"Greenville Cir., Meriwether Co., GA." *SCA*, 7-27-1838, p. 22.
"McDonough Cir., GA." *SCA*, 8-15-1851, p. 43.

Smith, Osborne L. (d. 1-24-1878)

*d. in *MPG* error; above *SCA* obit.
Prof. & Pres. of Wesleyan FC; Prof of Languages 1850; Pres. 1854;
Pres. of Emory College 1872.

"Report of the Pres. of Emory College." *SCA*, 1-22-1873, fp.

Smith, Peyton Pierce (d.5-15-1863)

son of Rev. John M. Smith. d. Fulton Co., GA.

"Leon Cir., FL." *SCA*, 9-29-1848, p. 66.
"Thomasville Dist., FL Conf." *SCA*, 7-5-1855, p. 19; 4-24-1856, pp. 186-187.
"Covington Cir., GA." *SCA*, 9-9-1837, p. 46; 10-21-1837, p. 70.
"Report on Greensborough Cir. Missionary Society." *SCA*, 7-13-1838, p. 14.
"Greensborough Cir., GA." *SCA*, 10-5-1838, p. 62.
"Gadsden & Quincy, FL." *SCA*, 3-29-1839, p. 162; 11-15-1839, p. 86.
"Baker Mis., GA." *SCA*, 6-14-1839, p. 206.
"Alachua Mis., FL." *SCA*, 8-16-1839, p. 34.
"Florida Dist.." *SCA*, 10-18-1839, p. 70; 7-17-1840, p. 18; 6-11-1841, p. 206.
"Quincy, FL." *SCA*, 9-10-1841, p. 50.
"Cherokee Dist., GA." *SCA*, 6-30-1843, p. 11; 10-6-1843, p. 67; 12-22-1843,
     p. 111.
"Madison Dist., FL Conf." *SCA*, 5-14-1863, fp; 9-18-1862, p. 143.
"Pastoral Address, FL Conf." *SCA*, 1-7-1858, fp.
"Progress in Apalachicola, FL." *SCA*, 2-25-1858, p. 155.
"The Tongue of Fire and Post Oak Circuit." *SCA*, 7-2-1857, fp.
"Missions in Thomasville Dist., FL Conf." *SCA*, 7-2-1857, p. 19.
"A New Conference Suggested." *SCA*, 10-22-1857, p. 83.

Smith, Samuel H.

Chaplain, 60 Reg., GA Vol., CSA.

"The Marietta Dist. Conf." *SCA*, 8-16-1871, p. 130.
"The 60th GA Reg., Army of VA." *SCA*, 3-31-1864, np; 5-19-1864, np.
"Revival in the Camp." *SCA*, 12-4-1862, p. 187.
"Soldier's Christian Society." *SCA*, 2-5-1863, p. 22.
"The Revival in the Army." *SCA*, 9-10-1863, fp.
"Who Will Help?" *SCA*, 2-23-1865, np.

Smith, Samuel L. (1828 - 10-30-1873)
*prob. same as above.

Chap. 16th GA Reg., CSA; proprietor of Cartersville *Standard & Express.*

Smith, Seaborn E.
bur. Smith's Chapel, Carroll Co., GA.

Smith, Sydney M.
LP 10-14-1835; son of Rev. John M. Smith; wife, Asenath Boring,
d. 10-7-1884; 7 chrn.

"Forsyth Cir., GA." *SCA,* 9-18-1846, p. 59; 10-16-1846, p. 75; 9-24-1857,
     p. 67.
"Temperance in Forsyth, GA." *SCA,* 7-16-1847, p. 22.
"Carrollton Mis., GA." *SCA,* 7-24-1840, p. 22; 9-18-1840, p. 54;
     11-20-1840, p. 90; 1-22-1841, p. 121; 9-17-1841, p. 54;
     11-12-1841, p. 86; 12-31-1841, p. 114; 7-9-1841, p. 14.
"Ft. Valley Mis., GA." *SCA,* 8-16-1850, p. 42.
"Culloden Cir., GA Conf." *SCA,* 10-25-1850, p. 79.

Smith, Wesley F.
son of Rev. Anthony Smith.

"Barnesville Cir., N. GA Conf." *SCA,* 10-25-1867, p. 170; 10-1-1869, p. 158.
"Culloden, N. GA Conf." *SCA,* 6-24-1870, p. 98.
"Warrenton Cir., N. GA Conf." *SCA,* 7-31-1872, p. 118; 11-5-1873, p. 171;
     8-12-1874, p. 126.
"Decatur Cir., N. GA Conf." *SCA,* 10-16-1877, p. 166.

Smith, Whitefoord
9-8-1832, recom. to Conf. by Columbia QC. (Wof.).

"Augusta, GA." *SCA,* 11-10-1837, p. 82.
"Letter from Athens, GA." *SCA,* 9-7-1838, p. 46.
"Centenary of Methodism." *SCA,* 11-23-1838, p. 90.
"Sermon." *SCA,* 1-10-1840, fp.
"Dist. Meetings in the SC Conf." *SCA,* 6-28-1867, p. 102.
"Letter from Spartanburg, SC." *SCA,* 10-11-1867, p. 162.
"Samuel Dunwoody." *SCA,* 6-7-1871, fp.
"Some Recollections of the Rev. Reddick Pierce." *SCA,* 12-6-1871, fp.

"Sanctification." *SCA*, 9-29-1875, fp.
"Fraternity." *SCA*, 2-20-1877, fp.

Smith, William P.

bur. Concord, Elbert Co., GA. (church from which he entered ministry).

"Carnesville Cir., Elberton Dist." *SCA*, 6-23-1875, p. 98; 8-18-1875, p. 130.
"Hartwell Cir., N. GA Conf." *SCA*, 3-21-1877, p. 134.

Stokes, A.J. "Typescript of His Life & Works, 1812-1893." (12-7-1898). (Wof.).

Snead, Tillman F.   (5-11-1786 - 5-3-1875)

b. Wilkes Co., GA; d. Baldwin Co., GA; vet. War of 1812; joined church at Bethel, Bush River Cir., SC Conf.; le 7-13-1813; lp 10-30-1813.

m/ 6-13-1818, Elizabeth G.B. Washington (5-19-1790 - 12-28-1871)
b. Edgefield Dist., SC; d. Baldwin Co., GA; dau. of Robert R. & Elizabeth Washington.

1829-1830, papers relating to his affair with Bolin Swearington. (Wof.).

Snow, Littleton A.

"Leesburg Cir., S. GA Conf." *SCA*, 9-18-1877, p. 150.

Solomon, D.

*not a preacher

"Gordon, GA." *SCA*, 9-28-1866, fp.

Solomon, John W.

"Sabbath-School Houses." *SCA*, 11-9-1866, p. 2.
"Sunday School Houses." *SCA*, 2-19-1869, fp.

Spain, Hartwell

dv. 3-9-1868

12-17-1836, communication to the Conf. (Wof.).

Sparks, James O. A.

Chap., Co. A, 4th GA Reg., CSA.

"Brunswick, GA." *SCA*, 3-16-1866,bp.
"Progress in the FL Conf." *SCA*, 6-21-1867, p. 98.
"A College in the FL Conf." *SCA*, 9-6-1867, p. 142.
"From Key West, FL." *SCA*, 3-5-1869, p. 38.
"Psalm CIV." (poem). *SCA*, 4-30-1869, fp.
"Letter from Key West, FL." *SCA*, 4-30-1869, p. 71.

Spearman, Gabriel Toombs   (9-26-1798 - 8-17-1868)
b. Wilkes Co., GA; d. Jasper Co., GA; son of John Spearman & Ann Dawson;
cvt. 1830; lp 1831.

Speck, John R.
"The Rev. J.R. Speck attempted suicide yesterday morning by cutting his throat
from ear to ear with a pocket knife and jumping into a little river at his home
near Woodstock. The wound was dressed by Dr. Lattimore, and he is resting
quietly. He is about 33 years old." *WCA*, 8-19-1885.

Speer, Alexander
"Columbus, GA." *SCA*, 8-30-1839, p. 50.
"Augusta, GA." *SCA*, 10-8-1841, p. 54.

Speer, Eustace W.
filled the chair of Belles Lettres at UGA after retirement. d. Athens, GA.

Speer, William H.
mv. Nov. 1882.

"Pleasant Hill Cir., N. GA Conf." *SCA*, 9-9-1874, p. 139.
"Morganton Cir., N. GA Conf." *SCA*, 5-7-1878, p. 70.

Speight, Thomas
"Perry Cir., GA." (Andrew Chapel). *SCA*, 11-3-1848, p. 86.
"Meeting in Perry Cir., GA." *SCA*, 4-26-1839, p. 178.

Spence, Charles C.
m/ 12-15-1870, Mattie F. Harper of Oxford, GA.

Spence, James
"Vienna Cir., S. GA Conf." *SCA*, 9-4-1872, p. 138.

Sprayberry, Uriah C.
(L) as listed in Ebenezer, Wesley Chapel folder, DeKalb Co., GA.

Stacy, James
10-24-1829, recom. to SC annual Conf. at Columbia for the itinerancy by Morganton Cir., Lincolnton Dist. (Wof.).

"Georgetown, SC." *SCA*, 7-15-1837, p. 14.
"The M.C. in Camden, SC." *SCA*, 11-20-1856, p. 99.
"Lexington Cir., SC Conf." *SCA*, 3-5-1857, p. 159.
"Carolina Female College." *SCA*, 8-13-1857, p. 43.

Stafford, Ellis (1809 - 4-17-1869)
b. Greensboro, NC; d. Grantville, GA; moved to Upson Co., GA; then to Grantville in 1851.

Stafford, James H.
12-19-1829, recom. to SC Conf. from Morgantown Circuit. (Wof.).

Standley, O.B.
nv. Stanley.

"Holmesville Cir., GA." *SCA*, 11-1-1850, p. 87.

Stanley, Augustin O.
Chap., 37th GA Reg., CSA.

Stanley, Thomas C.
Chap. 46th GA Reg., CSA.

"The 46th GA Regiment." *SCA*, 5-14-1863, fp.
"Col. Colquitt's 46th GA Reg." *SCA*, 7-16-1863, bp.

Stanley, Thomas W.
1816, plea to the SC Conf. at Columbia for a high school at Salem, GA, under the care of the Conf. (Wof.).

Stansell, Joel B.
Co. A, 18th GA Reg., CSA.

Stansell, Levi (1784 - 5-11-1869)
b. Abbeville, SC; d. Newton Co., GA; cvt. 1816; moved to Stanley Co.,

NC; m/ 11-4-1819 Charlotte Howell; joined NC CONF. 1818; moved to GA in 1831; wrote pamphlets on "Baptism" and "The Divine Providence."

Starr, David E.
Sgt. 60th GA Reg; 22nd Bttn., GA Heavy Artillery, CSA.

"Pardoned." (poem). *SCA*, 6-2-1859, fp.
"Scriven Colored Mis.." *SCA*, 7-30-1857, p. 37.
"Jonesboro Cir., N. GA Conf." *SCA*, 10-30-1872, p. 170.

Starr, John W.
"Montgomery Dist., AL." *SCA*, 7-16-1841, p. 19.
"Chattahoochee Mis." *SCA*, 5-27-1842, p. 198.

Starr, Trammell
listed on Spring Place Cir. 4-4-1888. *WCA*.

Steagall, Ivy F.
"Perry Cir., GA Conf." *SCA*, 10-1-1844, p. 65.
"Talbotton, GA." *SCA*, 8-27-1841, p. 42.

Steagall, William W. (6-25-1805 - 9-5-1884)
built the first church erected in Newnan, GA, out of poles.
See: 1860 Census, Heard Co., GA.

Stearns, Zechariah
wife Elizabeth H. S. Harris (1789 - 7-4-1869) b. Franklin Co., NC; d. Talbot Co., GA.

Steed, Wiley
"Sandtown Mis., N. GA Conf." *SCA*, 11-11-1870, p. 178.

Steele, Robert A.
"Liberty Campmeeting, Hinesville Circuit." *SCA*, 10-29-1841, p. 78.
"Meeting at Bethany." *SCA*, 10-29-1841, p. 78.

Stephens, Edward L.
"Factory Mis., Athens Dist., GA." *SCA*, 4-7-1848, p. 174; 7-14-1848, p. 22; 10-13-1848, p. 74; 11-3-1848, p. 86; 12-22-1848, p. 114; 11-1-1850, p. 86; 11-15-1850, p. 94.

Stevenson, William D.
dv. 1920. (obit. is in 1921 Journal. He did not die in Turin and is not bur. there).

Stewart, Alfred J.
Co. I, 10th GA Reg., CSA; deserted to the enemy 1865 and took the oath of allegience.

Stewart, Daniel McLachlan   (10-21-1791 - 1847)
b. Liberty Co., GA; bapt. 12-4-1791; son of Gen. Daniel Stewart; d. Alachua Co., FL; bur. Potosi, 10 m. s. of Newnansville.

LP in FL; preached at campmeeting at Taylor's Ck. CG, Liberty Co., GA in 1843.

Stewart, George
"Muscogee Cir., GA Conf." *SCA,* 8-16-1844, p. 39; 8-27-1847, p. 46.

Stewart, James R.   (3-21-1840 - 1-9-1864)
d. Sumter, GA; m/ Mary Rylander.

"Sumter Cir., GA Conf." *SCA,* 10-30-1862, p. 166; 9-4-1862, p. 132.

Stewart, Thomas H.
"From Gen. E.L. Thomas's Brigade." *SCA,* 5-19-1864, np.

Stewart, Thomas R.
"Ft. Gaines, GA Conf." *SCA,* 8-23-1855, p. 47.

Stewart, William   (1-27-1798 - 2-15-1863)
b. Newberry dist., SC; joined church on 3-15-1816; m/ 8-2-1819, Mary Kelly; moved to GA 1826; established Sardis Church near Oxford; class leader 4-15-1827; le 4-15-1835; entered ministry 10-19-1840; Deacon 1846; Elder (E) 1855; Elder 11-2-1856; in charge of Ladies Class at Oxford at time of death.

Stewart, William W.
Co. A, 12th GA Reg., CSA.

"Buena Vista, GA." *SCA,* 8-23-1871, p. 134; 8-20-1863, bp.
"Centreville Cir., GA Conf." *SCA,* 11-3-1864, np.
"Haynesville Cir., S. GA Conf." *SCA,* 10-1-1869, p. 158.
"Buena Vista Cir., S. GA Conf." *SCA,* 8-7-1872, p. 122; 10-14-1874, p. 162.

Stillwell, William R.
Co. F, 53rd GA Reg., CSA; lost a foot at Cedar Creek, VA 10-19-1864.

Stinchoome, G. W. (1835 - 7-7-1872)
d. Fayette Co., GA; lp 1868.

Stipe, John W.
m1/ Arminda Parker (1839 - 10-9-1868) dau. of Wm. H. Parker.

"Franklin Cir. & Henderson Mis." *SCA*, 9-2-1874, p. 138; 11-4-1874, p. 174.

Stockdale, James S.
"Saluda Cir., SC." *CA*, 11-5-1830, p. 38.

Stockton, J. T.
*see Stockton, Joseph H., *MPG*, p. 532.

failed of admission to the N. GA Conf. at its last session (1873) due to the crowded state of their ranks, assigned to a cir. in AR.

Stokes, David C.
Co. A, 7th GA Reg., CSA; Chap. 1864; was MPC preacher after the war.

Stokes, James M.
Chap. 3rd GA Vol., CSA.

"Army of Northern VA." *SCA*, 6-4-1863, p. 74.
"Testimony From the Camp." *SCA*, 9-4-1862, p. 134.
"Newnansville, FL." *SCA*, 7-26-1871, p. 118.
"From Gen. Lee's Army." *SCA*, 4-28-1864, np.
"The Work in Gen. Lee's Army." *SCA*, 2-11-1864, np.
"Sylvania Cir., GA Conf." *SCA*, 8-17-1866, p. 4; 9-7-1866, fp;
          11-30-1866, fp; 10-25-1867, p. 170.
"Letter from MO." *SCA*, 8-5-1870, p. 122.

Stone, George W.W.
Co. I, 9th GA Reg., CSA.

Stone, William
7-13-1827, letter to Chas. Hardy, Pensacola, FL, re church in Savannah. (Wof.).

Story, William
Co. I, 2nd GA Reg.

Strange, Leander A. (d. 1876)
(L) on Springfield Cir.

Strickland, John
Chap., 40th GA Reg., CSA.
widow Susan (1799 - 4-20-1869), Gordon Co., GA. 5 chrn.

"Ellijay Mis., GA." *SCA,* 10-3-1851, p. 70.

Striplin, B. O. (8-15-1788 - 6-19-1870)
b. York Dist., SC; d. Huntsville, AL; m1/ Elizabeth R. Steward; 1879
moved to Morgan Co., GA & Rehoboth Church, was le; 1834 moved
to Benton, now Calhoun Co., AL; 1835 lp; 1839 moved to Randolph
now Cleberne Co., AL. Only le in GA.

Stripling, David (9-4-1806 - 8-13-1882)
b. Carroll Co., GA; bur. Smyrna Church, Carroll Co., GA.m/11-23-1828,
Ann Mason (Dunn) Butler (5-11-1802 - 6-11-1876) of London, England,
dau. of Geo. & Ann Butler. Came to America 1826, d. Carrollton, GA;
chrn. Henry Marcus, 1830; Frances, 1832; Catherine H. (4-21-1834 -
7-18-1877); Mary, 1836; Rev. Robt., 1838; Rev. James W.G.,1840;
Martha, 1842.

An acct. of his death is found in Roberson, J.A. *Shiloh Campground
1867-1938.* bur. Smyrna UMC between Bowdon Junction & Carrollton, GA.
1870 Census of Carroll Co. mentions: Ann, 1802; Catherine, 1834; Martha,
1844; Mary, 1837; Josephine Bevins, 1861; Warren Thomas, 1850.

"Houston Mis., N. Ga Conf." *SCA,* 10-25-1867, p. 170.

Stripling, James (1808 - 8-7-1867)
b. Jones Co., GA; he formed the society at Concord, Carrollton Cir.

Stripling, Robert
See: 1860 Census, Heard Co., GA.

"Meriwether Mis., GA Conf. *SCA,* 5-14-1847, p. 194; 10-8-1847, p. 70;
8-11-1848, p. 38.

"Clarkesville Cir., GA." *SCA*, 10-18-1839, p. 70.
"Elberton Cir., GA." *SCA*, 8-19-1842, p. 39.
"Fayetteville, N. GA Conf." *SCA*, 11-20-1868, p. 186.

Strozier, Henry M.
educated, Emory College; m/6-2-1887, Lena Claude Armor (7-9-1862 - 11-14-1893), dau. of William Armor & Rebecca Winfield. chrn. Hallie, 6-28-1888; Alberta, 9-16-1890; Mary Nettie, 6-21-1892. m2/ 4-5-1896, Ola Teasley. chrn. William Alfred, 1-31-1897; Josiah Lewis, 4-12-1900; Henry Milton, Jr., 1-6-1906.

Stubbs, Samuel W.
"Trinity Cir., S. GA Conf." *SCA*, 11-13-1877, p. 182.

Sullivan, James N.
"Elijay Mis. N. GA Conf." *SCA*, 10-29-1869, p. 175; 2-11-1874, p. 22.
"Ellijay Cir. & Mis." *SCA*, 9-2-1874, p. 138.
"Spring Place, N. GA Conf." *SCA*, 8-11-1875, p. 126.

Summerhill, Warren   (4-23-1816 - 1867)
d. Paulding Co., GA, son of Jas. Summerhill, early settler of Cobb Co., GA who was mysteriously murdered ner his home. b. Sptbg. Dist., SC; joined church Oct. 1841.

Sutton, H. Howard
uv. as a Meth. minister.

"Protracted Meeting at Warsaw, Forsyth Co., GA." *SCA*, 11-29-1839, p. 95.

Swearington, Bolin
Papers relating to his affair with Tillman Snead, 1829-30. (Wof.).

Excerpts from the Memoirs of James Rowe Coombs, 1867-72, of Tarversville, Twiggs Co., GA, p. 30f. Original at Washington Mem. Library, Macon, GA.

(describes Swearington/Swearinger as a schoolteacher and a Meth. preacher of the primitive sort. Ends: "He stopped somewhere near Jackson, MS, where sad to tell, I know not whether by influences of the natural evil spirit, or whether by an unnatural distortion of temperment, caused by the fate of his sons. This old man deserted the ranks of Methodism, in which as a soldier he had fought many hard battles, and adorned his brow with many a wreath. And now, while even he was standing upon the verge of the grave side by side with his companion, he threw down the battle-axe of Methodism, and grasped the Sword, small though keen, of Universalism, standing side by side with those who had often withstood his powerful charge, while battling for the cause of Peter).

Sweet, Stephen S.
"Revivals in Burke Co., S. GA. Conf." *SCA*, 8-20-1869, p. 134.
"The Old & The New." *SCA*, 3-18-1870, p. 42.
"Our Philadelphia Letter." *SCA*, 8-5-1870, p. 122.
"Mt. Moriah Campmeeting." *SCA*, 9-30-1870, p. 154.
"Haynesville Cir., S. GA Conf." *SCA*, 9-27-1871, p. 155; 10-25-1871, p. 170.
"Henderson, S. GA Conf." *SCA*, 9-20-1871, p. 151.
"Another Year." *SCA*, 8-11-1871, p. 178.
"Quitman, GA." *SCA*, 5-1-1872, p. 66.
"Brunswick Dist. Conf." *SCA*, 5-8-1872, p. 70.
"Laying the Cornerstone." *SCA*, 5-15-1872, p. 74.
"Home Again." *SCA*, 6-12-1872, p. 90.
"Warm Weather Work." *SCA*, 6-26-1872, fp; 7-17-1872, fp.
"From the Low Country." *SCA*, 8-21-1872, p. 130; 5-7-1873, p. 70.
"Thomasville Dist., S. GA Conf." *SCA*, 10-29-1873, p. 167.
"East Macon & City Mis." *SCA*, 12-9-1874, p. 194.
"Savannah." *SCA*, 5-1-1877, p. 70.

Talbot, James C.   (d. 1840)
of Wilkes Co., GA. m/ 1829, Sarah A. Phillips, d. 12-21-1877, dau. of Geo. & Sarah Phillips of VA. 6 chrn. She m2/ Rev. Henry Morton, d. 1863.

Talley, Alexander
"New Home of the Choctaw." *CA*, 7-29-1831, p. 190.
"Choctaw Mis." *CA*, 5-27-1831, p. 154.
"West Choctaw Mis." *CA*, 11-25-1831, p. 50; 3-23-1832, p. 118.

Talley, John W.
attended school at Salem, Clarke Co., GA; siblings b. in VA were Wm. Southerlin, Alexander, Nicholas, Caleb & Elkanah; siblings b. in Greene Co., GA were Nathan & Elizabeth.

"Sandersville Cir., GA Conf." *SCA*, 8-8-1844, p. 33.
"Monticello Cir., GA Conf." *SCA*, 8-2-1844, p. 29.
"Eatonton Cir., GA Conf." *SCA*, 8-16-1844, p. 37.

"Twiggs & Wilkinson Cir., GA Conf." *SCA*, 8-30-1844, p. 45.
"LaGrange, GA, 3rd Quar. Meeting." *SCA*, 9-15-1848, p. 58.
"Troup Circuit, GA." *SCA*, 10-25-1850, p. 79.
"The Missionary Spirit in Newnan Cir., GA." *SCA*, 8-20-1851,
        p. 50; 4-30-1852, p. 190.
"Macon Dist., GA." *SCA*, 11-24-1843, p. 95.
"Sparta Cir., GA." *SCA*, 9-16-1842, p. 55.
"Springfield Cir., Scriven Co., GA." *SCA*, 6-7-1839, p. 203.
"Savannah Dist., GA." *SCA*, 10-28-1837, p. 74.
"Newton Cir., GA Conf." *SCA*, 9-30-1858, p. 71.
"Wheat's Campmeeting, Lincoln Co., GA." *SCA*, 8-7-1856, p. 39.
"Letter from Warrenton, VA." *SCA*, 10-23-1862, fp.
"Dry Pond Camp Meeting." *SCA*, 10-29-1857, p. 87.
"Reminiscences." *SCA*, 6-30-1875, fp.
"Lowndes & Echols Mis." *SCA*, 9-19-1876, p. 150.

Harrell, William A. (ed.). "Excerpts From The Writings Of
        The Reverend John W. Talley." *HH*, (in 6 issues,
        1981 - 1983, being parts of his journal).

Talley, Nathan
m/ Martha H. Travis, d. 7-12-1873, Clinch Co., GA.
m2/ 5-31-1874, Stockton, GA, Rachel Vanguson.

Talley, Nicholas
wife, Amy Ann Potter (12-7-1801 - 2-20-1873), b. Brunswick Co., NC;
bur. Washington St. Cem., Columbia, SC; dau. of Samuel & Ann Porter.

ref. to building a meetinghouse in 1816 called Bethlehem.
        see: Jenkins, James. *Experiences,* etc., p. 177.

"Quarterly Conference, Union Circuit, SC." *SCA*, 8-16-1844. p. 39.
"Greenville Cir., SC Conf." *SCA*, 8-30-1844, p. 45; 10-11-1844, p. 69.
"Newberry Cir., SC Conf." *SCA*, 10-11-1844, p. 69.
"Pendleton Cir., SC Conf." *SCA*, 10-11-1844, p. 69.
"Charleston Dist." *SCA*, 8-5-1837, p. 26; 11-17-1837, p. 86.
"Trinity & Cumberland St. Churches, Charleston." *SCA*, 8-24-1838, p. 38.
"Cokesbury." *SCA*, 7-16-1841, p. 19; 10-28-1842, p. 77.
"Reminiscences of Early Methodists in SC Conf." (series). *SCA*,
        2-24-1859, fp.

Talley, William R.
"Haw River Cir., AL Conf." *SCA,* 11-6-1862, p. 171.
"Greenwood Cir., GA Conf." *SCA,* 11-17-1864, np.

Tarpley, Joseph
2-25-1824, receipt of note. (Wof.).

Travis, Joseph. *Autobiography,* pp. 215-217.

Tarrant, John
12-7-1833, recom. by Saluda Circuit to itinerate; 10-25-1824,
recom. by Newberry Circuit same. (Wof.).

Tatom, Abel
"Orange Mission, FL." *SCA,* 10-22-1847, p. 78.
"Chattahoochee Mis., AL." *SCA,* 6-24-1853, p. 14.
"Chunnenuggee Mis. to Blacks, AL." *SCA,* 6-23-1854, p. 10.

Taylor, John H.
Chap., 35th GA Reg., CSA.

Taylor, John J.
"Telfair Circuit, GA." *SCA,* 9-13-1839, pp. 50-51; 12-6-1839, p. 99.
"Ossabaw Mission, GA Conf." *SCA,* 7-2-1841, p. 10.

Taylor, Thomas
"Spring Creek Mis., FL Conf." *SCA,* 7-2-1847, p. 186.
"Santatee Mis., FL." *SCA,* 10-31-1851, p. 86; 12-5-1851, p. 106.
"Hernando Mis., FL." *SCA,* 4-29-1853, p. 194.
"Gadsden Mis., FL." *SCA,* 5-28-1841, p. 198; 9-17-1841, p. 54;
      11-5-1841, p. 82.

Thigpen, Alexander M.
Chap., 6th GA Reg., CSA.

"Clarkesville Cir., GA Conf." *SCA,* 9-22-1859, p. 275.
"Clinton Cir., GA Conf." *SCA,* 11-13-1856, p. 95.
"From Gen. Colquitt's Brigade." (series). *SCA,* 5-19-1864, np.
"The Work Goes On." *SCA,* 7-21-1864, np.
"Rome, N. GA Conf." *SCA,* 9-27-1867, p. 154.
"West Point, GA." *SCA,* 9-24-1869, p. 155.
"Memoirs of our Deceased Ministers." *SCA,* 9-2-1870, fp.

"Greenville, GA." *SCA,* 11-18-1870, p. 182.
"The LaGrange Dist. SS Convention." *SCA,* 6-17-1874, p. 94.
"Newnan, N. GA Conf." *SCA,* 7-1-1874, p. 102.
"Cedartown, N. GA Conf." *SCA,* 10-3-1876, p. 159.

Thomas, Allen C.
m1/ 4-18-1872, Nannie H. Hubert of Warrenton, GA.

"Crawfordville Circuit." *SCA,* 5-3-1871, p. 70; 8-28-1872, p. 134.
"Payne's Chapel, Atlanta, GA." *SCA,* 6-17-1874, p. 95.
"Calhoun Cir., N. GA Conf." *SCA,* 6-16-1875, p. 94; 10-6-1875, p. 158.

Thomas, B.T.
"Hall Cir., N. GA Conf." *SCA,* 8-21-1872, p. 130; 9-25-1872, p. 150.

Thomas, Charles W.
went to the Episcopal Church. See: Burke, *Autobiography,* p. 103.

"Western Africa & Its Islands." (series). *SCA,* see: 9-23-1858, fp.
"Canary Islands." (series). *SCA,* 11-25-1858, fp.
"West Coast of Africa." (series). *SCA,* 12-23-1858, fp.

Thomas, George W.
wife, Mary Frances Payne, d. 8-23-1893.

"Subligna Cir., N. GA Conf." *SCA,* 9-23-1874, p. 150; 10-14-1874, p. 162.
"Dalton Cir., N. GA Conf." *SCA,* 10-27-1875, p. 171.
"Ringgold Cir., N. GA Conf." *SCA,* 11-21-1876, p. 186.

Thomas, James R.
"Wright's Improved Cotton Screw." *SCA,* 8-10-1866, p. 7.

Thomas, Joseph A.
"Sermon." found by preachers in the Centennial Anniversary of
Mt. Pleasant MC, Oglethorpe Co., GA. 1920, Atlanta, GA by
C.C. Cary. pp. 67-71.

Thomas, William H.
"Hiwassee Mis., GA." *SCA,* 6-22-1849, p. 10; 11-16-1849, 96.
"Murphy Mis., GA Conf." *SCA,* 7-19-1850, p. 26; 11-1-1850, p. 86.
"Ellijay Mis." *SCA,* 11-26-1852, p. 106.
"Clayton Mis., GA." *SCA,* 6-23-1854, p. 10.

"The Clayton Church." *SCA*, 6-28-1855, p. 15.
"Waresboro Cir., GA Conf." *SCA*, 9-22-1859, p. 275.
"Another Appeal For Clayton Church." *SCA*, 6-19-1856, fp.
"A Federal Raid." *SCA*, 2-26-1863, p. 32.
"Brunswick Dist., FL Conf." *SCA*, 7-27-1866, p. 5.
"Centervillage, S. GA Conf." *SCA*, 10-2-1872, p. 154.

Thomas, William Hannibal (1843 - 1935) (MEC)(N)
t/f Central Ohio Conf. 1872; 1872 principal of Rome Normal School, Rome, GA; 1873, Clark Theological Seminary; Oct. 1873, arrested for stealing money from the seminary.

Thomasson, William B.
Chap., 41st GA Reg., CSA.

Thompson, David
"Chattahoochee Mis.." *SCA*, 6-24-1842, p. 6.
"Burke Mis., GA." *SCA*, 5-12-1843, p. 188; 9-22-1843, p. 58.

Thompson, George C.
"St. Mary's, GA." *SCA*, 12-18-1877, p. 202.

Thompson, Robert
wife Milly d. 6-8-1867, Emanuel Co., GA.

Thomson, Thomas H.
"Finding The Unsought God." *WCA*, v101, n3, 7-16-1937, p. 9.

Thornburg, Amos
"Lookout Mtn. Cir. Again." *SCA*, 10-18-1871, p. 166.

Thornton, James A.
Co. A, 1st Reg., 1st Brigade, GA State Troops; Co. K, 54th GA Reg., CSA; Co. C, 1st Btn. GA Sharpshooters; wounded & disabled Chickamauga, 9-19-1863.

Thrasher, Alexander Barton (5-12-1824 - 6-29-1904)
son of Augustus Thrasher; school teacher, Judge, first Ordinary of McDuffie
Co., GA; m/ 5-5-1849, Mary Ann Smith, dau. of Mrs. Elizabeth (Blythe)
Smith who lived near Liberty, Greene Co., GA. bur. Thomson City Cem.
8 chrn., 3 lived to adulthood: Willie m/ James W. Boatright; Mamie m/ J.E.
Wilkerson; Alex.

"Warrenton Cir., GA Conf." *SCA*, 11-4-1858, p. 90.

Thrower, Osgood A.
"Cave Spring Cir., N. GA Conf." *SCA*, 2-5-1878, p. 18.

Thurman, John M.   (MPC)
bur. Smith's Chapel MPC near Bowden, GA; founded Mt. Pleasant MPC.

Ticer, Hugh   (1-3-1791 - 12-24-1870)
d. Warren Co., GA; cvt. Columbus, GA.

Tignor, Urban Cooper   (10-16-1809 - 9-2-1873)
b. Clarke Co., GA; d. Talbot Co., GA; son of Philip Tignor; m/ 12-23-1830,
Susannah Slaton; nv Susannah Rosamond (11-27-1805 - 9-14-1873),
b. Wilkes Co., GA; d. Talbot Co., GA.

lp 11-13-1841.

Tignor, Young F.
"Muscogee Cir., GA." *SCA*, 6-16-1843, p. 3; 8-18-1843, p. 39.

Timmons, B. E. L.
m1/ Lucy C.H. Menifee.

"Pleasant Grove Cir., S. GA Conf." *SCA*, 9-24-1869, p. 155.
"Cave Spring Cir., N. GA Conf." *SCA*, 10-20-1875, p. 166.

Timmons, D.F.C.
"Monroe Cir., N. GA Conf." *SCA*, 11-3-1875, p. 174; 8-14-1877, p. 130;
    2-19-1878, p. 26.

Timmons, Robert A.
"Hatchett Creek Cir., AL Conf." *SCA*, 9-10-1863, bp.
"Arbacoochee Cir., AL Conf." *SCA*, 7-28-1864, np.

Timmons, Thomas H.
m1/ 10-27-1870, Mary E. Booth of Madison, GA.
a wife d. in Sparta, GA, 5-1-1885. 5 chrn.

"Bowdon, N. GA Conf." *SCA*, 9-3-1869, p. 142.

Timmons, William   (1-18-1799 - 9-18-1877)
b. Hancock Co., Ga; d. Cave Spring, GA; father of BEL & TH Timmons; cvt.
under Lovick Pierce 1824; m1/ Mrs. P.A. Alford; m2/ Mrs. M.B. Ellison.
Co. G, 23rd GA Reg., CSA.

a charter member of Old Camp, Carroll Co., GA.

"Carrollton Cir., GA Conf." *SCA*, 9-17-1857, p. 63.

Tinley, James W.
The Influence of a Single Life. Pickett Pub., Louisville. 1902.
The Power That Prevailed. Pickett Pub., Louisville. 1906.

Todd, Alexander   (d. 1862)
d. Winchester, VA; Co. B, 22nd GA Reg., CSA.

Toole, Charles J.
m/ 1-17-1877, Loula P. Jones, dau. of Elias Jones, decd.

"The Altamaha Dist. Conf." *SCA*, 8-16-1871, p. 130.
"Swainsboro Cir., S. GA Conf." *SCA*, 9-25-1872, p. 150.
"The Macon Dist. Conf." *SCA*, 7-22-1874, p. 114.
"Macon Cir., S. GA Conf." *SCA*, 8-19-1874, p. 130.

Townsend, Joel W.
m2/ Maria Black, (1804 - 7-24-1875), Cokesbury, SC.

"Barnwell Cir., SC." *SCA*, 10-11-1839, p. 67; 12-27-1839, p. 111.
"Orangeburg Cir., SC." *SCA*, 9-16-1842, p. 55; 10-14-1842, p. 71.

Trammell, William H.
"Lincolnton Cir., N. GA Conf." *SCA*, 10-16-1877, p. 166.

Travis, John S. (3-10-1806 - 6-4-1876)
b. Warren Co., GA; d. Atlanta, GA; lp 6-30-1860; m1/ 1836, Eldesa
Parker, dau. of Rev. W.C. Parker; m2/ 9-29-1845, Elizabeth Smith of
Griffin, GA. bur. Griffin, GA.

Travis, Joseph
m1/ 5-1-1811, Elizabeth Forster, (d. 1843); dau. of Col. Foster of
Brunswick Co., NC. child b. 1812; Mary Ann Eliza (6-17-1817 -
1-25-1847). wife had a bro., Rev. Anthony Forster, Congregational
minister in Charleston, SC. m2/ 5-13-1845, Mary Smith Butler of
Giles Co.,TN, age 45.

"Our Book Concern." (series). see: *SCA*, 3-11-1858, p. 163.

Traywick, James W.
Chap. CSA.

Treadway, James M. (6-22-1813 - 6-16-1872)
le age 18; lived in Troup, Cherokee & Floyd cos., GA; in AL during War;
"after serving the church, he declined in piety, lived a wicked and worldly
life, and lived 4 years out of the church." Cpl. 51st GA Reg., CSA; d. in
prison. (or so says one source).

Triggs, John J.
"Waynesboro Cir., GA." *SCA*, 11-8-1839, p. 83.

Trimble, Isaac Newton
bur. Mt. Zion UMC, Carroll Co., GA. left autob.

Temple, Robert M., Jr. *Florida Flame*. pp. 31-32.

Trussell, Claiborne
bur. Wesley Chapel, Villa Rica, GA.

"Jackson Cir., GA Conf." *SCA*, 10-25-1850, p. 79.
"Powder Springs & Dallas, GA Conf." *SCA*, 10-12-1866, p. 5.

Tucker, Epps   (MPC) (CMC)
d. Chambers Co., AL; first Pres. of GA Conf., MPC.

Tucker, Reuben

12-30-1818, Camden committee to examine the opinions of his. Report respecting doctrines of original sin and sanctification. 2-8-1825, letter to SC Conf. at Willington containing charges against him. (Wof.).

Lawrence, Harold. *The Tucker Band.* Boyd PC. 1992.

Tucker, Summerfield N.

"Worth Mis., S. GA Conf." *SCA,* 8-19-1874, p. 130.

Tumlin, George W.

bur. Hollywood Cem., Tallaposa, GA. m/ Verlona Taylor (1-3-1871 - 9-28-1947)/

Tumlin, Jasper Milton

son of John Russell Tumlin; m/ Mattie Melissa Perkins; chrn. Winfred; Mattie May; Mozelle, b. 1885 (Meth. Missionary); Scott Asbury (12-14-1887 - 5-30-1888).

Tumlin, John Russell

entered as John B. on p. 563 of text; error accd. to family. b. Lumpkin Co., not Lincoln; son of Wm. H. Tumlin (1801 - 1860); chrn. William Liles (1855 - 2925); Sarah, 1856; Jasper Milton (9-8-1858 - 5-29-1945); George W. (6-27-1863 - 6-8-1928); John Calvin (1866 - 1935); Ellen Jane; Phobie; Florence.

Turner, Allen

m/ Martha Murray (1795 - 2-20-1874), d. Senoia, GA.

7-29-1822, acct. w/ book concern. (Wof.).

"Apalachicola, FL." *SCA,* 4-30-1847, p. 186.
"Little River Mis. among the Blacks in GA." *CA,* 12-16-1831, p. 62.
"Warrenton Cir., GA." *SCA,* 9-15-1848, p. 58.
"The Work In Madison, FL." *SCA,* 7-19-1855, p. 27.
"Letter From GA." *SCA,* 10-16-1856, p. 79.
"Covington Cir., GA Conf." *SCA,* 11-6-1856, p. 91; 10-1-1857, p. 73.
"Old Methodism Restored." *SCA,* 7-2-1857, p. 18-19.
"I Am Astonished Beyond Measure." *SCA,* 1-21-1864, np.

"Class Meetings." *SCA*, 2-16-1866, fp.
"Our Decline As A Church, The Cause." *SCA*, 3-2-1866, bp.
"Results of the Church's Defection." *SCA*, 4—6-1866, bp.

Turner, Isham
"Flint River Mis., GA Conf." *SCA*, 6-30-1848, p. 14.

Turner, Jackson P.
"Marietta Cir., GA." *SCA*, 8-14-1846, p. 39.
"Ellijay Mis., GA Conf." *SCA*, 6-8-1849, p. 2.

Turner, James R.
Co. C, 56th GA Reg., CSA. d. in service.

Turner, John W.
m/ 5-4-1869, Mary J. Hunnicutt of Coweta Co., GA.

"Palmetto Cir., GA Conf." *SCA*, 9-9-1858, p. 59.
"Hinesville Cir., GA Conf." *SCA*, 9-15-1859, p. 271.
"Gainesville Cir., GA Conf." *SCA*, 10-30-1856, p. 87.
"Our People Seem To Have Deserted Us." *SCA*, 3-19-1863, p.45.
"Dahlonega Cir., GA Conf." *SCA*, 10-29-1857, p. 87.
"Savannah Army Mission." *SCA*, 3-10-1864, np.
"The Desolations of War." *SCA*, 6-23-1864, np.
"Letter from Dalton, GA." *SCA*, 9-13-1867, p. 138.
"Sabbath School at Palmetto." *SCA*, 1-17-1868, p. 10.
"Griffin Dist. Meeting." *SCA*, 7-31-1868, p. 122.
"Fayetteville Cir., N. GA Conf." *SCA*, 10-1-1869, p. 158.

Turner, Joseph T.
"Chattahoochee Mis. to Blacks." *SCA*, 8-14-1846, p. 38; 8-6-1847,
      p. 34; 7-5-1855, p. 19.
"Chattahoochee Mis., GA." *SCA*, 6-30-1843, p. 10.

Turner, Julius C.
Co. C, 12th GA Reg., CSA.

Turner, Thomas
bur. Wesley Chapel MC, Villa Rica, GA. bro. of Jas. R. Turner.

"Carrollton Mis., GA." *SCA*, 9-23-1853, p. 66.

Turner, Thomas, Jr.
"Putnam Mis., GA Conf." *SCA*, 6-16-1848, p. 6; 9-15-1848, p. 58.

Turner, William K.
"St. John's Mis., FL Conf." *SCA*, 5-4-1855, p. 191.
"Hamilton Cir., FL Conf." *SCA*, 10-8-1857, p. 75.
"Micanopy, E. FL." *SCA*, 10-5-1866, p. 5.

Turner, William S.
"Elberton Cir., GA." *SCA*, 11-1-1855, p. 87.
"Oglethorpe & Traveler's Rest, GA Conf." *SCA*, 8-18-1859, p. 254.
"Newnan Cir., GA Conf." *SCA*, 9-18-1856, p. 63.
"Bellview Cir., GA Conf." *SCA*, 9-1-1864, np.
"No License in Dooly County." *SCA*, 4-27-1866, bp.

Turrentine, Morgan C.
"Cape Fear Mis., SC." *SCA*, 9-13-1844, p. 54; 8-14-1846, p. 38;
  9-3-1847, p. 50.
"Lynch's Creek letter. *CA*, 11-26-1830, p. 50.
"Bladen Cir., NC." *CA*, 1-13-1831, p. 78.
"Cape Fear Mis., SC." *SCA*, 9-17-1841, p. 54; 12-31-1841, p. 114;
  6-24-1842, p. 6; 9-30-1842, p. 62; 12-30-1842, p. 112.
"LaFayette Cir., AL Conf." *SCA*, 10-2-1862, p. 151.

Tweedle, A.W.
wife d. 8-3-1877, Gordon Co., GA.

Twitty, Peter S.
bur. Dublin lst UMC, Dublin, GA. 1Sgt. Co.K., 4th GA Vol. Inf. CSA.
m/ Rebecca Smith (5-1-1845 - 12-10-1903).

"Camilla & Newton Cir." *SCA*, 10-21-1874, p. 167.
"Fort Gaines & Blakely, S. GA Conf." *SCA*, 8-18-1875, p. 130.

Tydings, Richard M.
m/ 5-2-1860, Louisa H. Bryant.

"Bainbridge Station, FL Conf." *SCA*, 12-29-1859, p. 330.
"Ocilla Colored Mis., FL Conf." *SCA*, 5-6-1858, p. 195.
"Jacksonville Dist., FL Conf." *SCA*, 5-7-1857, p. 195; 7-30-1857, p.37;
  9-24-1857, p. 67.

"Waukeenah Cir., FL Conf." *SCA*, 11-22-1867, p. 186.
"Madison & Bellville Cir., FL Conf." *SCA*, 10-29-1869, p. 175.

Tyler, Henry (12-25-1812 - 10-4-1876)

b. Elbert Co., GA; d. Hart Co., GA; cvt. age 15; joined at Mt. Zion, Clarke Co., GA; 1831 CL; le 1832; lp 1833; lst sermon preached at Bethlehem, Walton Co., GA, 11-21-1833 on Matt. 5:16; his last was at Hartwell, 7-16-1876, on Heb. 2:8. m/1-19-1838, Patience S. Reeves of Anderson, SC. 3 chrn.

Tyner, E.S.

"Live Oak, FL Conf." *SCA*, 9-4-1872, p. 138-139.

Tyson, Isaac P.

"Paper on Evangelism." *WCA*, v102, n34, 2-17-1939, pp. 7, 11, 13.

Underwood, Marion L.

"Great Revivals in the Cleveland Cir." *SCA*, 8-20-1873, p. 130.
"Gainesville Cir., N. GA Conf." *SCA*, 8-12-1874, p. 126.
"Dahlonega, GA." *SCA*, 5-5-1875, p. 70.
"Douglasville Cir., N. GA Conf." *SCA*, 8-1-1876, p. 122.
"Ringgold, N. GA Conf." *SCA*, 4-30-1878, p. 66.

Urquhart, J. F.

"Albany, GA." *SCA*, 6-9-1864, np.

Varner, James O.

a preacher on the Marietta Circuit in 1852.

Venable, Gus F.

"Call of the World for Men & Women." found by preachers in the Centennial Anniversary of Mt. Pleasant MC, Oglethorpe Co., 1920. Atlanta, GA, by C.C. Cary. pp. 56-59, 62-65.
"Fire On Earth." *WCA*, v101, n38, 3-25-1938, p. 16.
"The New Financial Plan - Diagnosis." *WCA*, v99, n42, 1934, pp. 6-7, 15.

Vestal, John M.

"Marietta Cir., GA." *SCA*, 8-27-1841, p. 43.
"Fayetteville & Zebulon Cir., GA." *SCA*, 8-19-1842, p. 39.

Vickory, Green
nv. Vickery. bur. Bethel, Coweta Co., GA.

Vinson, John
m/ 1796, Margaret ? (1781 - 7-23-1856), b. MD. She moved to GA as a child; joined MEC at Smyrna, Hancock Co., GA. chrn. Tully, John, Ebenezer, Martha, Levinia, Louisa.

Wade, James
b. VA; a cousin of John B. Wade. age 51 in 1850 Franklin Co. Census. living w/ Nancy 46; Joshua A. 20; John F. 18; Sarah A.C. 15; Elizabeth 13; William P. 11; James B. 9; Martha 7; John W. 5; Thomas W. 2.

Wade, John B.   (4-23-1789 - 1874)
b. Bedford Co., VA; came to GA w/ his widowed mother 1801; cvt. 1801, Coldwater; le 1812; lp 1824; Deacon 1833; Elder 1853; Tribute Elbert Cir.

bur. Providence Cem., Hart Co., GA. Grave destroyed, date of death unk. Alive in 1850 (Franklin Co. Census), listed as b. in VA & living w/ Emilia 55, Wesley G. 30 & Elizabeth Mulkey 25. Son of Anne Wade (1764 - 6-18-1849) also bur. Providence.

Wade, John B.
*date does not conform w/ data on above entry.

m/ 6-11-1871, Mrs. Kizziah Pledger of Elbert Co., GA.

Wade, Peyton L.   (d. 1867)

Wadsworth, Willard W.
"Covington & Mt. Pleasant, N. GA Conf." *SCA*, 10-2-1872, p. 154; 9-30-1873, p. 138.
"Atlanta Dist. Conf." *SCA*, 7-9-1873, p. 106.
"Gainesville, N. Ga Conf." *SCA*, 2-19-1878, p. 26; 4-30-1878, p. 66.

Walker, J.G.   (6-8-1816 - 8-26-1893)
(L). b. Lincoln Co., GA; d. Spring Hill Cir.

Walker, Jackson   (d.10-12-1886)

Walker, Jeremiah S.
Co. B, 56th GA Reg., CSA.

Walker, Robert J.
"Cusseta Cir., N. GA Conf." *SCA*, 4-17-1877, p. 62.
"Cusseta Campmeeting." *SCA*, 9-11-1877, p. 146.

Walker, William D.
Co. K, 31st GA Reg., CSA.

Walton, Fletcher
m/ 12-23-1888, at the home of Frank Vonberg, Spring Place, GA, May Anderson of Spring Place.

Wardlaw, John B.
"Revival in Ft. Valley Cir." *SCA*, 7-26-1855, p. 31.
"Culloden Cir., GA Conf." *SCA*, 10-16-1856, p. 79.
"Buena Vista Cir., GA Conf." *SCA*, 9-3-1857, p. 55.
"Oglethorpe Cir., S. GA Conf." *SCA*, 8-5-1874, p. 122; 9-2-1874, p. 138; 9-16-1874, p. 147; 8-19-1874, p. 131.
"Cusseta Cir., S. GA Conf." *SCA*, 9-29-1875, p. 154.

Wardlaw, Joseph P.
"Meriwether Mis., GA Conf." *SCA*, 6-19-1846, p. 4.

Wardlaw, William J.
m/ 8-4-1836, Mary Poor (6-30-1820 - 2-11-1871), b. SC; d. Fulton Co., GA.

"Factory Mis., Columbus, GA." *SCA*, 4-21-1859, p. 187.
"East Point, GA." *SCA*, 9-23-1870, p. 150.
"Conyers Cir., N. GA Conf." *SCA*, 9-25-1872, p. 150.
"Bethel Cir. (Americus Dist.), S. GA Conf." *SCA*, 8-8-1876, p. 126.

Ware, James R. (9-5-1807 - 5-19-1893)
b. Wilkes Co., GA; d. Columbus, GA.

Ware, Nicholas C.
m/ Matilda ? (12-18-1818 - 1-31-1885) b. Lincoln Co., GA; d. Wilkes Co., GA.

"Two Classes of Ministers, Efficient & Inefficient." *SCA*, 2-15-1871, fp.
"Facts & Stubborn Things." (series). *SCA*, 2-7-1872, fp.

Warnock, J.
"Savannah River Mis." *SCA*, 6-19-1846, p. 4.

Warwick, Loy
"The Psalms In Human Life." *WCA*, v100, n43, 4-30-1937, pp. 11, 14.

Warwick, Wiley
1-23-1828, letter to SC Conf. (Wof.).

Waters, Andrew J.
"Silver Creek Cir., N. GA Conf." *SCA*, 9-4-1877, p. 142.

Watkins, Benjamin E. (8-18-1800 - 11-26-1876)
b. Whitly Co., KY; d. Colquitt Co., GA; cvt. Wall Ck. CG 1839; le 1840; preached 6-7 yrs. in KY; moved to AL where he organized many churches; moved to Colquitt Co., GA 1863.

Watkins, John W.G.
"Danielsville Cir., N. GA Conf." *SCA*, 12-5-1876, p. 194.

Watson, George, Jr. (12-24-1811 - 3-22-1868)
b. Maine; grad. West Point; le Newnansville St., FL; lp. 1839; teaching; 1851-60, lived in Roxbury, MD.

Watts, George (6-11-1796 - 4-18-1881)   (MEC)(MECS)
bv. 1-11-1796. b. Fairfield Dist., SC; m/ Jasper Co., GA, 4-4-1822, Mary Ann Dawson (1-29-1806 - 5-20-1881), b. Fairfield Dist., SC. One child was Rev. William M. Watts of FL Conf.

(L) GEORGIA CONFERENCE: 1843 Deacon (E); 1849 Elder (E).
joined MEC at Poplar Springs, Hall Co., GA.

Watts, William M.
"Sumter & Lee Colored Mis., GA." *SCA*, 7-28-1854, p. 30.
"Fayetteville Cir., GA Conf." *SCA*, 11-5-1857, p. 91.
"Liberty Cir., GA Conf." *SCA*, 7-27-1866, p. 5.

Weathers, Charles V.
m/ 12-28-1884, ? (9-24-1862 - 11-29-1934), b. Monroe Co., GA, a dau. of Azariah & Elizabeth Bostwick.

Weaver, Shelton R.
bur. New Hope, Miller Co., GA on 11-2-1888.

"Leon Cir., GA Conf." *SCA*, 10-16-1862, fp.
"Division of the GA Conf." *SCA*, 11-30-1866, p. 2.
"Florence Cir., S. GA Conf." *SCA*, 10-9-1868, p. 162; 11-12-1869, p. 183; 10-7-1870, p. 153.
"Geneva Cir., S. GA Conf." *SCA*, 8-11-1871, p. 179.
"Springvale Cir., S. GA Conf." *SCA*, 10-1-1873, p. 155.

Weems, David J.
m/ Lula L. Burch.

"Tilton & Resaca Cir." *SCA*, 10-18-1871, p. 166.
"Rock Springs Cir., Dalton Dist., N. GA Conf." *SCA*, 10-30-1872, p. 170.
"Ringgold Cir., N. GA Conf." *SCA*, 11-5-1873, p. 171.
"Dalton Cir., N. GA Conf." *SCA*, 11-25-1874, p. 186.
"Forestville Cir., N. GA Conf." *SCA*, 9-22-1875, p. 152.
"Powder Springs Cir., N. GA Conf." *SCA*, 9-18-1877, p. 150.

Wells, Elijah
"ME Church, Talbotton, GA." *SCA*, 8-2-1844, pp. 29-30.

Wesley, Robert M.
b. in either Newton or Henry Co. as Rockdale was not formed at his birth.

Weston, Joseph W.
m/ 12-5-1876.

"Trinity Cir., S. GA Conf." *SCA*, 8-26-1874, p. 130.

Westwood, John   (6-28-1791 - 4-9-1873)
b. London, England; d. Harris Co., GA; came to U.S. in 1818; lp 1824; m/ 1810, Mary Ann Ellaway of Shipston, England.

Wheeler, Thomas B.
LP, joined the church at Friendship Campmeeting & became a member of Coldwater.

Whitby, Thomas H.
"Carroll Mis., GA." *SCA*, 7-19-1850, p. 26.
"Troup Cir., GA." *SCA*, 11-10-1848, p. 91.

White, Benjamin D. (1811 - 3-19-1871)
(L). reared Jones Co., GA; d. Houston Co., GA; le 1861; 1p 1868;
member, Liberty Chapel, Houston Co., GA.

White, David L.
2-2-1818, letter w/ Samuel Hodge, Augusta, GA. (Wof.).

"St. Augustine, FL." *SCA*, 9-25-1846, p. 62; 1-15-1847, p. 126; 7-16-
1846, p. 22.

White, Edwin
"Burke Mis., GA." *SCA*, 9-28-1838, p. 58.

White, Miller H.
"Culloden Cir., N. GA Conf." *SCA*, 10-18-1867, fp.
"Thomaston Cir., N. GA Conf." *SCA*, 10-23-1872, p. 166.

Whitefield, David B.
bur. Hargrove Cem., Cobb Co., GA. m/ Sallie Power (12-9-1843 - 6-1-1936).

Whiting, Elbert M.
"Dublin Cir., S. GA Conf." *SCA*, 8-28-1877, p. 138; 10-9-1877, p. 162.

Wilburn, John, Jr. (7-23-1785 - 2-16-1841) (MPC)
b. VA; d. Randolph (now Jasper) Co., GA. A minister of MPC who served in
Greene, Newton & Randolph cos. cvt. 8-5-1827. Son of John Wilburn
(d. 1792), of Powhatan Co., VA, and Martha ? She m3/ John Deshazor &
left will in Greene Co., GA. m/ 10-19-1809, Elizabeth Jackson in Clarke Co.,
GA. dau. of Daniel Jackson, RS, of Clarke Co., GA. chrn. Samuel Jackson,
John Thomas, Albert, Jack Harrison, Percival Leonidas, Mary Jane, Elizabeth
Ann Brewer.

Wiggins, James A.
"Columbus Dist., GA." *SCA*, 10-23-1846, p. 79.
"Waukenah, FL." *SCA*, 10-15-1869, p. 166.

Wiggins, Lemuel R. G.
"Savannah Mis." *SCA*, 12-10-1844, p. 110.
"Colored Charge, Macon, GA." *SCA*, 10-23-1856, p. 83.
"West Point Cir., GA Conf." *SCA*, 10-15-1857, p. 79.
"The FL Brigade, Army of TN." *SCA*, 3-24-1864, np.

Wiggins, Robert L.

m/ Mary Hardee Goodbread (9-26-1846 - 5-24-1870); d. Quincy, FL.

"From Gen. Bragg's Army." (series). see: *SCA*, 2-19-1863, p. 30.
"The FL Troops in TN." *SCA*, 11-19-1863, fp.
"From Houston, FL." *SCA*, 4-27-1866, bp.
"Jacksonville Dist., FL Conf." *SCA*, 10-5-1866, p. 5.
"Cause of Inefficiency." *SCA*, 10-16-1868, fp.
"New Hope, Houston Cir., FL Conf." *SCA*, 10-30-1868, p. 174.
"Live Oak, FL." *SCA*, 9-10-1869, p. 146.
"Tallahassee FL Dist. Meeting." *SCA*, 4-29-1870, p. 66.
"Letter from FL." *SCA*, 6-14-1871, p. 94.
"Muscogee Cir., S. GA Conf." *SCA*, 8-28-1872, p. 134.
"Weston Cir., S. GA Conf." *SCA*, 9-23-1874, p. 150; 9-22-1875, p. 152;
9-29-1875, p. 154.

Wilkins, John H.

"Clinch Cir., S. GA Conf." *SCA*, 10-21-1870, p. 166.

Williams, Albert M.

m/ 1876, Lovena L. Brown.

Williams, Amicus Warren

son of William Williams (1-30-1812 - 6-6-1869).
m/5-23-1869, Alice C. Nance (1847 - 1919), of Clarke Co., GA.

"Cleveland Cir., N. GA Conf." *SCA*, 8-7-1868, p. 126.
"Letter from Louisiana." *SCA*, 10-16-1872, p. 162.
"Oconee St. Church, Athens, GA." *SCA*, 6-2-1875, p. 86.

Williams, Benjamin W.

m/ 11-5-1873, Laura Smith of Elbert Co., GA.

Williams, George Walton

"Nacoochee & Its Surroundings." (series). *SCA*, 9-10-1869, p. 146.
"Letters from Nacoochee." *SCA*, 7-22-1870, p. 114.

Williams, John L.

"Waynesville Cir., S. GA Conf." *SCA*, 10-9-1872, p. 158.
"Jesup, GA." *SCA*, 8-8-1876, p. 126.

Williams, Samuel L.
bur. Waynesboro, GA.

Williams, West (April 1792 - 5-2-1868)
d. St. James, Goose Ck., SC.

11-6-1825, letter to Conf. for elder's orders from Charleston Dist. (Wof.).

Williams, William S. (2-25-1807 - 1875)
b. Franklin Co., GA; joined church 1819; m/1-14-1830, Frances Winn of
Hall Co., GA. bur. old Mt. Zion Cem., Forsyth Co., Ga. on Hwy. 369
near Oscarville.

*a death date indicates 12-28-1865, Lunenburg CH, VA; not verified as to
being this same man.

"Dahlonega Cir., GA Conf." *SCA*, 8-8-1844, p. 33.
"Perry Cir., GA." *SCA*, 9-13-1839, p. 50.
"Dahlonega Mis., GA." *SCA*, 11-27-1840, p. 94; 6-18-1841, p. 2.

Williamson, Davidson
"Factory Mis., Athens Dist., GA Conf." *SCA*, 5-4-1849, p. 190; 10-5-
1849, p. 70.
"Sumter Mis., GA Conf." *SCA*, 5-29-1856, p. 207.
"Terrel Cir., GA Conf." *SCA*, 9-3-1857, p. 55.

Williamson, Robert F.
"Jamestown Cir., GA Conf." *SCA*, 11-13-1862, p. 175.

Williamson, Thomas J.
"ME Church, Woodville, AL." *SCA*, 8-30-1844, p. 45.
"Mission to Slaves in Burke Co., GA." *SCA*, 7-22-1837, p. 18.
"Mission to Slaves on the Chattahoochee." *SCA*, 7-20-1838, p. 18; 12-4-
1838, p. 102; 7-5-1839, p. 10.

Wilson, Francis M.
"Columbia Cir., FL Conf." *SCA*, 10-7-1858, p. 75; 11-11-1858, p. 94.
"Taylor Mis., FL Conf." *SCA*, 5-26-1859, p. 207.
"Holmesville Cir., FL Conf." *SCA*, 10-2-1856, p. 70.
"The Benefit of Class Meetings." *SCA*, 3-19-1857, p. 167.
"Blakely Cir., FL Conf." *SCA*, 12-4-1862, p. 187; 8-20-1863, bp.
"Newton Cir., FL Conf." *SCA*, 9-1-1864, np.

Wilson, John (d. 1860)
a Meth. preacher for 29 years; lived in Hancock Co., GA in 1808.

Wilson, Moses
dv. 1802. bur. at James Skinner's on Little Lynch's Ck. See: Jenkins,
  James, *Experiences,* etc., 1842.

Wimberly, Frederick D. (d. 1847)
m/ Sarah P. (1797 - 10-18-1875), b. Bladen Co., NC; d. Fort Valley, GA;
1833 moved to Stewart Co., GA; 1848 moved to Lumpkin Co., GA.

Wimbish, John
b. SC; in 1840, age 40-50, living in Chambers Co., AL; son of
Samuel Wimbish & Mildred Martin. lived in AL & LA. m/ Anna
Jane Car Bridges.

Wittick, Ernest L.
"The Bible." (poem). *SCA,* 1-5-1838, p. 116.
poem. *SCA,* 2-9-1838, p. 136.
"The Drunkard." (poem). *SCA,* 3-9-1838, p. 152.
"What Is Man." (poem). *SCA,* 7-13-1838, p. 16.
"Centenary in Madison, GA." *SCA,* 10-25-1839, p. 75.
"Kingston Mis., GA." *SCA,* 7-9-1841, p. 14; 9-17-1841, p. 54;
       8-5-1842, p. 30.

Wolley, V.
le Concord Church, 12-21-1825; lp by Warren Cir., 9-1-1826;
preached at Waynesville Camp Meeting, 1842.

"Satilla Mis., GA." *SCA,* 12-10-1841, p. 102.

Woodall, W.H.
"Talbot Cir., S. GA Conf." *SCA,* 11-11-1874, p. 178; 4-5-1876, p. 54.

Woodbury, Samuel
"Madison Cir., FL." *SCA,* 9-13-1850, p. 59.
"Monticello, FL Conf." *SCA,* 8-6-1857, p. 37.
"Leon Cir., FL Conf." *SCA,* 9-20-1867, p. 150.

Woodruff, Michael
"Stewards, Their Duties & Powers." *SCA,* 11-29-1867, fp.
"Watchmen, Stewards, What of the Night." *SCA,* 3-13-1868, p. 42.

"Can Christians Attend Operas?" *SCA*, 4-3-1868, fp.
"A Correspondent's Defense." *SCA*, 11-13-1868, fp.
"To the Stewards & Members of the Columbus Dist." *SCA*, 11-20-1868,
     p. 186.
"Opening the Year Right." *SCA*, 2-12-1869, p. 26.
"Our Position." *SCA*, 12-18-1868, fp.
"Prove All Things, Hold Fast To That Which Is Good." *SCA*, 5-21-1869, fp.
"Campmeetings." *SCA*, 7-9-1869, fp.

Woody, James
m/ 1832.

Woolridge, Andrew J. (6-3-1836 - 10-3-1871)
b. Franklin, TN; member FL CONF.; Grad. MD, Univ. of Nashville, 1855;
le July 1855; lp 9-22-1855; OT 1855; Deacon 1858; Elder 1860.

"Great Fire in Quincy, FL." *SCA*, 9-25-1868, p. 154.
"Leon Cir., FL Conf." *SCA*, 9-3-1869, p. 142.
"Tallahassee Dist., FL Conf." *SCA*, 6-17-1870, p. 94.

Woolridge, James M.
"Cusseta Cir., S. GA Conf." *SCA*, 8-27-1873, p. 134.

Wootten, William L., Sr.
G.G. Smith describes a visit to his place in *WCA*, 9-16-1885, p. 2.

Wootten, William L., Jr.
m/ 11-21-1876.

"The Lecture Craze." *WCA*, v58, n7, 2-14-1894, p. 8.
"Putnam Cir., N. GA Conf." *SCA*, 9-30-1874, p. 154; 8-11-1875, p. 126.
"Ringgold Cir., N. GA Conf." *SCA*, 2-20-1877, p. 30; 9-11-1877, p. 146.

Worley, James G.
"Lake Charles, LA." *SCA*, 11-6-1872, p. 175.

Wright, Alexander P.
"Ockmulgee Cir., S. GA Conf." *SCA*, 6-25-1869, p. 102.
"Waynesville Cir., S. GA Conf." *SCA*, 8-26-1870, p. 134.
"Centervillage Mis., S. GA Conf." *SCA*, 9-2-1870, p. 138.
"Morven Cir., S. GA Conf." *SCA*, 10-9-1872, p. 158.

"Lowndes & Echols Mis., S. GA Conf." *SCA*, 8-27-1873, p. 134;
    9-3-1873, p. 139; 8-26-1874, p.130.
"Grooverville Cir., S. GA Conf." *SCA*, 9-17-1873, p. 146.

Wright, John C.   (12-31-1803 - 3-4-1867)

(L) on Coweta Cir. b. Clarke Co., GA; educated at Salem, Clarke Co.;
le 1828; lp1828; served Houston Mis.; was a teacher after location.

Wright, Patrick A.

"Oglethorpe Mis., GA." *SCA*, 6-8-1849, p. 2; 11-9-1849, p. 90.
"Griffin, GA Conf." *SCA*, 9-22-1859, p. 275.
"St. John's, Augusta, GA." *SCA*, 10-26-1866, p. 5; 11-26-1869, p. 190.
"Griffin Station, 1871." *SCA*, 5-31-1871, p. 86.

Wyatt, Lorenzo D.

m/ 1-6-1835, Edith (11-3-1816 - 21-31-1876), b. E. TN; d. Gordon Co., GA.

Wynn, Alexander M.

"Thomaston, GA Conf." *SCA*, 8-9-1855, p. 39.
"Talbotton, GA Conf." *SCA*, 10-13-1859, p. 286.
"Columbus, GA." *SCA*, 7-9-1857, p. 23.
"The Christian Liberality, A Worthy Example." *SCA*, 2-12-1869, p. 26.
"The Yellow Fever in Savannah." *SCA*, 9-12-1876, p. 146.
"Wesley Monumental Church, Savannah." *SCA*, 7-10-1877, p. 110.

Wynn, Thomas L.

1-6-1830, letter against his conduct w/ bro. Few from Lexington GA.
Stewards. (Wof.).

Yarbrough, George W.

bur. Citizens Cem., Cobb Co., GA. m/ Mary Boyce Morris (9-12-1843 -
1-24-1915), b. Marietta, GA; d. Winder, GA.

"Lawrenceville, GA." *SCA*, 9-2-1858, p. 54.
"From Gen. Longstreet's Army." (series)., *SCA*, 2-11-1864, np.
"From Gen. Lee's Army." *SCA*, 7-28-1864, np.
"From the Army at Petersburg." *SCA*, 8-18-1864, np.
"A Birthday and a Dedication Day in Greene Co., GA." *SCA*, 4-17-1872, fp.
"Elberton Dist." *SCA*, 4-23-1873, p. 62; 10-14-1874, p. 162.
"To the Methodists of the Elberton Dist." *SCA*, 10-8-1873, p. 158.
"Griffin Dist." *SCA*, 10-10-1876, p. 162; 11-20-1877, p. 186.

Yarbrough, John F.
"Methodism in Gainesville." *WCA*, v100, n25, 6-19-1936, pp. 11, 18.
"Successors To The Apostles." *WCA*, v100, n28, 1-15-1937, p. 3.

Yarbrough, John W.
"Newnan Cir., GA Conf." *SCA*, 8-8-1844, p. 35.
"Newnansville Dist., FL Conf." *SCA*, 7-31-1846, p. 31.
"Coweta Mis." *SCA*, 5-28-1847, p. 202.
"Leon Cir., FL." *SCA*, 7-6-1838, p. 10; 12-28-1838, p. 110.
"Cassville Mis., GA." *SCA*, 5-24-1839, p. 194.
"Marietta Mis., GA." *SCA*, 5-15-1840, p. 190.
"McDonough Cir., GA." *SCA*, 9-30-1842, p. 63.
"Rome Dist. Preachers Too Modest." *SCA*, 12-1-1859, p. 315.
"Newton Cir., GA Conf." *SCA*, 10-8-1857, p. 75.
"Atlanta Dist., GA Conf." *SCA*, 9-17-1863, bp.
"A Farewell Letter." *SCA*, 3-9-1866, fp.

Yarbrough, Walter L.
m/ 11-30-1876, Laura Morton.

"Little River Cir., N. GA Conf." *SCA*, 9-4-1877, p. 142.

Young, William (d. 1902)
nv. William M. Young.

ADDENDUM

Birch, Edmund P.
"The Successful Appeal." WCA, 6-19-1895, p. 5

Boring, Jesse   (12-4-1807 - 1-29-1890)
d. Dixie, GA. m1/ 1843, Harriet E. Howard
(1816 - 1878); m2/ Mrs. Hattie Colquit.

Bryan, William
m/9-16-1873, Sarah Tarpley (1-25-1827 - 9-11-1894), who m2/
George N. Smith of Greene Co., GA.

Crumley, William. M.
wife, Julia A. Choate; d. 1895. bur. West View, Atlanta, GA

Duffey, Daniel   (1762 - 1838)
(L); b. Ireland; d. Crawford Co., GA.

Flournoy, Robert   (1797 - 4-6-1834)
d. Perry, GA.

Jackson, Charles A.
m/ Eliza Faison of NC, not Eliza Williams

Kelsey, Daniel
record of another marriage to Mrs. Mercy who d. 1-7-1842.

Mathews, Moses   (1773 - 1833)
d. Roanoke, Stewart Co., GA; formerly of Monroe Co., GA.

Miller, R.F.
"Extracts From Diary, 1878." WCA, 10-9-1895, p. 8.

Mixon, J. Fletcher
m/ 2-14-1895, Addie Harper, Elberton, GA

Ogletree, Absalom (2-11-1811 - 7-21-1861)
m/ 1832, Matilda Stewart (2-4-1814 - 5-19-1910). chrn: Mary Jane, 2-3-1833; William T., 1835, Philemon, 7-7-1836; James M., 4-20-1839; Nancy Elizabeth Victoria, 11-2-1840; John Fletcher, 4-8-1843; Sarah F., 1846; Absalom Hardy, 1850; Robert David, 1853.

Ogletree, Absalom Hardy (1850 - 1-23-1892)
m/ Mary Bell

Pearce, Gadwell J.
wife, Eliza Ann Glenn (6-26-1821 - 9-3-1895), b. Jackson Co., GA; d. Decatur, GA.

Powell, William
(d. 1894);   died at his home in Cairo, Thomas Co., GA.

Robinson, Wingfield W.
wife, Susan Ellison, sister of Rev. Wm. H. Ellison, d. Opelika, AL.

Sinclair, Elijah
(d. 12-20-1841); d. Anson Co., NC; recently a merchant of Savannah, GA.

Smith, Eli
m/ Helen Trimble (5-28-1856 - 6-10-1895), b. Bartow Co., GA, dau. of A.C. & Adeline Trimble. She m2/ his brother, J.F. Smith of Buford, GA. She was almost blind since age 14.

Smith, Osborne L.
m/ 12-12-1843, Amanda Lawrence. bur. Oxford, GA.

White, John M.
wife, Rachel C. Frances Lenora A. Lyon (11-10-1844 - 1-11-1921), dau. of James P. Lyon (12-20-1826 - 11-11-1892) and Elizabeth T. Cherry (4-18-1828 - 2-11-1898).

INDEX

This is an index of the articles in the *Christian Advocate* and *Southern Christian Advocate* which reference the particular churches, charges or circuits described by preachers and/or others in these church papers. Every reference to a particular entry may not describe the same place. For instance, there may be 9 entries about Bethel which may describe two or more locations; the entry Washington may refer to the town in Wilkes Co. or to the county by that name. In some instances, the same place entries may be listed in more than one state. Many appointments in FL were also in GA. They are listed under both.

In most instances the reference is to circuits rather than to specific churches, though there are a few churches named which are clearly not the names of circuits. Names of counties and circuits are given together in the entries which may not be the same. If the reader will check the reference, many of these explanations will be made obvioius.

AL

Andrew	165
Arbacoochee	188
Chambers	165
Chattahoochee	185
Chunnenuggee	185
Columbia	29, 52
Dog River	52
Eufaula	58
Gaston	18
Harpersville	123
Hatchett Ck.	188
Haw River	185
Lafayette	193
Lineville	113
Macon	102
Mobile	30, 127
Montgomery Dist.	178
Ochesee	65
Pea River	52
Pikeville	165
Rembert Hills	18
Russell	102
Selma	165

Talladega Dist. 120
Tuskegee 30
Uchee 159
Wetumpka 57
White Water 52
Woodville 201

AR
Batesville 57

FL
Alachua 91, 173
Albany 61, 123
Alapaha 77, 127
Altamaha 75
Apalachicola 61, 173, 191
Aucilla 74
Bainbridge 67, 193
Bainbridge Dist. 98
Bellville 194
Benton 107, 148
Bethel 117
Black Ck. 12
Blakely 201
Brooksville 69
Brunswick 65, 98
Brunswick Dist. 187
Centreville 86
Chicachatta 49
Clinch 112
Colquitt 8
Columbia 16, 89, 115, 201
Concord 98
Decatur 66, 86, 162
Fruitland 67
Gadsden 25, 148, 173, 185
Hamilton 193
Hernando 92, 185
Holmesville 12, 109, 201
Houston 200
Isabella 92
Jacksonville 41, 110

Jacksonville Dist.	98, 193, 200
Key West	46, 56, 65, 66, 107, 154, 158, 176
Leon	17, 25, 33, 56, 66, 71, 86, 87, 115, 148, 173, 202, 203, 205
Liberty	96
Linwood	148
Little River	14, 191
Live Oak	194, 200
Live Oak Dist.	52
Madison	82, 86, 98, 191, 194, 202
Madison Dist.	86, 123, 173
Marion	109, 141, 148, 154
Micanopy	66, 98, 107, 193
Milford	37
Monticello	202
Morgan	37
Morven Dist.	133, 148
Middlebury	12
Nassau	167
New Hope	200
Newnansville	41, 70, 82, 91, 154, 180
Newnansville Dist.	205
Newton	201
Ocean Pond	107
Ocilla	193
Orange	141, 185
Pensacola	163
Pilatka	107
Quincy	4, 27, 52, 91, 149, 173, 203
Quitman Dist.	133
Randolph	91
St. Augustine	107, 125, 154, 167, 199
St. Illa	154
St. John's	193
St. Mary's Dist.	67, 98
Santee	185
Satilla	12, 123, 141, 154
Spring Ck.	185
Sumter	123
Tallahassee	5, 33
Tallahassee Dist.	52, 56, 66, 91, 154, 200, 203
Tampa Bay	49

Tampa Dist.	41, 107, 127, 148
Taylor	201
Thomasville	85
Thomasville Dist.	173
Troupville	57
Union	50
Valdosta	133
Wakulla	33
Waldo	67
Waresboro	121
Warrior	109, 141
Waukenan	57
Waukeenah	87, 194, 199

GA

Acworth	9, 46, 49, 80, 95, 121
Albany	41, 62, 110, 125, 194
Alexander	125, 161
Alpharetta	8, 11, 66, 78, 81
Altamaha	7, 75, 123
Altamaha Dist.	126, 189
Americus	8, 35, 44, 53, 98, 107, 113, 116, 164
Americus Dist.	36, 49, 84, 113, 133, 151, 171
Andrew Chapel	39, 65, 100
Antioch	151
Appling	62
Asbury	43, 47, 98, 164
Athens	19, 30, 53, 60, 81, 99, 102, 134, 135, 138, 147, 174
Athens Dist.	1, 16, 22, 29, 68, 82, 87, 106, 135, 136, 137
Atlanta	11, 43, 51, 54, 89, 84, 92, 98, 103, 106, 116, 128, 137, 153, 164
Atlanta Dist.	1, 13, 22, 57, 61, 81, 124, 137, 195, 205
Augusta	9, 17, 45, 47, 60, 99, 134, 171, 174, 176
Augusta Dist.	17, 60, 81, 99, 116, 137, 147
Baldwin	64
Bainbridge	22, 32, 48, 108, 135
Bainbridge Dist.	35, 48, 123, 124, 143
Baker	54, 173
Barnesville	53, 140, 149, 157, 174
Bartow	129
Beaver Dam	96

Bellview	193
Belton	136
Berlin	62
Bethany	23, 178
Bethel	1, 23, 26, 82, 94, 114, 115, 129, 196
Bibb	116
Black Ck.	25
Black Riv.	17, 48, 70, 118, 162
Black Swamp	59
Blackshear	73, 115, 128
Blakely	193
Blairsville	3, 36, 41, 56, 57, 149
Bold Springs	135
Bowdon	54, 117, 141, 189
Brandon's Chapel	101
Brooks	167
Broad Riv.	32, 43, 49, 82, 95, 124, 149
Brunswick	40, 65, 80, 110, 115, 133, 143, 145, 176, 183
Brunswick Dist.	128, 138, 165, 167
Bryan	39, 96, 114
Buena Vista	2, 41, 58, 141, 151, 179, 196
Bulloch	114, 115
Burke	18, 48, 61, 62, 65, 79, 94, 133, 151, 152, 183, 187, 199, 201
Butler	15, 26, 93, 107, 151
Cairo	2, 102
Calhoun	9, 19, 77, 119, 145, 150, 153, 168, 186
Camden	9, 158
Camilla	2, 105, 151, 193
Campbellton	20, 94
Canton	3, 26, 76, 103, 109, 111, 134
Capers' Chapel	72
Carnesville	31, 56, 69, 87, 119, 130, 132, 149, 175
Carroll	53, 198
Carrollton	2, 12, 53, 54, 117, 149, 171, 174, 189, 192
Cartersville	60, 101
Cassville	2, 47, 94, 120, 138, 143, 167, 205
Cataula	99
Cave Spring	34, 76, 82, 129, 153, 155, 164, 188
Cedar Ck.	97
Cedar Springs	85
Cedartown	103, 152, 186

Centervillage	203
Centerville	150, 179, 187
Chatham	79, 114
Chalybeate Springs	95, 107
Chattahoochee	24, 123, 147, 178, 187, 192, 201
Cherokee	70, 77, 128
Cherokee Dist.	68, 120, 136, 173
Cherokee Hill	148
Chesterfield	79
City Mission	27, 116
Clarkesville	34, 69, 87, 88, 182, 185
Clayton	14, 19, 22, 36, 43, 49, 158, 186, 187
Cleveland	119, 134, 170, 194, 200
Clinch	200
Clinton	22, 23, 24, 50, 53, 113, 115, 124, 185
Colquitt	147, 158
Columbia	10, 54
Columbus	2, 35, 41, 60, 76, 116, 143, 162, 176, 204
Columbus Dist.	13, 19, 34, 35, 83, 84, 85, 113, 120, 199
Columbus Factory	24
Concord	129
Conyers	72, 196
Cooper's Ck.	31
Coosa	153
County Line	101, 124
Cove	116
Covington	1, 8, 13, 61, 81, 82, 106, 129, 133, 137, 167, 168, 173, 191, 195
Coweta	205
Crawford	45, 165
Crawfordville	2, 186
Culloden	24, 40, 64, 92, 174, 196, 199
Cullodenville	77
Cumming	30, 92, 134, 135, 140
Currihee	119
Cusseta	131, 196, 203
Cuthbert	14, 23, 40, 51, 53, 95, 114, 133, 171
Dade	3, 17, 22, 114, 149, 152
Dahlonega	3, 12, 24, 34, 50, 66, 115, 132, 192, 194, 201
Dahlonega Dist.	8, 13, 43, 76, 142, 146, 168
Dallas	2, 34

214

Dalton	1, 16, 53, 87, 88, 103, 114, 117, 129, 145, 153, 162, 167, 186, 192, 198
Dalton Dist.	1, 16, 22, 34, 164
Danielsville	197
Darien	10, 26, 80, 100, 128
Davisboro	25, 33, 45, 86
Dawson	23, 35, 36
Dawson Dist.	128
Dawsonville	128, 136
Decatur	15, 18, 47, 68, 70, 72, 105, 126, 133, 152, 174
Desoto	95
Dole's Chapel	100
Dooly	62, 131, 193
Douglasville	27, 194
Dry Pond	60
Dublin	57, 63, 109, 114, 146, 161, 199
Dublin Dist.	84
Ducktown	32
Duluth	56
East Macon	183
East Point	49, 196
Eatonton	16, 17, 53, 72, 98, 101, 109, 152, 183
Echols	133, 184, 204
Edgewood	22
Effingham	128
Elbert	94, 126
Elberton	38, 42, 74, 87, 114, 156, 167, 182, 193
Elberton Dist.	87, 95, 136, 204
Ellaville	15, 23, 45, 93, 102, 123, 151
Ellijay	24, 71, 76, 102, 142, 149, 181, 182, 186, 192
Emanuel	63, 70
Etowah	47
Evan	78
Evan's Chapel	54
Factory Mission	38, 43, 73, 82, 178, 196, 201
Fairburn	21, 45, 73, 129
Fairhaven	70, 79, 114
Fayette	55
Fayetteville	36, 66, 130, 140, 172, 182, 192, 194, 197
Flat Shoals	59
Fletcher's Chapel	164
Flint River	24, 55, 148, 192

Florence	45, 198
Flowery Branch	160
Forrestville	156, 198
Forsyth	8, 14, 36, 40, 42, 43, 47, 50, 53, 65, 80, 86, 99, 129, 152, 167, 174
Fort Gaines	44, 113, 141, 179, 193
Fort Gaines Dist.	137
Fort Valley	3, 10, 18, 22, 23, 36, 37, 42, 50, 55, 90, 94, 106, 117, 162, 174, 196
Franklin	20, 36, 107, 136, 180
Franklin Springs	56
Fulton	37, 121, 129
Gainesville	13, 23, 28, 43, 66, 157, 192, 194, 195, 205
Gainesville Dist.	134
Geneva	198
Georgetown	63
Gibson	33, 102, 161
Glen Alta	84
Gordon	153, 163, 175
Griffin	1, 16, 65, 82, 91, 98, 160, 192, 204
Girffin Dist.	22, 40, 82, 97, 204
Grantville	22, 42, 95, 109
Green Hill	116
Greensboro	9, 42, 61, 87, 141, 166, 173
Greenville	50, 87, 99, 113, 118, 120, 152, 164, 171, 172, 186
Greenwood	185
Grooversville	86, 102, 204
Grove Level	1
Gwinnett	11
Hahira	165
Hall	13, 37, 136, 186
Hamilton	48, 93, 106, 107, 120, 135
Hampton	72, 97
Hancock	28, 34, 94, 95, 113, 127, 137, 169
Haralson	130
Harris	163
Hartwell	11, 129, 175
Hawkinsville	19, 108, 126, 151, 159
Hawkinsville Dist.	108
Haynesville	19, 179, 183
Henderson	180, 183

Hinesville	20, 57, 129, 178, 192
Hinesville Dist.	167
Hiwassee	166, 186
Hogansville	21, 125
Holmesville	177
Homer	19, 57, 149
Houston	94, 181
Irwin	68, 77, 138
Irwinton	63, 109, 138, 147
Isabella	7, 115
Isle of Hope	35, 48
Jackson	76, 82, 115, 130, 136, 149, 190
Jacksonboro	71
Jacksonville	39, 41, 64
Jamestown	201
Jasper	78, 89
Jefferson	10, 32, 35, 118, 134, 145, 171
Jeffersonville	33, 51, 162
Jeffersonville Dist.	43
Jenkin's Sch. H.	17
Jesup	35, 200
Jones Chapel	167
Jonesboro	58, 129, 136, 137, 155, 178
Kingston	14, 43, 53, 63, 94, 112, 152, 202
Kirkwood	103
Knoxville	10
LaFayette	3, 34, 57, 71, 76, 101, 153, 161
LaGrange	16, 39, 42, 60, 61, 80, 98, 103, 120, 137, 138, 184
LaGrange Dist.	1, 8, 47, 82, 113, 117, 171, 186
Lawrenceville	9, 26, 61, 71, 92, 93, 101, 109, 117, 119, 152, 204
Lee	197
Leesburg	9, 175
Leon	198
Lexington	1, 16, 57, 129
Liberty	132, 197
Lincoln	53
Lincolnton	17, 74, 189
Little River	13, 101, 205
Loganville	15, 59

Lookout Mtn.	167, 187
Louisville	26, 50, 61, 80, 84, 127
Lowndes	58, 133, 138, 170, 184, 204
Lumpkin	10, 47, 49, 82, 93, 116, 135, 159
Lumpkin Dist.	47, 122
McDonough	24, 55, 72, 78, 121, 150, 152, 172, 205
McIntosh	26
McLemore	16, 34
Macon	34, 53, 60, 63, 94, 116, 189, 199
Macon Dist.	8, 9, 84, 86, 91, 100, 171, 184, 189
Madison	53, 63, 132, 163
Magnolia	23
Manasses	53, 57, 60, 129
Marietta	1, 40, 42, 64, 69, 84, 89, 93, 96, 97, 151, 165, 170, 173, 192, 194, 205
Marietta Dist.	162
Marshallville	22, 106
Meriwether	119, 181, 196
Milledgeville	1, 65, 86, 171
Millen	46, 160
Milner	106
Monroe	38, 61, 81, 111, 124, 161, 167, 188
Monticello	15, 47, 72, 97, 127, 138, 183
Montezuma	62, 68, 78
Morgan	64, 82, 141
Morganton	11, 31, 103, 176
Morven	18, 32, 165, 203
Mossy Ck.	90, 149
Moultrie	14
Mt. Gilead	164
Mt. Moriah	35, 183
Mt. Pleasant	13, 59, 195
Mt. Vernon	63, 84, 115
Mt. Zion	15, 17, 35, 165
Mulberry	119, 127
Murphy	32, 36, 43, 107, 149, 151, 186
Muscogee	97, 179, 188, 200
Nacoochee	22, 200
New Bethel	22
Newnan	13, 61, 120, 184, 186, 193, 205
Newnansville Dist.	15
Newton	25, 61, 71, 78, 105, 136, 151, 184, 193, 205

Norcross	31, 95, 101
North Lincoln	31
Oak Grove	116
Oakland	78
Oakmulgee	24
Ocapilco	116
Ocmulgee	55, 115, 130, 134, 158
Ocklocknee	61, 203
Ocilla	43
Oconee	67
Oconee St.	200
Ogeechee	27, 41, 70, 148
Oglethorpe	15, 89, 93, 123, 147, 166, 168, 193, 196, 204
Olivet	80
Oostanaula	101
Oothcalouga Valley	166
Ossabaw	185
Oxford	1, 17, 22, 47, 121, 136, 137, 168
Palmetto	20, 75, 79, 109, 192
Payne Chapel	37, 53, 82, 152, 186
Perry	36, 37, 48, 51, 65, 80, 100, 102, 118, 137, 141, 159, 176, 178, 201
Pearce Chapel	99
Pierce Chapel	60
Pike	25, 71
Pine Grove	115
Plattville	147
Pleasant Grove	188
Pleasant Hill	171, 176
Pope's Chapel	100
Powder Springs	2, 103, 190, 198
Prospect	48, 170
Pulaski	38
Putnam	63, 93, 100, 122, 132, 166, 193, 203
Quitman	19, 82, 106, 109, 183
Randolph	107, 123, 133
Rehoboth	21
Reidsville	3, 38, 44, 146
Resaca	198
Reynolds	74
Richmond	9, 17, 62, 74, 164
Ringgold	81, 167, 186, 194, 198, 203

Rock Fish	106
Rock Spring	103, 198
Rome	8, 40, 45, 61, 95, 106, 130, 134, 153, 185
Rome Dist.	1, 8, 40, 53, 80, 81, 101, 103, 130, 138, 146, 156, 167, 205
Roswell	2, 38, 76, 118, 134, 158, 170
Salt Springs	149
Salem	132
Sandtown	72, 138, 148, 178
Sandersville	8, 62, 100, 129, 162, 172, 183
Sandy Springs	44
Satilla	45, 123, 202
Savannah	1, 48, 60, 62, 96, 116, 134, 171, 183, 184, 192, 199, 204
Savannah Dist.	25, 84, 86, 100, 117
Savannah R.	56, 72, 197
Schley	92
Scriven	47, 71, 151, 162, 171, 178
Senoia	46, 88
Shiloh	49
Silver Ck.	197
Skidaway	35, 48
Smithville	9, 106, 131
Snow Springs	51
Social Circle	22, 47, 72
S. Lincoln	72
Sparta	1, 64, 90, 94, 98, 106, 117, 139, 184
Spring Ck.	87, 162
Spring Hill	40, 45, 102
Spring Place	81, 87, 92, 103, 130, 145, 146, 182
Spring Vale	93, 125, 198
Springfield	38, 78, 80, 84, 86, 89, 102, 116, 125, 128, 184
St. James	1, 137
St. John's	60, 83, 204
St. Luke's	60, 99
St. Mary's	26, 33, 98, 187
St. Paul's	51
Starkville	39, 80
State Line	10, 71, 107
Statesboro	115
Stewart	45, 51, 78, 116, 147, 153, 167
Stone Mtn.	49

Subligna	22, 34, 38, 112, 151, 186
Summerville	39, 53, 54, 109, 145, 152
Sumter	179, 197, 201
Swainsboro	20, 102, 125, 129, 184
Sylvania	28, 86, 114, 115, 121, 131, 180
Talbot	39, 41, 65, 120, 152, 163, 202
Talbotton	35, 41, 50, 100, 106, 137, 159, 178, 198, 204
Taloola	62
Tatnall	100
Taylor's Ck.	8, 40
Tazewell	37
Telfair	33, 41, 185
Terrell	34, 58, 201
The Ridge	100
Thomaston	15, 44, 79, 97, 153, 159, 204
Thomasville	40, 113, 133
Thomasville Dist.	10, 108, 183
Thomson	54, 109, 199
Tilton	198
Toccoa	172
Toogalo	119
Trinity	43, 60, 61, 116, 164, 182, 198
Trion	53
Troup	23, 42, 57, 59, 61, 62, 71, 80, 119, 120, 184, 198
Tunnel Hill	145, 154
Turtle R.	59, 74
Twiggs	184
Upson	40, 71, 131, 136, 153
Valdosta	68, 115
Van Wert	64, 95, 104
Vienna	51, 58, 176
Villa Rica	8, 9, 93, 128, 162
Walton	71
Waresboro	64, 90, 115, 187
Warm Springs	171
Warren	41, 50
Warrenton	47, 53, 87, 91, 94, 105, 114, 117, 164, 174, 184, 188, 191
Warrior	25
Warsaw	182
Washington	15, 28, 33, 45, 52, 84, 130

Watkinsville	18, 22, 29, 44, 68, 79, 80, 101, 127, 129, 132, 167
Wayne	35
Waynesboro	42, 52, 65, 133, 190
Waynesville	200, 203
Wesley Chapel	19, 35, 70, 98, 99
Wesley Monumental	117, 204
West Point	114, 137, 162, 185, 199
Weston	122, 123, 131, 151, 200
Wheat's CG	184
White Plains	109, 141
Whitesburg	135, 168
Whitesville	42, 43, 80
Whitfield	92, 155, 167
Wilcox	38
Wilkes	34, 104, 152
Wilkinson	11, 184
Winterville	31, 38
Worth	19, 49, 191
Wrightsville	148, 150
Zebulon	51, 55, 94, 117, 140, 149, 164, 194
Zoar	129

LA
Lake Charles	203

MS
Bethel	145

NC
Bladen	193
Charlotte	21
Rockingham	146
Yadkin	9

SC
Ashepoo	37
Bamberg Dist.	15
Barnwell	189
Beaufort	37, 124
Black R.	161
Black Swamp	44

Blackville	15
Camden	30, 90, 177
Cape Fear	193
Charleston Dist.	13, 30, 184
Chesterfield	21
Cokesbury	44, 55, 184
Cokesbury Dist.	13
Columbia	55, 98
Columbia Dist.	119
Combahee	37
Congaree	119
Cooper R.	125
Cumberland St.	184
Cypress	55
Darlington	125
Deep R.	21
Edgefield	55
Edgefield Dist.	55
Fairfield	55
Flatwoods	125
Georgetown	177
Greenville	44, 184
Lancaster	145
Laurens	124
Lexington	177
Lincolnton Dist.	44
MacKannan	126
Marion	44, 70, 126
Montgomery	21
Mt. Vernon	55
Newberry	124, 184
Orangeburg	44, 189
Peedee	100, 161
Pendleton	184
Pickens	170
Providence	13
Saluda	180
Santee	13, 16, 37, 44, 83
Sharon	44
Smyrna	44
Spartanburg	39, 50, 174
Sumpterville	44

Trinity	184
Union	184
Waccamaw Neck	14
Washington St.	119
Wachita	
Lehi	146

www.ingramcontent.com/pod-product-compliance
Lightning Source LLC
Chambersburg PA
CBHW061727270326
41928CB00011B/2139